Cyberprotest

MANCHESTER
UNIVERSITY PRESS

© Hinze/Scratch! Media (www.scratch.com.au)

CYBERPROTEST

Environmental activism online

JENNY PICKERILL

Manchester University Press
Manchester and New York

distributed exclusively in the USA by Palgrave

Published by Manchester University Press
Oxford Road, Manchester M13 9NR, UK
and Room 400, 175 Fifth Avenue, New York, NY 10010, USA
www.manchesteruniversitypress.co.uk

Distributed exclusively in the USA by
Palgrave, 175 Fifth Avenue, New York,
NY 10010, USA

Distributed exclusively in Canada by
UBC Press, University of British Columbia, 2029 West Mall,
Vancouver, BC, Canada V6T 1Z2

British Library Cataloguing-in-Publication Data
A catalogue record for this book is available from the British Library

Library of Congress Cataloging-in-Publication Data applied for

ISBN   0 7190 6394 9   *hardback*

First published 2003

11 10 09 08 07 06 05 04 03   10 9 8 7 6 5 4 3 2 1

Typeset in Palatino with Frutiger
by Servis Filmsetting Ltd, Manchester
Printed in Great Britain
by Biddles Ltd, Guildford and King's Lynn

Contents

Acknowledgements

This book would not have been written without the involvement of the eighty or so interviewees, from a broad range of environmental groups, whose time, energy and interest are reflected throughout. Many of them also provided me with group literature, arranged access to meetings and contacts, facilitated my participant observation in their projects and gave feedback on my analysis. Their enthusiasm and inspiration were essential to the completion of the book. I am indebted to them all.

The research was undertaken through funding provided by the Economic and Social Research Council and the Leverhulme Trust. I am also grateful to the University of Newcastle and to Curtin University, Australia, for providing quiet writing spaces. The initial outcomes of the research were published as chapters in *Culture and Politics in the Information Age*, edited by Frank Webster (Routledge, 2001), and *Fibreculture Reader: Politics of a Digital Present* (Fibreculture Publications, 2001) and as an article for *Peace Review*, vol. 13 (2001), no. 3. I thank the publishers for allowing me to reproduce some of this work.

Thanks must also go to Chantal Bourgault, Graeme Chesters, Brian Doherty, Rachel Gibson, Tim Gray, Graham Meikle, Jayne Rodgers, Bron Szerszynski, Neil Ward, Stephen Ward, Frank Webster, Michele Willson and David Wood for their academic guidance and thoughtful discussions. My special thanks go to Alastair Bonnett, of the University of Newcastle, for his years of patience, encouragement and enthusiasm. Finally, for their continuous support and good humour, thanks are due to my family and friends without whom the process would have been a far more sobering experience.

Jenny Pickerill
Fremantle

Abbreviations

ATA	Alternative Technology Association
CAT	Centre for Alternative Technology
CB	citizen-band (transmitter–receiver)
CMC	computer-mediated communication
CRI	chemical release inventory
DAM	digital alternative media
DiY	do-it-yourself
EA	Environment Agency
ECD	electronic civil disobedience
EF! AU	*Earth First! Action Update*
EF! UK	Earth First!
FoE	Friends of the Earth
GMO	genetically modified organism
GSN	Green Student Network
HSA	Hunt Saboteurs' Association
HTML	hyper-text markup language – the language used to write web pages
ICT	information communication technology
IRC	internet relay chat
ISP	internet service provider
IT	information technology
J18	international demonstrations held on 18 June 1999
MNC	multinational corporation
MO	Mobile Office
N30	30 November 1999 anti-globalisation actions, mainly in Seattle
NGO	non-government organisation
NSM	new social movement
NVDA	non-violent direct action

RCC	regional campaign co-ordinator
RTS	Reclaim the Streets
SEN	Student Environmental Network
SMO	social movement organisation
WTO	World Trade Organisation

Introduction

On 18 June 1999, in the City of London, a protest occurred which centred around a 'Carnival Against Capitalism'. Linked to a global day of action aimed at the banking and financial centres of the world, the protest had no clear leaders, spokesperson or discernible plan. Despite the majority of participants remaining peaceful, violence erupted and caught the attention of Britain's media.

The mainstream media coverage over the ensuing days was dominated by images of riot police clashing with protesters, injured civilians and the trail of destruction left behind. However, newspapers also focused on the role of the internet. Headlines from both the broadsheet and tabloid newspapers included; 'A Riot From Cyberspace', 'Internet Message Sets Off A Rampage' and 'Virtual Chaos Baffles Police'. Journalists portrayed the J18 demonstrations as a 'new departure for protest' (*Daily Express*, 19 June 1999, p. 10). The defining difference was use of the internet which enabled activists to plan, plot and co-ordinate actions with low costs, anonymity (from police detection) and speed. At the same time they were apparently able to reach a wider audience of potential participants than ever before, and thus were able to spark a 'rampage'.

The internet is rapidly permeating the everyday lives of many British citizens. By 2002, almost one-third (19 million) of the British population had access to the internet, with 15 million having direct access from home (*Which?Online* 2002). The internet is widely available in public libraries, cyber-cafés (of which there is usually at least one in each city or large town), at universities and colleges, and increasingly in schools (Bingham, Valentine and Holloway 2001).

The politics of cyberspace is of importance both for the future use of computer-mediated communication[1] (CMC) and within traditional political arenas, commerce and society itself. As illustrated with the J18 protests, the incorporation by political activists of CMC within their repertoire will influence not only their own campaigning abilities, but the responses required by governments and security forces.

Technological changes in communication have long been recognised as important to the development of cohesion between dispersed individuals and within activist movements. Innovations in transport as well as in the media – in telecommunications, radio, film and television – have both enabled and shaped the agendas and organisation of social movements and allowed individuals with similar views to come together. With the advance of CMC, there have been numerous and passionate polemics about the implications of the technologies for society. A key debate concerns the notion of electronic, or 'cyber', democracy by which CMC would enable the inclusion of a greater variety of often-marginalised voices, thus strengthening the democratic process. Kellner (1999: 101) argues that CMC has significant potential to aid the development of 'a radical democratic technopolitics that will use new technologies to advance the interests of oppositional social groups and movements that have been excluded from mainstream media and political debate'. The controversy over the advancement of this technopolitics in the contested terrain of cyberspace, and its relation to existing political structures, provides the focus of this book. Much of the public debate over the implications of CMC remains utopian or dystopian. Both these visions tend to be futuristic, simplistic and only weakly based on empirical evidence; moreover, they fail to engage with the complexities of CMC use. Thus there is a need for empirical analyses which would explore in detail the ways CMC is actually politically employed.

Within Britain there are many different political groups that have a presence online and utilise CMC, including for example members of the far right, human rights advocates, religious groups and environmental activists. Environmental activists have been chosen as the focus of this work for several reasons. The importance of the environment has been acknowledged by public bodies at the national, regional and international levels. The environmental movement in Britain is large, varied and heterogeneous. It includes several large and wealthy non-governmental organisations (NGOs) – for example Friends of the Earth and Greenpeace – and also visible direct action groups – such as Earth First! and Reclaim the Streets. There has been much debate about groups which undertake non-violent direct action (NVDA) to prevent environmental destruction through, for example, road-building (Twyford Down, 1992, Newbury, 1995–96), the planting of genetically modified crops (Genetix Snowball demonstrations) or airport extensions (Manchester Airport, 1998). There is a need to understand these visible and dynamic groups and relate them to the wider arena of British environmental politics and to other more established environmental lobbying associations (Doherty 2002). Moreover, many environmental activists have been using CMC for years and theirs were among the first political groups on the web. This fusion of high-technology use and environmental activism at first seems paradoxical because environmental political philosophy has been characterised by a scepticism about the evolving technological society. This tension adds a further dimension of interest to the use of CMC by this sector of political activism.

This book examines the relationship between the strategies of environmental activist movements in Britain and their use of CMC; it explores how environmental activists negotiate the tensions and embrace the opportunities of CMC, and analyses the consequences of their actions for the forms and processes of environmental politics. It serves as a disjuncture from some broader critiques of the implications of CMC for society as a whole (see, for example, Slevin 2000), concentrating on unpacking what CMC means for activists engaged in social change. Within this broad aim there are three specific objectives: first, to evaluate how CMC provides opportunities for political expression and mobilisation; second, to examine whether CMC use has different implications for established environmental lobbying organisations than it does for the non-hierarchical fluid networks of direct action groups, and thus to identify what challenges the technology poses for activism; and, third, to elucidate the influence of CMC on campaign strategies and consequently on business, government and regulatory responses to environmental activism.

Environmentalists' use of CMC

> The Internet has become a major organizing and mobilizing tool for environmentalists around the world, raising people's consciousness about alternative ways of living, and building the political force to make it happen. (Castells 2001: 280)

Although there is a growing body of work documenting political activists use of CMC (see for example, Walch 1999; Meikle 2002), there has been little work specifically on the possible implications of CMC on environmental movements. Several authors have identified that increased information exchange and communication resulting in new social networks and new space for communication could have profound implications for all the components of a social movement (Rheingold 1994). CMC could enable more diverse associations than those in place-based communities and reduce the costs of co-ordinating collective action. These properties have improved the campaigning ability of environmental groups, increasing international collaboration and easing internal communication problems (O'Lear 1997; Zelwietro 1998). In particular, White (1999) argued that CMC use was facilitating the creation of a more connected movement, one within which individuals not affiliated to particular groups were able to take on greater roles

than previously. Activists would also be able to bypass traditional hierarchies, such as that of the mainstream media, to distribute their ideas to a
broader audience (Warf and Grimes 1997; Atton 2000).

These studies have a common emphasis on adducing international collaboration through CMC use, and many have identified CMC use as an
increasingly important component of political activism (see Doherty
1999a; Chesters 2000a; Redden 2001; Terranova 2001). However, few have
engaged in case-study in-depth examinations that might illuminate some
of the complexity of CMC use and, in particular, the implications of CMC
use for groups' capacity to enact environmental change through more
effective organisation, tactics and mobilisation.

Research in action

Research into the implications of CMC use has moved on from the initial
phase of optimistic euphoria versus dystopian paradox to the cynical (if
not necessarily pessimistic) works that highlight the specific constraints
and limitations of this technology. Many technologies have, with time,
been treated similarly, from the telegraph to the television. First there is
utopian excitement tinged with dystopian gloom, and then criticism and
complexity. While the study of technology and its relation to society have
received significant academic comment, the role of agency has been often
ignored – the basic questions of detail, of how and why people use technology to pursue their goals, and how this use leads them to transform
other aspects of their lives.

As technology develops and becomes more integrated with individuals'
daily lives, people are able to reflect more incisively upon it and move
beyond the utopian–dystopian discourse. Current literature is able to interrogate examples in exploring how CMC is actually used (as opposed to the
mere speculation and 'personal experience' that littered the early field of
internet studies) and what problems are involved. Yet much research stops
at that point and fails to examine how these constraints and opportunities
are *negotiated* and *embraced* by users. Furthermore, there is a lack of research
that considers how CMC is used within specific social contexts.

Such questions can be answered only through detailed empirical examination of the ways in which specific technologies are used by particular
population cohorts. It is only through such close examination that the dominant ways of interpreting technology use (traditionally juxtaposed
between utopic and dystopic discourse) can be challenged and the actual
complexities, viewing technological change as a *social process* and CMC as a
media which is constructed through use, be brought to light (Edwards 1995).

Environmentalists' use of CMC is influenced by a host of circumstances, including their attitude towards technology, their chosen ideology, group dynamics, skills, perception of surveillance, their experience of opponents' counter-strategies and their ability to innovate tactics. All these components need to be examined in any consideration of their use of CMC as they all intertwine to produce the *outcome* seen as the surface of the environmental movement – the resulting demonstrations and actions, the media stories of 'riots of cyberspace' or a government's moves to increase surveillance of insurgent use of CMC. The ways in which environmentalists negotiate around the constraints they are faced with, and perhaps their failure to address some adequately, are crucial in facilitating an insightful understanding of how CMC is used *and* shaped by political activists.

There are several approaches that can be taken to researching CMC use: in-depth interviews, the observation of technology use and participation through online interaction (Kendall 1999). Observation of online interaction through email discussion lists or attempts to reach the online audience of websites, as well as general integration with online activities and regular observation of websites, are essential to an understanding of CMC use (Mitra and Cohen 1999). At the same time these methods alone provide little data with which to place CMC use into the wider background of an individual's activities. Only through in-depth interviews or observation of the actual interface between activists and their computers can all influences on their use be examined adequately. Moreover, to examine the nexus of inter-relations between environmentalists and CMC a case-study approach is the most appropriate because it enables consideration of all the factors that may influence people's use of the technology, including a group's organisational structure, facilities and available skills.

This book is based on analyses of a number of case studies, encompassing a variety of British groups and environmental campaigns, and on an examination of the differences between (and within) groups' uses of CMC and a consideration of the reasons for those differences. To enable this, groups were selected which employed dissimilar organisational structures, were composed of discordant population cohorts, worked at differing scales (local to international), had alternative political aims and were at contrasting stages of CMC implementation. Thus there was an empirical emphasis on multifarious types of environmental body (such as direct-action groups, formal political lobbying organisations and student activists). In order to ensure that a broad perspective of CMC use was attained (and any significant practices not ignored) contact was also made with individuals who were not associated with the case studies.

'Environmental activist' is defined quite broadly in this book. The term represents far more than the limited stereotype which denotes short-term physical action. Rather an 'activist' is one who takes any form of action, ranging from direct physical acts to minute lifestyle adjustments, and also

includes simply voicing concern or opinions through letter writing or discussion (via an email discussion group, for example) (Norris 2002). As
Maxey (1999: 199) suggests, 'activism is not something that can be clearly
bounded, marked as separate from everyday life'.

Research often raises ethical concerns (Katz 1994). The imbalance of
power that sometimes occurs between researcher and researched can
produce in those taking part in a study feelings of a lack of control over how
information about them is acquired, used and distributed. To address that
imbalance information in this study was acquired through the author's
direct participation in both case-study interviews and the environmental
movement itself, and the results carefully disseminated (as recommended
by Opie 1992 and Kobayashi 1994). Although social studies academics hold
a specific position in the field, empathy, membership and participation in
the processes being researched can complicate that position by blurring
divisions between the researcher and those being researched. Furthermore,
involvement in environmental activism was substantially a consequence of
undertaking the research, which meant that as a researcher I had to deal
with the 'politics of integration' (Fuller 1999). This enabled access to many
who otherwise were not interested in talking to academics and facilitated a
prolonged engagement with most of the case-study groups (cf. Maxey
1999). Without this process of integration access to several crucial components of the data-set would not, perhaps, have been possible and the
research would, as a result, have been less comprehensive. Consequently
this book is written not from within the movement, but from a level of
involvement in some aspects of environmental activism.

Seven case studies were chosen because each represented a distinct style
of organisation, its campaign defined by organisational aims, capacity and
funding. The organisations were: Friends of the Earth (FoE) UK; the Centre
for Alternative Technology (CAT); Green Student Network (GSN);
McSpotlight; *SchNEWS*; Save Westwood, Lyminge Forest campaign; and
the Mobile Office (MO). They were, respectively: an international NGO; an
environmental centre; an email-based network; a campaign structured
specifically around the internet; a weekly environmental and social justice
newsletter; an on-site autonomous protest; and an office in a van which has
worked on several protest camps. A balance was sought between case
studies which were significant (in size or notoriety) and those which represented differing aspects of the environmental movement. Thus this
selection combines well-known cornerstones of the British environmental
movement (such as FoE and CAT) with those of more transient notoriety
(such as McSpotlight) and with such lesser-known groups as GSN, MO
and the Save Westwood, Lyminge Forest campaign. Essentially, despite the
inclusion of FoE and CAT, most of these groups are concerned with radical
political change as opposed to reformist demands.

The rapidly changing nature of the technology dictated that the research was situated within a specific time-frame; thus a snapshot was taken of CMC use between June 1997 and June 1999, and this is the time period referred to throughout the book. Participation was possible with some case studies, while with others access was restricted to individual interviews. The informal in-depth interview was chosen as the cornerstone of the research as this format provided an environment where the interviewee could speak freely about and around the topic of CMC use.[2] Overall 80 interviews were conducted[3] (65 within case studies, 15 others[4]). For each case study between 3 and 14 interviews were conducted with individual members or staff[5]. One of the aims of the book was to enable activists' voices to be heard and for them to speak for themselves about the value of CMC and the challenges its use poses. Thus, their statements are relied upon to provide an understanding of their experiences as direct participants in the social processes of CMC use.

It was found appropriate to contact also corporate and governmental bodies, often the adversaries of environmentalists, to ascertain their response to activists' use of CMC – often to target their own companies and organisations. The aim was to incorporate a broad range of the targets of the case studies. Thirteen companies and three governmental agencies were contacted via post, email or phone. Governmental responses to environmental activists' use of CMC were ascertained through interviews with the Environment Agency, Kent County Council and correspondence with the Metropolitan Police. Corporate stances were restricted to four email responses to the formal letter requesting their opinions, and two interviews with Shell and Nestlé. Other corporate bodies declined to be involved in the research.

To set the context for the case-study groups and their participants, they are introduced here. A brief outline of their online operations also aids understanding of their detailed CMC use, discussed in later chapters.

Centre for Alternative Technology

CAT is an international environmental visitor centre near Machynlleth, Wales. The aim of the centre is to 'inspire, inform and enable society to move towards a sustainable future' (CAT 1997a). CAT attempts to achieve this by educating, experimenting and through living example. In particular CAT demonstrates that it is possible to live using renewable forms of energy generated by water, wind and sun, and the majority of the power on site is derived from those sources (CAT 1997b). The site contains a number of visitor attractions, such as the water-powered cliff railway, organic gardens, displays illustrating wave, solar and wind power, self-build houses and compost toilets.

CAT's website (www.cat.org.uk) was first launched in 1995, and has been re-launched several times since. CAT utilises CMC to advertise the centre and encourage visitors. It also provides those unable to visit the centre with access to ideas about alternative technology (such as tip-sheets about using sustainable technologies). The website answers many of the most frequently asked questions about alternative technology, deflecting work away from the (sometimes overstretched) information centre. CAT has developed several innovative features on its website – a virtual tour, an online shopping service and the Alternative Technology Association Secret Garden. The website has been constructed and influenced by a number of people at CAT, but it owes much to Martin Donnelly, a long-term volunteer. The construction and maintenance of CAT's website has been achieved without external funding, relying instead on the use of free servers, initially by courtesy of FoE, and then IIP (a multimedia company in Swansea), and the work on the site is performed for free by volunteers (Anon, 1998a). Access to email and the internet has been somewhat sporadic at CAT. Each department has organised its own access and consequently many have used different ISPs, accessing them via their personal modems. A lack of resources meant that not all staff have had internet access at work and CAT did not have an intranet.

Friends of the Earth UK

FoE UK is one of the biggest and most influential of the UK's NGO environmental groups (Rawcliffe 1998). Although FoE's perspective is rooted in the belief that radical political and social changes are required in order to avert further environmental destruction, its aims and tactics prevent it from being a radical environmental group (Lowe and Goyder 1983; McCormick 1995; Wapner 1995). FoE's aspiration to appear professional can conflict with its attempts to resist the forces of institutionalisation and maintain an element of informality (Rawcliffe 1998). FoE has had to respond to the tension between the centralising forces of UK politics and the decentralising demands of local activism by developing a regional structure comprised of elected regional board members, and eight regional offices (Maynard 1998). FoE's ability to adjust its tactical style rapidly has frequently caught adversaries by surprise. Though it supports the notion of direct action it rarely actively takes part (Schwarz 1994). Initially, FoE was a confrontational group willing to 'wage an all out war' (Blair 1971: 326) on those causing environmental degradation; now it is perceived as less confrontational and more inclined to use its discreet political influence.

FoE launched its website (www.foe.co.uk) and email system in December 1994, and claimed to be the 'first environmental campaigning organisation with a presence on the Internet' (Pipes 1996: 63). The website contains several hundred pages of information about campaigns and publications, press releases and how to join. FoE employed a full-time web producer to co-ordinate the website and another to co-ordinate the intranet.

Green Student Network[6]

GSN was a network of students in British universities who were interested in environmental issues. Its purpose was to exchange information and co-ordinate campaigns. The email network for GSN was set up 1992 and the website (no longer available) was established in 1995. It contained information about the purpose and structure of GSN, summaries of past gatherings, copies of newsletters and details of how to join the email discussion list. Its email list appears to be the only aspect of GSN that remained functional into the new millennium. The number of participants has varied from 120 in 1995 to 119 in January 1998, dropping to only 67 in January 2000. Its function also changed from being an email discussion group to being more information based, with many of the users complaining that GSN was not a particularly dynamic list in terms of its discussions.

CMC appears to be vital to GSN's survival, as it is the main avenue through which its participants communicate. GSN is not a cohesive group (by late 1999 it was little more than a discussion list with a fluid membership), and the network amounts to a collection of individuals involved in a variety of projects, groups and campaigns who may have nothing in common other than that they subscribe to the same email discussion list. Thus, rather than examine GSN as a group with collective aims, ideals and policy, the network is probed as to why and how these individuals are part of the network, and why and in what ways they use CMC for it and their other activities. Unlike many of the other case studies (where there is a common goal or project), GSN acts as a locus where individuals with a diversity of views and aims can interact and discuss environmental activism.

Save Westwood

Protesters occupied Westwood, Lyminge Forest, in east Kent, in March 1997 to prevent its sale to Rank for a holiday complex development. The activists' occupation was in support of the local community action group which had opposed the sale of the wood for several years. Opponents to the development objected to the potential scale of environmental damage, loss of important wildlife, noise and light disturbance, and increased air pollution in the area (Greensword 1997; Parsons 1997). By the end of 1999 most protesters had left the forest and were claiming victory as Rank's planning permission expired.

The campaign has had several websites and there have been eviction alerts and requests for support sent out over a number of email networks.

Only one of these sites (http://westwood.enviroweb.org) was under the direct control of the on-site protesters, and it had information about why the development needed to be prevented, the local environment, how the reader could help, a wish list, a map, details of Rank's plans, a discussion of sustainability, use of alternative energy sources and the practice of permaculture, a links page, a contacts page and a form to complete and send to their chairman in protest. Within this protest only a few individuals actually had access to CMC, and so had influence on the website. CMC was used to provide information to other activists and supportive individuals in order to encourage them to visit the forest in person, give their support and to generate interest at national and international levels.

McSpotlight

McSpotlight's website (www.mcspotlight.org) was launched on 16 February 1996 in support of the McLibel defendants who were being sued by McDonalds for allegedly distributing libelous material (Mills 1997). McSpotlight was just one aspect of a varied strategy co-ordinated by the McLibel Support Campaign. This campaign was initiated in 1990 (after writs had been served by McDonalds) and included mass leafleting, media focus, pickets outside McDonalds' stores and international days of action, with links to residents' opposition groups and disgruntled McDonalds' workers. The website posted up the original leaflet, alleged by McDonalds to be libelous, and maintained extensive coverage of the three-year-long trial.

The site quickly gained notoriety internationally and received a huge number of hits, was often referred to in internet magazines as an example of a high quality activist site, and earned significant mainstream media attention, which raised the profile of the McLibel trial. The anti-McDonalds campaign had been in existence for ten years in the UK prior to the website, and means other than CMC had been used to distribute the information (such as a paper-based mailing list). However, the website, and the media attention it received, prevented McDonalds from silencing its critics, raised the profile of the McLibel case and illustrated the potential of CMC for activist campaigning. Such publication was technically breaking British law, but as the site was hosted in the Netherlands the legal situation was unclear, providing a loophole which McSpotlight utilised.

The Mobile Office

The MO was set up by activists after the A30 protests at Fairmile, Fort Trollheim and Allercombe, Devon, early in 1997. It actually was a mobile office: a collection of equipment which fitted into a van which moved between protest camps where it could be stationed on site (eradicating the need for protesters to travel to the nearest telephone). It offered use of a computer with internet access, printer, digital camera and photocopier, TV and video, telephone, citizen band (CB) transmitters, and acted as a press office and a resource base. It was used in several direct-action site occupations – such as during the anti-quarrying action at Teigngrace, Devon, in August 1997 and in the campaign to save fifty-six poplar trees in Canbury Gardens, Kingston-upon-Thames, London, in March 1998.

MO had two laptops and one desktop computer. Internet access from the MO van was set up early in 1998 using a modem and a mobile telephone to connect the laptop. Email was then used directly from the office and the internet could be surfed (although mobile telephone costs were quite prohibitive), but the MO campaign websites were not updated from the van directly. HTML scripts were emailed to another activist who uploaded the new pages to the website. The internet was used by the MO as an information provider, and email to receive digital versions of activists' newsletters, as well as to keep in contact with other activists (nationally and internationally) and the 'mainstream'[7]. CMC was also used to send press-release faxes digitally (including using photographs from a digital camera) and to act as an additional medium through which the MO could publish and distribute its flyers and information. MO's activities appeared to diminish after 2000.

SchNEWS

SchNEWS is a weekly newsletter which appears every Friday and is produced by Justice?, a direct-action collective based in Brighton. It is 'a scrappy bit of A4 with a no advertising – no compromise policy' (Anon 1999a), which began by covering the Criminal Justice Act in 1994 and covers a range of environmental and social justice issues. *SchNEWS* typically consists of a cover story about a particular event or a report of a political item, shorter stories, a round-up of weekly news, forthcoming events and the 'crap' arrest of the week. Its coverage extends from the local (Brighton and south-east England) to the national and international arenas. In November 1999 there were 500 subscribers to the paper copy, and 2,000 copies were distributed to various places around Brighton, but up to as many as 4,000 copies are printed each week (Anon 1999a).

SchNEWS began using CMC in 1996, by launching a basic website and email. The website (www.schnews.org.uk) was re-designed and re-launched in 1998. *SchNEWS* used internet and email to ease and widen its distribution network, as a space for additional material and links, and to source stories (especially on international issues). Thus *SchNEWS* uses CMC to help prepare the document itself, to distribute it and to archive it. In April 1998, 500 people were subscribed to the email service of *SchNEWS*; by the end of 1999 this had grown to 3,000. The *SchNEWS* website has five sections: the latest *SchNEWS*, additional articles, archive, past copies of *SchNEWS*, a diary of forthcoming events, and a contacts database.

Mapping the implications of internet activism

Environmentalists' activities online provide an opportunity to examine the way in which social movement actors can utilise new technologies. Environmentalists are engaged in a struggle over cyberspace, a practical resistance to any corporate domination of CMC to ensure that the technology can be used to their advantage. This struggle is a reflection of the wider discord surrounding the use of new technologies and represents a microcosm of the broader debates about the future of technopolitics and society. The ways in which environmental activists overcome the barriers and utilise the communication opportunities afforded by the technology (such as reduced costs of communication, increased speed of interaction, mobilisation possibilities and anonymity, to name but a few) illustrate the complex uses to which cyberspace is put as a site (and form) of resistance.

Chapter 1 outlines a theoretical framework by which activists' use of CMC can be explored. By delineating what constitutes the politics of cyberspace and alternative approaches to the study of political activism, social movement perspectives are highlighted as a productive framework. Several implications of this framework for activists' use of CMC are proposed; the rest of the book is structured around an analysis of these implications. Each chapter explores one of the five broad themes: the paradox of technology use; access; mobilisation; tactics; and surveillance.

First, despite a recognition of the tensions between technology and environmentalists, their labelling as Luddites, and work on why other groups have shunned CMC use, there has been little consideration of how environmentalists have used CMC while retaining their critical stance on the use of advanced technology. This tension appears to arise out of a contradiction between environmentalists' ideologies and their actual practice. The ways in which this tension has been resolved are crucial to understanding the environmentalists' use of CMC. Thus, chapter 2 explores the ways in which environmental activists view and navigate this paradox, and the consequences of this negotiation for techno-environmentalism.

Second, extent of access is of integral importance to any consideration of CMC use, as with minimal access not only is its use restricted but its influence upon others is curtailed. There has been a general push within British society to increase access to CMC (Wills 1999). This has included the increase of public access points at libraries and cafés, and provision at schools, colleges and places of work. There remain, however, stark differences in access determined by locality, age, income, gender and social class

(Jordan 1999a; Walch 1999). Access to CMC is particularly important to environmentalists who espouse the increased provision of information and the participation of all individuals in decision making. Thus, chapter 3 examines how environmentalists' attitudes to inclusion are translated into their use of CMC and explores the ways in which they have secured access to CMC, the problems they have encountered and how they have tackled them. The effects of organisational form on CMC use, and the effects of CMC on organisational forms are also considered.

Third, the use of CMC in mobilising participation could fundamentally alter environmentalists' capacity to protest. As CMC enables an international audience to be reached, at relatively low cost and at speed, activists can co-ordinate world-wide protests or share ideas and solutions with international activists. Chapter 4 examines the use of CMC to mobilise participation in, and facilitate the networking of, environmental activists. This includes an examination of the impediments of using CMC for mobilisation and networking – such as the prerequisite of access, the problems of dealing with a diffuse audience, the poverty of online engagements and the privileging of word of mouth as the most valued form of communication.

Fourth, despite the tensions involved, the access limitations and threats from surveillance and regulation, CMC use by environmentalists still holds much potential for extending the repertoire of action. Despite significant work on action repertoires and, separately, on cyberactivism, there has been little consideration of CMC's influence on repertoires of action. Furthermore, CMC use could irrevocably alter the ways in which alternative media are produced and disseminated. Chapter 5 explores ways in which environmentalists could extend their use of the technology to developing CMC as a tool of protest. This includes substituting CMC use for a reliance on mainstream media and employing CMC in the production of a digital alternative media.

Finally, environmentalists, especially those who undertake radical direct action, have at times had an acrimonious relationship with the state and with corporate adversaries (Rowell 1996; Beder 1997). The examination of how environmentalists perceive and react to the threat of surveillance using CMC is important as it poses a significant potential restriction on environmentalists' use of CMC. Chapter 6 examines environmental activists' understandings of, and reactions to, online surveillance and counter-strategy and the implications of these threats for perceptions of CMC as a space for activism. The chapter also documents the responses of the State and of corporate bodies to environmentalists' CMC use.

This book employs an ethnographical focus to enable the voices and the views of activists to be heard.[8] It attempts to interrogate the quandaries and implications of environmentalists' use of CMC, and therefore involves an examination of many of the key issues of activism, such as participation, hierarchies and forms of organisation, tactics and opponents' responses. The contribution of CMC to all of these might also help to resolve existing problems and illuminate continuing areas of tension. This book aims to contribute to the understanding of environmental movements as heterogeneous, influential and innovative, as well as to the continuing debates about the value and challenges of internet activism.

Notes

1 The preferred term for internet-based technologies is computer-mediated communication (CMC). Other terms with a similar meaning include information communication technologies (ICTs), new communication technologies (NCTs) and network technologies. ICT is often used to refer to internet technologies, but encompasses a wider variety of technologies than CMC, covering as it does the more general fusion of telecommunications and computing technology.
2 Surveys were also used to gather supplementary information. A questionnaire was attached to the Save Westwood, Lyminge Forest, website to gain an indication of its readership. Over the seventeen-month period that it was online forty three responses were received. An email questionnaire was sent out to the GSN to contact potential interviewees and to gain a sense of views across the group; there was a 22 per cent response rate.
3 Names have been given as requested by the interviewees – thus those at FoE and CAT suggested use of full names, while others used just their first name or pseudonym. Unless otherwise indicated an interviewee was a participant in the case study rather than holding a formal position of responsibility. Although interviewees undertook particular roles, few categorised or delineated their positions and preferred for all participants to be viewed as equal.
4 These individuals tended to be affiliated to some sort of environmental group. Often they had multiple affiliations; sometimes they were only tenuously involved in a group. These groups included Cornerstone Co-operative, Earth First!, Hunt Saboteurs' Association, Newcastle Green Festival, North-East Green Party, Peace Action, Reclaim the Streets, (S)hell, Squall and Urban75, details of which are given as such individuals are referred to in the text.
5 Recruitment occurred until it was either perceived that a significant number of voices had been represented and redundancy (in terms of a lack of new themes) was occurring, or that the key players in each group had been interviewed and no further access to individuals was possible.
6 In 1998 GSN officially merged with SEA (Students for Environmental Action) to produce SEN (Student Environmental Network), though the email list maintains the original GSN name and few other changes appear to have occurred.
7 It was unclear whether participants were referring to the mainstream media only, or more broadly to the 'mainstream' of society.
8 Throughout the text interviewees' statements are quoted to enforce a point – though these quotations are representative rather than a cohesive picture of all that was said.

1

Politics, social movements and technology

According to Resnick (1998), the politics of cyberspace can be conceptualised in three distinct ways: *politics within cyberspace* – involving the internal operation of cyberspace and those who are online; *politics which impacts upon cyberspace* – the policies and legislation which affect cyberspace; and *political uses of cyberspace* – how the technology is used to affect political life offline. All three aspects need to be taken into consideration for they are all intertwined and all of them impact upon environmentalists' use of the technology.[1]

As Froehling (1997: 293) notes, cyberspace alters the nature of all politics: 'Its very existence changes human relations inside and outside the internet through the flow of information, whether people worldwide are directly connected or not.' Consequently, analysis needs to go beyond studying only those who are online (cf. Hill and Hughes 1998) and to include a broad examination of all the influences upon, as well as those of, the politics of cyberspace. The use of CMC might contribute to the formation of new forms and processes of politics, or cyberspace itself may become normalised, its politics merely reflecting offline politics. It is noteworthy that the importance of online interactions are examined for their offline implications because environmentalists are rooted in a concern for that which is offline – the earth. Moreover, it is in this interaction that the greatest potential of CMC lies.

In order to examine the political components identified by Resnick, and thus the different influences upon activists' use of CMC, a broad understanding of the processes of, and the pressures upon, environmental activism is required. In particular this approach needs to be applicable specifically to the British environmentalist scene. Social movement perspectives provide a framework which usefully informs and shapes such analysis, and the justification for such a choice is explored later in the chapter.

Furthermore, the implications of technological change are not predeter-
mined. Technology is of our own making and the use to which we put it a
result of social (and, to some extent, political) processes. Based on this
understanding of technology, the political uses of CMC can be more accurately explored than if a less constructionist approach was adopted. This
perspective and its implications also are explored in relation to other
approaches later in the chapter.

Using these understandings of activist and technological processes in
combination with existing research on internet activism makes possible a
number of assertions about the likely implications of CMC use for environmentalists. These claims are used to shape the analyses conducted
throughout the book, with theoretical suggestions being supported by the
empirical evidence in particular chapters. Thus, the first concern of this
chapter is to outline the most suitable theoretical framework for the analysis of environmentalists' activities and to establish a coherent understanding of technological change. These theoretical underpinnings are
then used for the second aim of the chapter – to identify possible implications of CMC use for environmental activists.

Understanding political activism

Social movement theories explain the formation, nature and workings of
social movements, and explore the how and the why of their actions and
their impact upon civil society. A social movement is more than just an
interest group and will be comprised of more than a single organisation: it
incorporates a whole range of networks into a specific social dynamic.
Until recently, the pressure- (or interest-) group perspective was dominant
in analyses of environmental movements (Rüdig, Mitchell, Chapman and
Lowe 1991). This approach categorised environmental groups' role as the
application of pressure on the political system and it measured their
success by the extent of their inclusion within the formal political structure
(Grant 1989; Baggott 1995). However, this approach focuses on the relationship between groups and the formal political system. It is therefore less
able to examine the relevance of the 'subterranean networks' (Melucci
1989: 41) of environmental activists which can motivate and give meaning
to individuals' political activism.

Then, in the 1990s, the do-it-yourself culture perspective emerged. The
term 'DiY Culture' was coined to represent an approach which examines
the ways in which politics merges with culture to produce a counter-
culture: 'DiY Culture, a youth-centred and -directed cluster of interests and
practices around green radicalism, direct action politics, new musical
sounds and experiences, is a kind of 1990s' counterculture' (McKay 1998: 2).

The rise of innovative forms of activism (illustrated by the tactical inventiveness of tree-sits, lock-ons, etc., utilised during anti-roads protests), coupled with a plethora of alternative lifestyles, led some commentators to argue that a DiY Culture had emerged. This counter-culture was typified by disillusionment with traditional politics and a preference for alternative forms of participation and direct democracy (McKay 1998). Although the DiY Culture perspective does incorporate these wider influences upon environmental activism, it is little more than a broad descriptive category that offers no framework for further analysis of the operation of environmental politics. Furthermore, its emphasis upon youth and radicalism provides for only partial consideration of other participants in environmentalism.

Of these three approaches, social movement perspectives, such as those advanced by Melucci (1994, 1996), Castells (1996), Tarrow (1998a), and Della Porta and Diani (1999), enable a greater depth of analysis of the actions of diverse social movement participants. They facilitate consideration of all the components (and their related aims) of the environmental scene, from those involved in 'counter-culture', to NGOs which aim to have their views represented in government policy. All levels of action (personal, cultural and political) need to be examined in order to understand fully the processes that yield the tangible products of social movements in, for example, non-violent direct action, protest events or political lobbying. Many of these functions remain hidden to other approaches, but they are vital for a full understanding of political activist processes. Furthermore, social movement theories provide concepts (analytical tools) through which detailed analyses of the implications of CMC are possible.

It is perhaps necessary at this stage to explore in a little more depth what is meant by the use of social movement perspectives and then to outline their applicability and usefulness to an understanding of British environmental activism. Among social movement theorists there is a broad division between examinations of 'old' social movements and the 'new' manifestations. Of the four main trends, three – the collective behaviour perspective, resource mobilisation theory (RMT), and the political process perspective – provide a framework for analysing different structural aspects of the 'old' social movements. The collective behaviour approach defines social movements as characterised by loose organisation with shifting and indefinite memberships rather than by 'organisational' and 'institutional' behaviour (Turner and Killian 1987). RMT places greater emphasis upon the role of resources and organisational factors in transforming a set of beliefs into collective action. In contrast, the political process perspective has focused upon the relationship of the emergent social movements to the established polity, and how actors attempt to gain access to political power-holders (Tilly 1978).

A fourth trend – the 'new social movements' (NSM) approach – contrasts with these earlier approaches by concentrating on the *why* rather than the *how* of collective action (Melucci 1989). Furthermore, NSMs are differentiated from old social movements because they appear no longer to be centred around the conflict over capitalism, between workers and employers, or conflict around existing political structures. Rather NSM theory tries to relate social movements to large-scale structural and cultural changes of the so-called 'information age' (Castells 1996). NSMs are concerned with adjusting the logic of the system. They want more than simply a reallocation of resources, more than mere political representation: they question the whole system and its codes, and propose new cultural codes in their place (Melucci 1994). In this sense, NSMs assert their ability to produce new meanings and new forms of social life, and aim to change societal values in a paradigmatic battle with the dominant model of society and existing concentrations of power. This 'systematic effect of making power visible is the characteristic function of social movements on societies increasingly based on information. Thus, the movements enable society to recognize and face the larger questions affecting human life in contemporary complex societies' (Melucci 2000: 98).

Although diverse social movements have emerged since the 1960s, of which many appear merely to request political incorporation rather than challenge the prevailing system, Melucci (1994) has convincingly illustrated that movements such as the women's, peace and ecological movements do fundamentally challenge the dominant logic of society. NSM theory emphasises the cultural sphere as an important area of conflict (which challenges the political process perspective's concentration on political movements). Increasingly, social movement analysts are focusing on the importance of the development of counter-cultures and self-transformation. In other words, increasing attention is being paid to the importance of personal needs and lifestyle choices in activism. For Chesters (2000a: 20), NSM theory

> stresses a need to analytically distinguish between the differing levels at which such protest actions are meaningful – personally, culturally and politically – and to articulate the processes which are often hidden from view, but which energise and facilitate protest events, such as the construction of a collective identity through everyday interactions, dialogue and shared activities.

Drawing on the assertions made by NSM theorists and on broader interpretations, a definition of what constitutes a social movement is sought through which CMC use can be examined. As the applicability of NSM theory to the British environmental movement is still under debate (see Wall 1999a), and because the approach has been criticised for being insufficient (Scott 1995; Lentin 1999), a broader understanding of the processes of political activism is required to prevent relevant aspects or processes being ignored.[2] Furthermore, the aim of this chapter is primarily to outline a useful framework through which to analyse the implications of technology use. To do this there needs to be a clear understanding and delineation of the structures and processes we are examining.

Diani (1992: 11) has proposed a useful synthesis of the different social movement perspectives to produce a general definition of what constitutes a social movement. He proposes that a social movement is a network of informal interactions between a plurality of individuals, groups and/or organisations, the boundaries of which are determined by the collective identity shared by those involved, whose 'actors are engaged in political and/or cultural conflicts, meant to promote or oppose social change either at the systematic or non-systemic level'. Diani also proposes that social movement action occurs within and outside the institutional sphere (cf. Doyle and McEachern 1998).

What is especially useful about this definition is that Diani is careful to exclude neither the earlier approaches to the study of social movements nor the possibility that groups may seek inclusion into political structures at the systematic level while simultaneously critiquing the dominant logic of society. This definition is also constructive in enabling the analysis of both institutional bodies and loose structures of organisation that are present concurrently in many political movements. For analysis of the implications of technology use this is a vital inclusion as part of the aim of this book is to compare CMC use between differing organisational forms that are likely to have different resources available with which to employ the technology. Such a broad definition also incorporates the three conceptualisations of the politics of cyberspace advanced by Resnick (1998) by including a wide variety of organisational forms. This definition then will be used to shape the choice of processes to be explored in detail for the implications of CMC use.

Using this definition and drawing upon many of the NSM theory assertions, the British environmental scene can best be conceptualised as a social movement. It has a tendency towards informal participatory democratic modes of organisation, a fluid structure of networks and a mix of non-institutional and institutional politics. Combined with its counter-hegemonic aim towards changing societal values, it fits within the definitions of a social movement proposed by Diani and many other theorists.

Social movement analysis is being increasingly applied to the British environmental movement. Wall (1999a) utilised many of its concepts in his examination of Earth First!, and Chesters (2000a) has argued that NSM theory is the most appropriate way to probe the underlying processes of radical environmentalism. The British environmental scene is vigorous and vibrant, yet also diverse and composed of disparate factions (Bosso

1991; Merchant 1992). It incorporates a range of groups from the large established NGOs to smaller non-hierarchical groups or local interest groups. These groups differ not only in their organisational structure and resources, but also in their aims. There is a broad dichotomy between 'reformists' – who accept the present system and parliamentary democracy – and 'radicals' – who want fundamental change (Pepper 1996).

Rüdig and Lowe (1986) have argued that there is an absence of a strong radical ecological movement in Britain. Furthermore, Rüdig, Mitchell, Chapman and Lowe (1991: 139) argue that

> the chances for any new social movements to emerge as an independent entity are thus very slim. Where such movements emerge and refuse any association with the interests dominating British society, they remain marginalised. More frequently, grievances which do not find a 'respectable' expression, in terms of an integrated interest group, appear to find their expression in unorganised, spontaneous collective actions such as inner-city riots or football hooliganism.

Events in the 1990s, however, illustrate the inaccuracy of such an assertion. Many components of the radical British environmental scene have managed to remain non-partisan, to resist integration; and yet they still trigger significant changes in environmental attitudes and policy. Large-scale actions such as the J18 demonstrations in London were more than 'unorganised, spontaneous collective actions': they were acts of very 'organised spontaneity' (Scott and Street 2001), which were well co-ordinated and had a clear political message.

Since the early 1990s there has been an increase in non-violent direct action (NVDA) protest – such as the occupation of development sites and large-scale urban street protests (Doherty 1999a). Although neither the size of these specific groups nor their particular undertakings are representative of the views of the majority of the population, their actions have been acknowledged by governments and by their adversaries, and they have generated influence disproportionate to their size. Furthermore, their use of NVDA has influenced the more established groups. Although the more established NGOs, such as FoE and Greenpeace, began as radical groups in the 1970s, they had entered a process of increasing professionalism and institutionalism by the 1990s. The rise of new groups like Earth First!, Reclaim the Streets and many smaller local groups has challenged the existing NGOs' position, and has triggered some, for example FoE, into supporting and undertaking NVDA once again (Lamb 1996). The dismissal by Rüdig, Mitchell, Chapman and Lowe (1991) of the possibility of the emergence of a radical environmental movement further ignores the fact that radical direct action groups have no intention of getting *inside* political process or of developing into pressure groups (Grant 1989). Nor do they appear to be threatened by marginalisation, a threat which can trigger the adoption of extreme terrorist tactics (Della Porta and Diani 1999).

In general, the British environmental movement is well publicised, has mobilised significant resources and draws support from a wide population cohort which includes people from diverse social locations. In terms of exerting political influence (resulting in the enactment of environmental laws such as the Wildlife Act), capturing mainstream media attention, increasing membership of large NGOs, and having a significant and well-known profile, the British environmental movement has been highly successful.

Thus the composition of this environmental movement can be delineated as the sum of all the different structural forms that exist within the environmental scene: the individual, the network, the informal group and the formal organisation (Doyle and Kellow 1995). Many of the individuals involved in networks or informal groups (Earth First!, for example) abstain from electoral politics and instead promote DiY politics, normally through direct action (Doherty 1997). This kind of DiY politics is seen as informal, participatory, all-inclusive, non-hierarchical and a challenge to the dominant political order. In contrast, organisations tend to be more formalised and are involved in both the politics of non-institutional social movements and the institutional politics of government. They are often classed as NGOs – permanent and well defined by a constitution (Byrne 1997). They are by and large autonomous from government and operate at local, regional, national and transnational[3] levels (Charlton, May and Cleobury 1995; Willetts 1996). Princen and Finger (1994) and Jordan and Maloney (1997) class NGOs, such as FoE, as separate from social movements as they do not practise participatory democracy. As will be shown in chapter 3, where the issue is explored in greater depth, FoE UK does not use participatory principles in its operations as much as some of the more radical groups; however, it has rooted its philosophy in the importance of participation. Furthermore, in Britain the significant integration of NGOs within the movement – in terms of communication between differing environmental groups and co-ordination of joint campaigns between NGOs such as FoE and radical direct action groups – demands their inclusion in an analysis of the operations of that movement (Doherty 1996). However, NGOs are included only as one component of the much larger network of diverse groups and individuals which constitute a *movement*, as outlined above.

Interpreting technology

Any examination of CMC use by activists requires not only an understanding of the processes of political activism but a framework through which technological change can be conceptualised. As was said earlier, technology is of our own making and its use a result of social processes. Technology is socially constructed: designed, built and implemented by us. It involves the construction of knowledge and organisation surrounding its implementation. Thus it is important when examining uses of technology to include all aspects of their social organisation and cultural value:

> '[T]echnology' does not just refer to the physical form, the pieces of metal, the electronic components, the chemical compound. Technology refers to the way in which the parts are organised, through the application of knowledge, to realise their particular purpose . . . it is also a set of decisions about how that technology ought to work. (Street 1992: 8–9)

Returning to Resnick's 1998 elucidation of the three concepts of the politics of cyberspace, there have been important debates about the implications of CMC for society which have dealt with the politics within cyberspace, political impacts upon cyberspace and political uses of cyberspace. Much of the analysis of these has fallen into the utopian–dystopian dichotomy. Utopian writings seek to suggest that technology will solve almost all of society's problems – ethical, economic or political (Graham and Marvin 1996). Utopian visionists, such as Rheingold (1994) and Mitchell (1996), paint a picture of cyberspace as a communitarian haven of equality and decentralised community organising. In contrast dystopian theorists often predict negative consequences of technology use (cf. Boyle 1997). Both these visions are futuristic, simplistic and a form of 'myth-information' (Winner 1988). They fail to examine the complexities of technology use, are rarely grounded in empirical evidence and thus seem somewhat optimistic. These debates, however, are useful in that they highlight issues (and possibilities) that might be of relevance to environmentalists – such as the possibility of online communities (within cyberspace) or the threat of surveillance (political impacts upon cyberspace).

Much of the utopian and dystopian hyperbole surrounding the use of CMC casts the technologies as socially and politically determinative (Friis 1996). Technology is seen as an autonomous agent of change, its inherent capabilities causing things to happen independently in an inevitable unidirectional process that can be projected (Marx and Roe Smith 1994; Mackay 1995). In this vein, CMC is predicted to directly bring about fundamental changes in society, changes to which society can only react, but which it cannot alter (Grint and Woolgar 1997).

Conversely, social constructivists argue that 'technology does not spring, *ab initio*, from some disinterested font of innovation. Rather it is born of the social, economic, and technical relations that are already in place' (Bijker and Law 1992). This is supported by evidence that the same technologies have produced alternative outcomes when used in different situations. Technology becomes appropriated and reinterpreted by its users – and their use of it is not always as foreseen by its designers and developers (Feenberg 1999). Thus social constructivists examine the micro-level social processes which shape cyberspace. Deterministic assumptions are challenged by an awareness that technology is not a discrete artefact which operates externally to *impact upon* social relations, and through a methodology which seeks to explore the complexity and two-way relationship between technology and the user. The social relations which construct the use of a technology can be studied via an in-depth empirical examination of the way in which CMC is viewed and used by different groups of individuals.

A danger of such an approach, however, is that social constructivism overplays the importance of social agency and underplays the role of industry and science in technological developments (Escobar 1994). This can to some extent be resolved by a consideration of some aspects of technological development as advocated by political economists. Their perspective suggests that technology is inextricably tied into capitalist modes of production and the associated societal relations of capitalism. Thus, CMC will serve to reproduce the political and social relations of capitalism (Graham and Marvin 1996). This is a view held also by some environmental activists, as will be discussed further in chapter 2. For example, the production of computer systems by large companies like Microsoft would influence the ways in which environmentalists could make use of the technology.

On its own this approach ignores the possibility of a subversive use of CMC by, for example, environmental activists, to curtail the prevailing model of capitalism. However, such considerations should be combined with a social constructivist approach to produce a more comprehensive understanding of the influences at work upon technology construction and use. Inclusion of the importance of some aspects of technological development from the political economist perspective enables a clearer analysis of political impacts upon cyberspace, such as multinational ownership or government regulation of its uses.

Furthermore, the way in which CMC is constructed is liable to have a significant influence upon the way in which it can be controlled. Using an alternative interpretation of 'code' to that of Melucci (who explored the dominant code of society), Lessig (1999a) has explored how the architecture of CMC is rooted in code in examining how CMC is structured and consequently is controllable. Thus Lessig claims that governments and business interests could easily legislate and regulate CMC by controlling the code that is written. Until recently, with the emphasis upon simplistic utopian or dystopian analysis, the complexity of what this might mean has been ignored. However, activists are beginning to move beyond simply thinking of the technology as a tool to be used with hardware they could own, to taking control of the code too. The proliferation of open source

software (and activist websites based on open code) challenges governments' ability to regulate such CMC use (see also Castells 2001; Levy 2001).

The structure of cyberspace has been likened to that of a rhizome
(Escobar 1994; Wark 1994; Froehling 1997). While this concept does not
provide a comprehensive framework with which to examine the implications of technology for society, it can be used to help understand the organisational structure of CMC and consequently how groups using CMC are
able to interrelate. Deleuze and Guattari (1987) have used the concept to
develop an alternative way of viewing space. Its form has no definite
beginning or end, and grows in all directions (Shurmer-Smith and
Hannam 1994). A rhizome has no centre, no points or positions, just lines
and intersections, so that everything is fully interconnected and consequently non-hierarchical. Space is thus represented as smooth, open and
nomadic. Furthermore, a rhizome may be broken or shattered, but then 'it
will start up again on one of its old lines, or on new lines' (Deleuze and
Guattari 1987: 9).

This nomadic, interconnected, space of multiplicities can be used to
describe how political activists use CMC. Cleaver (1995) and Froehling
(1997) liken the way the Mexican Zapatistas (and their supporters) use
CMC to this understanding of the rhizome. Environmental activists' form
of organising using CMC could reflect this rhizomic structure – with no
core or root, but infinite connectibility and a resistance to connections
being broken or lost. If cyberspace reflects such rhizomic form, then its use
by political activists poses a distinct threat to their opponents. Furthermore, a rhizomic structure provides multiple entryways, facilitating
potential participants' entry into environmental activism through connection into their rhizomic online network. This interpretation of rhizomic
structures, however, tends to relate more to how technology is used rather
than aiding understandings of what technology is or how technology is
constructed through social agency.

Returning once more to Resnick's concepts, it is clear that any of these
theoretical approaches towards the study of technology taken alone is both
limited and limiting in understanding the three processes of the politics of
cyberspace. Each perspective is too narrow in its consideration of the
factors that influence our understandings of technology (Feenberg 1999).
To be able to adequately consider the influences upon CMC use, a combination of the social constructivist and political economist perspectives has
been employed throughout the book. This acknowledges that technology
is the result of an interplay between a variety of factors (Dosi 1982). While
environmental activists are able to socially construct their use of technology, the wider political system and its ownership by multinational companies also shape CMC.

In support of the use of a combined approach, Fischer (1985: 294) called for the use of more detailed empirical work which avoids 'sweeping meta-phors, assumptions of homogeneity and of linearity . . . the same technol-ogy may be used differently by different people in different ways to different effect'. As a result, this combination enables a sensitivity to the diverse processes which impact upon environmentalists' use of CMC, and is reflected throughout the book by an examination of the different factors that play on their technology utilisation.

This approach towards technology is combined with the use of social movement perspectives. Social movement theories frame the processes of collective action, providing a useful structure through which to examine the variety of factors that influence technology use. As each chapter explores an aspect of activism, the detail of the influences on CMC use can be examined – the situations that shape individual environmentalist's use of technology combined with the broader forces of governmental or multi-national activities.

CMC and the changing nature of political activism

Having outlined a framework with which to examine political activism and technology it is now possible to elaborate on the range of assertions about environmentalists' use of CMC which will be examined using empirical evidence in the rest of the book. There has been relatively little attempt to examine the implications of CMC use within social movement debates. This is surprising in view of the considerable literature on the forms of social movements, and the prognosis that such new forms of communication are likely to particularly affect groups involved in non-institutional politics (Melucci 1996; Castells 1997a, 2001; Tarrow 1998a). Diani (2001) has explored the implications of CMC use for mobilisation potential and Tarrow (1998b: 193–4) has identified an area of research but has yet to offer an answer:

> Is the new technology of global communication changing the forms of the diffusion of collective challenges or only the speed of their transmission? . . . we will need to follow some of the recent campaigns that have been assisted by electronic communication to find out whether it increases the movement's power or merely changes how it frames its message.

Castells (2001: 164) is one of the few who has begun to answer such a ques-tion. He asserts that the internet is indispensable to those social move-ments concerned with cultural values, organising in a non-hierarchically loose form, and for those wishing to retain their local roots and yet acting on a global level. In comparison to social movements' extensive and inno-vative uses of CMC, Castells also calls attention to the lack of interaction offered online by formal political parties. In general, he asserts, activists are able to benefit greatly from CMC use, despite cyberspace being a contested terrain: 'by relatively levelling the ground of symbolic manipulation, and by broadening the sources of communication, it does contribute to democratization'.

This book aims to continue this dialogue about social movements and their use of CMC. As previously defined, social movements contest and create cultural patterns in relation to the prevailing model of society. Communication is vital for this to take place – both within the social movement itself and outwards to other movements, political decision-makers, the media and the public. Accordingly, social movements historically have been concerned with access to, and use of, communication technologies, such as the printing press, television and radio, citizen-band transmitters–receivers, mobile phones, photography and video. In this context the use of CMC could be viewed as simply an additional form of communication technology. However, CMC is more than just an extension of existing media[4]: it has the potential to trigger fundamental changes in social movement processes. Indeed, Melucci (1996: 194) has suggested that the use of CMC could develop into a site of conflict:

> On the one hand, there can be observed a concentration of power, with very few core centres that control the world in terms of the world-wide transmission and distribution of ideas, languages, programmes, and the like; on the other hand, we can see emerging symptoms of resistance to this trend, manifest in, for example, the action of hackers, information pirates, self-managed networks, and so on.

Here Melucci is alluding to the use of CMC as a form of resistance to the those influencing the dominant logic of society – governments and large corporations. This resistance could take the form of self-organised communication networks campaigning for social change or hackers' disruption of the systems that their opponents rely upon. In effect the conflict would revolve around control of the means of communication, transmission and distribution.

Furthermore, Melucci's notion of the production of 'codes' (which come to represent the dominant logic of society) can be considered in terms of CMC. In a programmed/technocratic world, much of society revolves around the production of information and communication resources. Conflict arises around that production, and social movements form to challenge the apparatuses that govern the construction of information (principally by their opponents – the government and corporate interests) in order to reveal that the dominant system of meanings is not neutral but reflects vested interests and unequal forms of power. Thus social movements are seeking to 'recast the language and cultural codes that organise information' (Melucci 1994: 102). This is achieved through a number of channels, with some groups attempting to use mainstream media, while others prefer to project their message through alternative media and CMC. Codes are also culturally challenged by exemplifying alternative lifestyles and through visible protest. CMC potentially increases social movement participants' ability to communicate because it is low cost, enables editorial control and potentially offers access to an international audience.

In this respect then, even at the most basic level, advances and changes in the form of communication technology that are adopted by movement activists may well aid their capacity to form and project alternative codes to the wider public and their political adversaries. Whether their adversaries will benefit to the same extent from communication technology advances, and thus nullify any movement advances, will also be explored.

CMC use has the potential to impact upon many social movement activities, and its influence can be examined in detail by considering these processes and functions separately. Thus, CMC may alter the social movement processes of organisation operation and mobilisation, collective identity and the formation of solidarities, and the development of repertoires of action. Furthermore, CMC use may modify both the role of movement intellectuals and how public space is created for debate. Each of these aspects will now be examined in more detail and assertions made as to the possible implications of CMC use, which will be re-examined using empirical evidence in the chapters that follow.

Social movement organisations, networks and mobilisation

There tends to be heterogeneity and plurality in the forms of social movement organisation (SMO), a constant process of 'adopting, adapting, and inventing' (McCarthy 1996). SMOs tend to favour decentralisation, participatory democracy, internal solidarity and *ad hoc* short-lived leadership. Organisational models have been differentiated by Doyle and McEachern (1998) according to degree of organisation and distribution of power, and in the level of commitment required from participants. These potential differences have resulted in a panoply of organisational forms, such as: local nuclei; umbrella organisations; party models; public interest groups; movement associations; and supportive organisations.

Movement networks are often viewed as the cornerstone of any attempts at mobilisation (Oliver and Marwell 1992). Research to date has concluded that recruitment and mobilisation are reliant upon individuals' inclusion and integration within social movement networks (McAdam 1988; Wall 1999a). Usually that initial inclusion in social networks is reliant upon face-to-face interaction. It is not just the existence of a social tie which is important but the *type of link* and the intensity of the tie. The intensity of

social ties necessary to mobilise action increases proportionately with the
associated costs of the action (measured by the personal risks and personal
transformation required). Furthermore, a strong identification with the
cause, previous membership of political organisations or involvement in a
strong counter-culture are also necessary (McAdam and Paulsen 1993).
Jasper and Poulson (1995), however, have been able to show that
'strangers' can be recruited into collective activism in the absence of social
networks, through 'moral shocks'. Movements use both mechanisms for
recruitment – existing social networks and moral shocks.

CMC is likely to contribute to these forms of mobilisation in a number
of ways. CMC could serve as a useful technology through which to articulate moral shocks to a wider audience than previously possible, serving
as a new medium through which to frame activists' concerns. There
remains doubt, however, as to whether participation is likely to occur
without previous interaction (Wall 1999a). Diani (2001) has argued that the
usefulness of CMC in mobilising participation is dependent upon the
types of resource that organisations are attempting to mobilise. Those
mobilising professional resources (such as FoE) are expected to gain in
terms of efficiency of communication – but this is not likely to impact upon
identity building, as there is little need to mobilise for direct action.

For those mobilising participatory resources (such as direct action
groups), mobilisation is likely to remain reliant upon existing linkages.
Thus, Calhoun (1998: 383) argues that CMC may facilitate actors' participation through 'the maintenance of dispersed face-to-face networks', but
that these networks would have to pre-exist for meaningful virtual interaction to take place. In this way it is unlikely that purely virtual ties will
result in sustained collective action. However, virtual interaction has led
to formations of online 'communities', though the strength and depth of
many virtual community networks remains contested (Rheingold 1994;
Virnoche and Marx 1997). Critics have doubted the durability of social ties
created through virtual communication alone, and have described the relationships developed as 'thinner' than those within traditional communities (Fernback and Thompson 1995; Kolko and Reid 1998; Willson 2002).
Meikle (2002: 31) also distinguishes between different forms of interactivity possible via CMC, identifying conversational interactivity as the only
form likely to result in productive debate: 'Only with conversational interactivity do we get to the idea of a two-way communication flow, with both
partners producing and inputting their own information, and, often more
than this, working to create something.' Thus, online communication
needs to be examined with respect both to who is communicating and to
how they are communicating to determine the implications that CMC
might have for fostering ties strong enough for mobilisation.

Social movement organisations link to each other through both official consultation channels and through the multiple affiliations of their activists. CMC use is likely to improve the effectiveness of this communication in terms of increased speed, reduced costs, persistent accuracy of the original message, increased interaction between branches of organisations and the possibility of connecting a geographically dispersed set of individuals into a united aggrieved population (Myers 1994). It is to be doubted, however, that increased communication possibilities alone can overcome existing matters of contention between SMOs, as technology has rarely been shown to solve social issues (Kyrish 1994).

Use of CMC may also affect the 'strength' of movement networks in that communication becomes simultaneously both easier and more fragmented. Those who are connected are able to communicate with others who are connected more quickly, easily and cheaply than before. For those who are not, the use of CMC by other groups can actually begin to exclude them as they become left out of conversations, and communication with them without using CMC appears to become relatively harder. Although clandestine groups have long existed effectively within many social movements, CMC facilitates not only their anonymity but also their connections to other SMOs without revealing themselves. CMC use may increase communication between the different types of groups by providing yet another medium for communication.

Technological development is likely to change the form of organisations (Tilly 1978). CMC use offers speed in terms of response, information gathering, networking ability to groups and reduction of co-ordination costs, which in turn might alter their organisational capabilities. The utilisation of CMC may reduce the need for highly structured organisations, in that it is now possible for a 'lightweight' one to get a message across (Scott and Street 2001). Although the uses of CMC require some technical proficiency, they also afford more flexibility to groups which can benefit from the lack of editorial control. This once again reinforces the proposition, supported by Castells (2001), that CMC may facilitate the development of less rigid and formal organisational forms (and reduce the push towards professionalism), enable smaller groups to voice their views more successfully and perhaps trigger mobilisation. However, although in principle evolution towards institutionalisation may be challenged by the use of CMC, as Washbourne (1999a) argues, it is more likely that this process would have been challenged anyway by internal and external forces calling for greater accountability and democratisation.

Identity and solidarities

The creation and shaping of identities within social movements is said to be important in the successful mobilisation of collective action and to the maintenance of the movement through periods of inactivity (Johnston, Larana and Gusfield 1994; Castells 1997a). CMC could facilitate the building of collective identity and solidarity, by increasing the ability of individuals to communicate with like-minded activists in a form of *direct* communication, strengthening feelings of identity even across dispersed networks. However, whether virtual interactions have a capacity to formulate identities similar to those of face-to-face interactions is still under debate (Willson 2002). A key aspect may be a required level of mutual trust, which is essential for mobilisation purposes. The problem is how mutual trust is created through virtual interaction (Tarrow 1998b: 193). In interactions activists seek some form of validation of the individual or the group, for example, through word of mouth or through linkages from websites of which activists approve. This validation–approval of sources has also been sought in social movements from printed media and alternative media sources.

CMC use may also facilitate a cross-movement, cross-cultural, interaction and thus change an individual's view of their identity (McAdam and Rucht 1993). For example, they may move from being primarily concerned with local environmental issues, but through internet use begin to view themselves as political activists with wider concerns. Similarly, an environmental activist may begin to interact, through CMC, with computer hackers. As a result each could acquire new skills and develop new identities. Finally, CMC use may affect activists' identity as perceived by their opponents and critics as modern, non-luddite, pro-progress and innovative by using a technology with which many of the general public are not adept.

Repertoires of action

The 'repertoire of action' of a movement refers to the set of strategies, tactics or forms of protest which are employed by its participants. Repertoires of action are strongly influenced by historical traditions, the diffusion of ideas from other social movements or cultures, movement leaders' choices and political opportunity structures (Tarrow 1998b). A repertoire of action is also finite, limited by both time and space, such that techniques of protest evolve slowly, limited by tradition, adapted from previous forms, and this in turn might actually limit innovation to the margins: 'people tend to act within known limits, to innovate at the margins of the existing forms, and to miss many opportunities available to them in principle' (Tilly 1986: 390).[5]

Repertoires can also be exclusionary, as they depend on the resources available to certain groups or develop in response to police or political adversaries (Doherty 1999a). The use of CMC is only possible given acquisition of the technology and the development of a certain level of skill; thus innovation using CMC may in turn appeal only to a particular section of the environmental movement and may actually be exclusionary in its development.

However, this use of CMC also extends the existing protest repertoire in terms of affording another tool to be utilised during protest organisation and campaigning. In particular, CMC use is likely to affect the need to gain public attention via coverage by the mainstream media. Traditionally media coverage has been an important way to reach a broad audience. However, gaining media attention is particularly difficult, primarily because moderate actions are not newsworthy, yet extreme acts will be condemned and, even when coverage is given, actions are often represented without explanation of the proposed message (Rochon 1988; Smith, McCarthy, McPhil and Augustyn 2001; Scalmer 2002). The use of CMC could radically alter this search for media representation by enabling self-representation to a wide audience. Traditionally, many choices of repertoires of action have been based on the assumption that their actual deployment will be mediated by the media and more powerful actors. The use of CMC challenges this assumption as it enables the activists themselves to mediate their message, and provide as much detail and content as they wish.

In addition, the use of CMC enables the development of radical new forms of action not previously possible, such as the use of electronic civil disobedience – transposing the traditional tactics of street activism to cyberspace, turning the physical occupation by sit-in into a virtual occupation, for example – and could aid in the diffusion of information about the construction and operation of tactics. Such information previously would have to have been distributed through underground publications and word of mouth (Rucht 1993). Furthermore, the use of CMC may do more than simply enable new forms of action to be developed at the margins of existing repertoires, such as adapting extant notions of civil disobedience to the electronic sphere. It may also enable the merger of previously distinct sets of action into new forms, such as the use of online tactics simultaneously with street tactics, and could change the focus and the characteristics of the repertoire of action more fundamentally.

Movement intellectuals

Movement intellectuals are often the source of new ideas and critiques of modern society. Intellectuals contribute to 'the existence of a vocabulary and an opening of ideas and actions which in the past was either unknown or unthinkable' (Gusfield 1981: 325). Movement intellectuals help determine a social movement's ideological direction and influence the use of resources – cognitive, material and affective – in the mobilisation processes (Bagguley 1992). However, the movement intellectual is increasingly less an ideological leader, and more a spokesperson, facilitator, interpreter and synthesiser (Eyerman and Jamison 1991). Such intellectuals could advocate new ways of viewing and utilising technology – to those within the movement and to the general public – ways that might be inconsistent with commercial desires for the technology.

Intellectuals' ideas need to be communicated and social movements have increasingly adopted more professional tactics and employed (sometimes non-committed) professionals in order to better communicate their message both to those within the movement and to those outside. Communication has been 'technified' with the rapid development of new hardware through which to communicate, such as radio and television, the computer and video phone. Through such developments communication is increasingly technically mediated (Eyerman and Jamison 1991). The use of CMC contributes to, and challenges, this process of mediation and professionalisation. It enables movement intellectuals to bypass mediation through the mainstream media, by communicating directly with the masses, and to an extent to bypass the requirement for professional skills. Through CMC, movement intellectuals' ideas may be able to be more freely distributed and consumed within the social movement and thus increase their ability to stimulate protest.

At the same time, use of yet another form of hardware contributes to the mediation of the message through technology, and any use of technology requires a certain level of skill. There is a risk that if the intellectuals are some of the better educated in the movement, and they have an important role to play in tactical choices, then they may advocate the use of such a complex technology that not all are able to participate. Also, although use of CMC facilitates the wide distribution of people's ideas, there is still an emphasis on the written word. Emphasis on CMC may exclude those intellectuals less able to articulate their ideas through text and detracts from the emotive force of a public speech.

Although it may be argued that *all* activists in a social movement are 'movement intellectuals' because they contribute to the collective identity, some individuals are more *visible* than others as the organising forces, leaders or spokespersons. This visibility is enhanced by the mainstream media (Eyerman and Jamison 1991). The use of CMC, however, can reduce the divide between these visible movement intellectuals and other social movement actors. The interactive capacities of the technology enable more individuals to converse more easily and to critique the intellectuals' written text and ideas. Such increased interaction, and the potential for more ideas to be shared could result in a movement more closely aligned with the ideals of participatory democracy – where the future of the movement is decided by genuine discussion within the movement and not simply handed down by intellectuals to the masses. This also raises the question of whether the notion of a 'movement intellectual' is still relevant when CMC use can reduce their role, and given that their existence runs counter to the decentralised and non-hierarchical desires of many social movement organisations.

Public and private spheres

One of the goals of many social movements is to widen the public sphere and increase the area for public debate. The 'public sphere' is being constantly restricted by state and corporate encroachment, and there are increasing attempts to control the private sphere by the government (Lyon 2001). Access to the public *agora* and the fight for the space to communicate thus become central issues for any social movement: 'control of the media and of symbolic production therefore becomes both an essential premise for any attempt at political mobilization and an autonomous source of conflict' (Della Porta and Diani 1999: 40).

Social movement activists may use CMC as their own form of symbolic production unrestrained by the corporate control of the mainstream media – using CMC to broaden the public sphere (O'Donnell 2001).[6] This could be achieved by using CMC to organise protests to voice concerns, or in terms of using the virtual space of cyberspace as a new form of public sphere. Furthermore, CMC could be used by activists to regain some of the privacy that has been threatened by government surveillance.

These assertions illustrate that CMC use has the potential to alter many aspects of social movement activities. It is also important to consider the impact of CMC at each level or process of a social movement. It is clear that use of technologies by social movements is in itself not new; but careful consideration is required to determine how CMC use might affect and alter their processes, and this will be explored in the context of the specific case studies over the following chapters.

Summary

Any comprehensive examination of the politics of cyberspace needs to consider the diverse influences on the medium. The politics within, impacts upon and political uses of cyberspace can be analysed using a social movement approach combined with understandings of technology as socially and politically constructed. Using these as the theoretical framework for analysis, a number of assertions have been made about the potential implications of CMC use for environmental activists in Britain.

Primarily, there is likely to be an increased efficiency of operation. CMC use offers speed in terms of response, information gathering and networking ability to SMOs, which in turn might alter their organisational capabilities. Use of CMC might enable less-hierarchical forms of organisation to be more effective than previously and thus reduce the pressure towards professionalisation and oligarchy that many SMOs face. There are possibilities for new forms of recruitment and identity formation (though this is limited by the apparent need for face-to-face interaction). There is also potential for the wider diffusion of ideas, the sharing of ideologies and tactics across social movements and geographical areas, which may strengthen existing networks.

CMC also offers opportunities for new forms of tactics to be developed using the technologies. Movement intellectuals' ideas may be able to be more freely distributed and consumed within the social movement and thus aid their ability to stimulate protest. At the same time, however, CMC enables a vast number of individuals freely to distribute their ideas and to critique current intellectuals, and thus enable new intellectuals to develop and the movement to move further towards participatory democracy. Finally, activists can use CMC to assert the importance of the public sphere. It could be used both as a medium through which to organise protests, and as a virtual public sphere.

The aim of this book is to explore whether environmental activists are actually able to operate – and benefit from – CMC use in the ways outlined above. Furthermore, examination is required of the ways in which they negotiate the problems they encounter in using CMC.

Chapter 2 begins the exploration by illustrating how activists have resolved the tensions inherent in using a potentially environmentally damaging technology.

Notes

1 It is important to note that 'cyberspace' and CMC are not necessarily one and the same: 'cyberspace' tends to be restricted in its meaning to the online virtual space visited by users accessing the internet. In contrast, this book is more broadly concerned with CMC – which incorporates this online space, but also the offline hardware, software and social context through which communication is operated.

2 It is also pertinent that many social movement theorists have begun to look beyond the use of NSM, or indeed any one particular approach, to develop syntheses with which to work towards more integrated perspectives (see for example McAdam, Tarrow and Tilly 2001).

3 The British environmental movement is tied into the international environmental scene through collaborations between international NGOs or skill sharing between direct action activists (Wall 1999a).

4 CMC is more than just an extension of existing media not just in enabling interactivity but in providing space for files, audio, video etc, to be easily shared.

5 Tarrow (1998b) also proposes that forms of collective action change over time through the 'protest cycle' – which goes from incubatory stages with a small base to its height where there is an increased pace of innovation and rapid diffusion of collective action to new participants – followed by a routinisation and subsequent disillusionment. Each cycle widens the repertoire of collective action.
6 CMC is simultaneously both private and public in nature, and there has been extensive debate linking ideas of the public sphere to cyberspace (Poster 1997).

2

Negotiating the tensions of techno-environmentalism

This is the classic dilemma for activists – the tools we use for the job of opposition may not be the ones we wish to become dependant on in a free society.
Just like money – we need to raise it and use it now, but it would be a great
relief when it is finally abolished in the future. (Dave Morris, McSpotlight)

Technology has historically been viewed with scepticism by environmentalists. This scepticism can also manifest itself as a tension *between* environmentalists who advocate differing approaches to, and uses of, technology
(Pepper 1996). Techno-environmentalism refers to those environmentalists
who advocate the use of particular types of 'appropriate' technology, such
as wind turbines, to overcome some resource issues in contemporary
society, thus justifying the use of certain types of technology while still
opposing others (Lewis 1992).[1] This is in contrast to those who argue for
the dismantling of all complex technologies (Rifkin 1989; Glendinning
1990a; Tokar 1992).

This debate has resonance historically, but has been brought to the fore
as many environmentalists have eagerly adopted CMC (Clark 1996). Their
utilisation of such technologies sits uneasily within traditional environmental philosophy. CMC requires the use of high technology, the production and use of which have extensive environmental and social
consequences. Not surprisingly, its use results in tensions between environmentalists' theories and practices, for not only is CMC technology environmentally damaging, but it is that very technology which facilitates the
functioning of environmentalists' adversaries and aids those processes of
corporate globalisation that many environmental activists are attempting
to curtail (Wall 1999a).

Examination of this paradox enables analysis of CMC's impact on
society to move beyond the utopia–dystopia debate – characterised by
utopic authors such as Rheingold (1994) and dystopic writers such as

Boyle (1997) – to illustrate the complexity of CMC use. There are both strengths and weaknesses, advantages and disadvantages, in environmentalists' use of the technologies, and their use of CMC has compelled many to confront the quandary of using an environmentally destructive technology. This negotiation is a continuation of an existing process: for example, many environmentalists have had to grapple with justifying their use of automobiles or 'white' goods, or, more broadly, how to live a sustainable lifestyle in a modern environment.

The ways in which environmentalists seek to use CMC technology to justify or overcome this paradox will, in turn, affect the messages they are attempting to deliver to society. If environmentalists cannot resolve this paradox, will some of the impact (or importance) of their message become lost in a mesh of contradictions? It is perhaps indicative of such a process that an article in the *Independent on Sunday* allied the use of high technology to a weakened environmental philosophy: 'Eco-warriors go soft and opt for the telly. Environmental protesters . . . are no longer prepared to put up with life's hardships for the sake of their green beliefs' (Nuthall 1997: 12).

This chapter explores the ways in which environmental activists view and negotiate the paradox of using the potentially environmentally damaging technology of CMC. By negotiating the quandaries, many activists are able to resolve their tensions. The different ways in which they do so can be isolated into main tendencies, but such classification illustrates some of the basic diversities (and incompatibilities) between participants of the British environmental movement.

The chapter is structured into four parts. It begins with an appraisal of the attitudes to technology espoused by environmentalists, then more specifically explores their views on CMC and their understandings of the environmental consequences of computer usage; the third part of the chapter details the ways in which environmental activists have sought to resolve the paradox of using CMC; and, finally, the consequences of this negotiation of techno-environmentalism are examined.

Critiquing the technological fix

There is a general suspicion of technology on the part of environmentalists that can be encapsulated by the claim that the 'wholehearted acceptance of any form of technology disqualifies one from membership of the dark-green canon' (Dobson 2000: 84). Green attitudes tend to favour the natural world over the 'surrogate' world of man-made technology. These attitudes incorporate those who are anti-technology altogether ('primitivists'), those who support only the use of alternative technology, and those who are willing to be pragmatic and utilise high technology as the need arises

(MacKenzie and Wajcman 1985; Lewis 1992; Pepper 1996). The majority of environmentalists advocate the use of 'intermediate, appropriate and democratically-owned technology' (Pepper 1996: 11) and are opposed to advanced technology, but 'only the most extreme eco-radicals oppose all forms of modern technology' (Lewis 1992: 117).

Technology termed 'alternative', 'appropriate', 'intermediate' or 'soft' has historically been adopted by some members of the environmental movement (Boyle and Harper 1976; MacKenzie and Wajcman 1985; Dobson 2000). This is in contrast to hard, high or advanced technology which constitutes highly polluting, large energy input, ecologically unsound technologies. Motivated by profit generation, high technologies are capital intensive, mass produced and involve non-reversible use of resources (Dickson 1974).[2] Alternative technologies (AT) can be defined as including small-scale constructions, within a local environment, that can be produced largely by recyclable, recycled or cheaply and easily accessible parts by a local labour force (Schumacher 1973; Boyle and Harper 1976; Lewis 1992; Volti 1992). They are intended to be easy to use (and repair) and to be non-reliant on a knowledgeable elite. In this way they are meant to be 'directly' democratic, minimising relationships that are hierarchical.

Some environmentalists cast doubt on the adoption of any technology; for them 'even appropriate use of technology is a holding operation rather than an assault on the principal issues' (Dobson 1995: 98). They even critique the use of AT as being part of a belief in a 'technological fix', a practice that would need major technological innovations in order to solve all the world's problems. There are those who propose instead that social change would be more appropriate. If AT is seen to be the 'fix' to problems, then this assumes that the problem with advanced technology was simply that it was designed and used inappropriately. Pepper (1996) also argues that attributing the problems of advanced technology to ownership and thus striving for AT to be communally owned (as suggested by Schumacher 1973), or asserting that the difficulty lies in large-scale production and thus advocating small-scale construction, is not an adequate analysis of the failures of high technology. AT 'merely complements' (Pepper 1996: 97) existing large-scale capitalist development and actually provides the conditions for small-scale enterprise to grow into large-scale capitalism. Thus AT becomes part of the problem rather than its cure.

Among those interviewed, some felt that technology and environmental destruction were interwoven. However, few regarded technology as the sole source of environmental destruction or were entirely anti-technology. Rather, many were opposed to the system within which modern technology is designed, owned and operated. Such activists did not argue for the destruction of the technology *per se*, but for an alteration in the whole operation of society: 'There's nothing wrong with being anti-technology ... No environmentalist is "anti-progress" – they are in favour of social and environmental progress and therefore critical of the alienation and domination of modern technological systems and ideas' (Dave Morris, McSpotlight).

While such views left open the option for interviewees to adopt other technologies, deemed more appropriate, such beliefs also formed part of a critique of the 'techno fix'. In other words, if fundamental social change was the only path to creating a better society, then tinkering with different types of technology would not aid such social change: 'No liveable future can be imagined unless we change our social relations and the circulation of information before simply improving our technical apparatuses' (Melucci 1996: 163).

Many of the interviewed activists who were critical of technology use were particular about the type of technology with which they disagreed and advocated the use of alternative technologies. Thus, CAT's principal aim was to encourage the adoption of technology that would enable society to maintain its standard of living, but would reduce its environmentally damaging impact (Harper 1995). In other words, some use of technology is justifiable:

> I am a bit of a technophobe, and a bit of a Luddite. I sort of avoid machinery if I can, including car use, but it's interesting at CAT that their whole perspective is that if you are going to have technology, then use it appropriately, so I'm moving towards that idea ... but without taking it too far as well. You don't need technology for everything. (Kirsty Sunderland, information volunteer, CAT)

There is, however, some debate between environmentalists as to what actually constitutes AT. Volti's definition (1992) of AT includes the use of other 'high' technologies in an attempt to overcome some existing problems, such as the use of carbon filters on cars or microprocessor monitoring systems of office environments. In contrast, Lewis (1992: 117) refers to AT as excluding 'virtually every innovation made over the past century – if not the past five millennia'. He aligns AT with the rejection of all complex technologies, including electricity production, television, cars, battery-run products and the computer. Within this understanding of AT, the development of solar and wind power would also be rejected, technologies which have traditionally been used as prime examples of AT by environmentalists such as Porritt (1984). This debate was also reflected by interviewees, where the specifics of which technologies are acceptable as 'alternative' remained unresolved, with some even distinguishing between different forms of 'high' technology:

> Photovoltaic cells are exceptionally highly polluting ... extracting all these complex minerals out of the centre of the earth and then making them into a

highly complex technology that only the West controls . . . I much prefer the idea of wind power: people should have windmills in their back gardens. (James, Earth First![3])

For CAT, the task was to make the environmental impact of daily activities as small as possible, while still enabling life to continue in a bearable way. Thus, in addition to the supporters of AT, some interviewees (including some of those at CAT) chose to be pragmatic about their use of environmentally destructive technology. As Mike (Lyminge Forest) noted: 'At the end of the day, living is environmentally unfriendly and you just have to do your best at being as sustainable as possible.' Steve Jones (former ATA co-ordinator at CAT) related the question about technology to the dilemma about using cars while simultaneously campaigning against their use:

> Should environmentalists use cars? Everybody should try to use cars as little as possible, but living in a remote area, it's not possible, you're just making your life more difficult. And if only the people who are aware of the issues respond to the issues by limiting their lifestyles, then we're just not going to be able to communicate the message. [If we adopt the attitude] 'We're eco, we're not going to use computers', then no one will get our message. [Instead] if we use our message and say, 'Think about the consequences of everything you do, including computers', then we're fulfilling our mission statement.

In this way Steve has had to compromise some of his beliefs in order to be practical about what is possible. Consequently he uses a car but also tries to limit its environmental impact: 'As much as possible, I share it with other people – I'm not the sole user.' Interviewees' willingness to accept the need for the use of high technology reflects their broader lifestyle choices and the extent to which they have chosen to, or are able to, make sacrifices: 'It depends on what you're trying to do, if you're trying to change things then I think it's okay to use stuff like high technology and things that are around at the moment. But if you're trying to live a lifestyle that is totally green, I don't [think it's okay]' (Peat, Lyminge Forest).

Thus, while Jon Ivar (former list co-ordinator at GSN) regarded himself (as one who has campaigned for sustainable transport and an end to nuclear power) as a deep ecologist who believed that 'we cannot separate ourselves from nature, and . . . small, self-governing communities are the most appropriate form of political organisation', he simultaneously had few environmental qualms about using computers, because 'it's an essential part of my work'.

Interviewees' views of technology were heavily influenced by the control they were able to exert upon it. In this they assert that technology is not neutral, being to some extent infused with the objectives of those who design and produce it; and it becomes more acceptable if they have some say in its use. Thus Charles Secrett (director of FoE), when talking about genetic engineering, asserted that 'technology isn't some pure thing stolen from the gods by Prometheus and given as a gift to man. It is owned by corporations. It is regulated – or not – by government. It can be used for good or ill' (Secrett and Cochrane 1999: 2). What is clear is that, while there are some distinct differences in environmentalists' views of technology – such as between those who are opposed to the use of all modern technology and those who argue that forms of AT are acceptable – an individual's position is often not so clear cut. Such views of technology have been further complicated by the increasing adoption of CMC by activists.

Uses of computers: advocates and detractors

> [T]here are two kinds of technology – the enabling, democratic sort, that allows people to swap information and ideas by circumventing the powers that be, and the other technocratic sort that allows only top-down, one-way communication. In the former corner we have the telephone . . . the photocopier, Citizen Band radio – and the internet. In the other corner we have cinema, television, mass media. One allows for passive participation, the other active. One is centralised, the other is strongly decentralised, with no one in control. If we have to have technology at all, I know which I'd prefer. (Thorpe [formerly of CAT] 1995: 12)

In utilising CMC one is engaging with complex technologies,[4] many aspects of which correspond to Dickson's 1974 categorisation of 'hard' and 'high' technology. This is technology which traditionally has not been acceptable to many environmentalists, even to those who advocate the use of AT. Computers are mass produced, often in foreign countries by low-paid workers. The software is often supplied by multinationals (such as Microsoft or Oracle) and is quickly obsolete. A large quantity of power is consumed in their construction and the processes produce several toxic pollutants. Furthermore, ownership is private and for-profit rather than free and shared (Young 1993; Sale 1995). Given that environmentalists are increasingly utilising CMC, there is a tension between their views about technology and their use of computers. Some environmentalists have taken an anti-computer stance: 'It's hypocritical, they argue, to claim that computers can be used in an environmentally responsible way; no product of high technology can possibly be harmless, and all should be eliminated' (Anzovin 1994: 11).

In particular, the neo-Luddites[5] oppose using computer (and other) technology as they are highly sceptical of its advantages (Sale 1995). They argue that the alternatives (such as books, typewriters, pens and stamps) are perfectly adequate and do not result in as much environmental pollution

(Birkerts 1995; Ethical Consumer 1996; Henderson 1996). Furthermore, Glendinning (1990b: 52) asserted that computers 'cause disease and death in their manufacture, enhance centralized political control, and remove people from direct experience of life'. In a similar vein, Mander (1994a: 24) suggested that computers 'empower corporate global-scale development processes a thousand times more than they do the individual', with dire consequences for the environment.

Given the hesitancy with which many interviewees advocated the use of technology, it is interesting to note the sheer variety of technology employed by different factions to aid their campaigning – such as telephones, mobile phones, printing presses, camcorders and computers. This association with certain technologies has also come from many sources. In the early 1990s many environmental activists joined with others, such as participants of the (illegal) rave culture and new age travellers, against the Criminal Justice Bill and in turn shared both skills and dance culture's inventive use of technology (in the latter's case, for organising raves) (Collin and Godfrey 1997).

Unlike primitivists, many interviewees argued that technology is not intrinsically bad but claimed that 'it's the way that you use technology that counts' (David Blake, IT systems support, Birmingham FoE). Historically there has been an anti-technology streak running through parts of the environmental movement, and this, in some cases, constrained activists' adoption of computers: 'We tried to get the internet going from about Issue 4 [December 1994], I think, but initially people didn't even want to use computers – they wanted to use typewriters' (Jo Makepeace, *SchNEWS*).

In time, however, people like Dave Morris (McSpotlight) came to be 'persuaded by the effectiveness of what the McSpotlight people were doing'. Thus he managed to negate his view that 'technology in general is elitist and oppressive and environmentally damaging', so long as the technology was used in circumstances which helped a campaign and, in particular, was able to achieve successes which would not have been possible without using the technology (such as in reaching an international audience quickly and cheaply). Thus, 'even two years ago a lot of campaigners weren't online, and they were Luddites [who] firmly believed that technology was bad and it was all in control of the fat bastards . . . And now they realise that it's a tool . . . and it's a powerful tool, so now most of them are online' (Bob, McSpotlight).

This is not to say that all interviewees were enthusiastic about computers, but that there is no simple shared antagonism towards them. For example, just within CAT,

> there's three groups: [one] there's some that are quite indifferent to it, they don't mess with computers at all; [two] some are really, really pro . . . and

then [three] there's a few that – well, they've realised now that you've got to have it. . . . So I don't think there's anybody saying, 'No, we don't need a website', but there's a few that are a bit dubious about it. (Martin Donnelly, website volunteer, CAT)

This doubt about computers is further expressed as cautiousness towards the extent to which CMC is used. Some have a fear that virtual interaction can begin to take precedence over face-to-face interaction, and 'we have to be wary of the tendency of email, newsgroups and IRC [internet relay chat] to replace personal contact, and of the abstract world of the internet to replace physical contact with nature' (Jon Ivar, GSN), the result of which is that the environmental campaign loses some of its value: technology

> disconnects us from our immediate surroundings – the earth, face-to-face community interaction – and focuses on the abstract (online/virtual) reality; intellectualises the campaign which could alienate/reduce the involvement of those who do not have access to/knowledge of/interest in technology; sanitises the concept of direct action as a committed 'hands on' experience. (Lyminge Forest questionnaire respondent no. 26[6])

Finally, there are some who still doubt whether any new technology will, ultimately, serve to benefit environmental activists, given the prevalence of the view that 'it has uses, but I don't know if those uses outweigh the enormous growth of power and centralisation this technology have given to the corporations. If you think about the way this stuff is marketed it's pretty obvious who it is designed for. I think maybe on balance the advantage goes to our enemies' (Andy, GSN).

Awareness of the environmental paradox of computer use

> It's a dirty industry in terms of how it's manufactured. It feeds on the same fears as car manufacture in terms of you always want to upgrade, you're always getting faster and you always want another one . . . At the end of the day, it's still like buying a car. (Bob, McSpotlight)

Despite the scepticism about technology use there appears to be a lack of concern specifically about the tension generated by the paradoxical use of computers by environmentalists. Much of the rhetoric surrounding the environmental movement has focused on the potential advantages offered by CMC. Use is often advocated by discussion of how inexpensive, secure, fast and uncensored CMC is (Jackson 1995; Schwartz 1996; RoadAlert 1997). Its global reach, communication capacities, information dissemination uses and its value as a campaigning platform are often cited (Lamb 1996; Pipes 1996). Porritt (1984: 166) argues that 'with modern communications technology, there need be no fear of a return to the mean-minded parochialism of pre-industrial Britain', suggesting that environmentalists can use CMC to aid the favoured practice of localised and decentralised politics (see Dobson 2000). Such advantages to campaigning are presented as if they outweigh any environmental consequences and CMC is often optimistically described as the answer to many existing campaign limitations. When environmentalists do critique CMC[7] it is quite often not from the perspective of the environment, but because of issues of access or utility. For example, early on in activists' use of CMC RoadAlert! (1997: 25) stated that the internet is 'undoubtedly fairly elitist, as you need expensive equipment and technical know-how'.

Thus it is instructive to establish to what extent the interviewees themselves recognised the paradox. Activists White and Merlin (Lyminge Forest), and Debbie Bell (former Yorkshire and Humber RCC, FoE) had no environmental qualms about using computers, and suggested that it was not a significant issue: 'I am not specifically aware of any major environmental concerns'. David Blake (Birmingham FoE) thought that the computer industry had improved its environmental record recently and that 'the industry has done quite a lot to improve its use of materials. Virtually all the software houses print their support material on recycled paper.' Participants of GSN, faced with the question: 'How concerned are you about the environmental consequences of computer manufacture and use?', responded as follows: 10 per cent were 'very concerned'; 50 per cent were 'mildly concerned'; 5 per cent were 'not at all concerned'; and 25 per cent were 'not sure'.[8] Such response percentages indicate that while those who were not concerned at all constituted a minority, only double that number expressed mild concern.

The majority of interviewees, however, identified at least one environmental and social concern that they had with the technology. CMC is facilitating the processes of corporate multinational globalisation to which many environmentalists are reacting. Thus 'the irony is that the same tools that enable capital to disregard borders and produce commodities thousands of miles away from their markets, the internet and cheap air travel, are the same tools which are helping global social movements to meet and work with each other' (Anon 1999b: 11).

Lyminge Forest questionnaire respondent no. 31 felt that their use of CMC symbolised 'being seen as part of (and endorsing) the consumer, technocratic society, rather than providing an alternative'. The use of computer hardware and software predominately produced and controlled by 'mega-corporations . . . is something we are not happy with' (Tony Canning, IT technical and support manager, FoE). Furthermore, these 'mega-corporations' are able to take advantage of the international distribution of labour (and some countries' lack of environmental regulations) by locating within developing countries and thus employing workers on low wages. Dave Morris (McSpotlight) emphasised the poor working conditions of these computer component factories:

> [Computers] mean massive profits for huge multinationals who form the materials, who control the materials that go into making the computers, who exploit the workers who compile or construct the internal works, and, of course, who control the distribution of those computers in the market . . . The majority of workers engaged in constructing the inner works of computers are working in poor conditions for very low pay, often with dangerous chemicals.

In terms of pollution from these processes, Tony Canning (FoE) believed that '90 per cent of the environmental problems of computers are in the manufacturing stage'. Richard Weatherley (former IT manager, FoE) identified several sources of pollution from computer manufacture including toxic gas discharges and air pollution, groundwater contamination with methyl chloroform, trichloroethylene, benzene and other hazardous chemicals, and the use of CFCs in production. He also suggested that there were health problems for computer industry workers created by exposure to solvents, acids, caustic substances, heavy metals, plastic films and emulsions, and epoxy resins (Weatherley 1994: 97–8).

The energy consumed by computers during use also gave concern for some activists, especially as this electricity in Britain is often sourced from nuclear power stations: 'No one ever mentions the amount of power needed to keep the telecommunications infrastructure [telephones, internet] going' (Richard Weatherley, FoE). Health concerns about computer use were less often voiced, though Mike Birkin (South West RCC, FoE) mentioned the social and health aspects of spending hours in front of a computer screen. Richard Weatherley also identified health concerns about the low-frequency electromagnetic radiation, and radio-frequency interference (as possibly precipitating cancers and other diseases), ozone from printers, sound pollution, eye strain, and stress and strain injuries (Weatherley 1994: 97–8).

Finally, many were concerned with the 'throw-away aspect of computers, the built-in obsolescence and people being encouraged to upgrade' (Tony Canning, FoE). The constant updating of computers made machines rapidly redundant, and their packaging also added to waste landfill pressures (Weatherley 1994). Lyminge Forest questionnaire respondent no. 21 suggested: 'There are not many schemes to recycle and re-use them – industry should be made responsible for this excessive creation of waste.'

Resolving the tensions

Aware of the paradox, many environmentalists have sought to resolve the tensions between their scepticism of technology and their CMC use. The resolution is often a compromise between articulating a justification and employing ways to reduce the environmental impact of the technology.

'The ends justify the means': activists' need to communicate

Many interviewees sought to justify CMC use by arguing that the benefits of using the technology outweighed any resultant environmental damage. In other words, the ends justified the means:

> It would be somewhat hypocritical to say McDonald's [is] ruining the atmosphere, ruining the planet and happily go on using a plastic and metal contraption that was made using CFCs . . . But I think their use can be justified under certain circumstances . . . The environmental unfriendliness of computers is offset to some extent by the fact that they are being used for a 'good' purpose. (Gideon, McSpotlight)

Such justifications were used by many activists. Their computer use was a compromise in an imperfect world. This attitude reflects the deeper desires of some interviewees for a situation in which they had no need to make such trade-offs, but were able to live a fully sustainable lifestyle:

> I wish computers had never been invented, I wish the industrial revolution had never happened, I wish everyone still lived in nice little communities and everyone worked on the land . . . I know a lot of people can't deal with using the internet because it's the weapon of capitalism . . . but pragmatically it's important that people balance any Luddite [opinion] against using the high technology, against the potential benefits of using it. (Toby, *SchNEWS*)

Any environmental damage incurred through the use of such technology was, furthermore, defended by three sets of explanations, all of which use the pretext that the benefits 'outweigh' the disadvantages: fighting a war of minds; trading-off the environmental damage; and maintaining control.

One of the key justifications asserted for using CMC, despite its environmental impact, was the need to be effective in the 'war' that many interviewees perceived themselves to be waging against their adversaries. In order to have any influence in this battle, many argued, they had to have effective tools and needed to appear 'modern'; technology use was warranted because it was only temporary (for the duration of this crisis period) and/or because the availability of computers required that they should at least be put to 'good' use. In this battle, CMC has been touted as capable of levelling the playingfield for environmentalists. Using the technology, interviewees claimed that they were able, at least, to compete with their opposition: 'In some sense it's an arms race . . . We feel that we are up against the power of global corporations, with all their technical resources . . . and, to some extent, if they are tooled up, we've got to be tooled up. We've got to be at least as good as them' (Tony Canning, FoE).

By using the technology of their opponents, interviewees could attempt to 'rupture the system from within' (Bonnett 1999: 25), rather than abstain from the struggle: 'You can't get into arguments about abstaining from things that there are problems about, or else you end up being in a cave, somewhere, weaving your own yoghurt' (Laptop Mike, RTS[9]). Activists have in the past used all the tools available to them even when it involved using technology that they were actively campaigning against. This was illustrated during many of the anti-roads protests where 'I used the motorway to get to Twyford Down to protest about the motorway. One has to make sacrifices or else you can't beat them' (Worzel, Lyminge Forest). Consequently, compromises are made in order to be effective, and to be able to communicate their message to as many people as possible:

> If you live on the Internet and you want to be campaigner that's a compromise. You've just got to say we are going to be more effective by sharing ideas with people, or opening up peoples' minds to new ideas than we would be by being a good example. Because you can go and live in the country and be sustainable and be wonderful but if nobody knows about it you are not part of the problem, but you are not part of the solution either. (Chris, (S)hell[10])

Furthermore, use of modern technology also helps crack the image of activists being primitive hippies living in a past age. As Foley explained: '[T]hese people are media-friendly, technology-literate and unencumbered by outdated ideological baggage' (quoted by Brass and Poklewski Koziell 1997: 98). In this way environmentalists can be seen to be educated, intelligent citizens whose views should be listened to: 'If we didn't have it, I think we'd be seen as very behind the times and I think we have to fight that image . . . We have to be very careful to be seen using cutting-edge technology . . . and it also makes us look professional and modern' (Charlotte Cosserat, information officer, CAT), a view that reflects a perception of the public as valuing modern technology and respecting those who have skills and act in a professional manner.

A further justification for CMC use was that some perceived themselves to be engaged in a temporary (all be it protracted) battle. When this battle was won, they argued, there would no longer be a need to use CMC.[11] Their current use of it was only transitory and was therefore warranted in facilitating the progression to a better society: 'I don't think there's a place for them in an ideal world, but I recognise them as an extremely useful tool in creating the world I would like to see' (Devin, McSpotlight). Thus 'the day we get what we want that device goes out of the window' (Michael, EF!). Whether, in fact, it would ever be possible entirely to dispose of a technology which was used in the creation of such a society, however, is open to doubt.

This argument was also applied more specifically to the crisis period of a protest. Andy (GSN) suggested that those at Lyminge Forest could use computers because to do so was a short-term action: 'You can't really start laying the infrastructure for a proper community. All you can have is a few benders, a fire – and so obviously you've got to prop it up with other things.' Activists are unable to establish any long-term sustainability or community infrastructures while in a protest camp, and thus need to maintain links with wider society. However, if they were able to stay on the land permanently, many suggested, they would reduce their use of technology.

Finally, some interviewees proposed that, in this battle, it was illogical not to use technology which already exists: 'We should use existing technologies to our own ends . . . The computer explosion has happened anyway, and we are not promoting it, we're just taking advantage of it' (Steve Jones, CAT). As activists were not able to 'un-invent things' (Ben, Lyminge Forest), they had little option but 'to say: "OK, they exist." It would be a completely disastrous allocation of resources to try and fight [technologies]: there are much more important things to fight, like genocide in Indonesia' (Chris, (S)hell).

In addition to their belief that they were in a state of conflict with adversaries, many interviewees argued that the environmental damage resulting from computer manufacture and use could be off-set. Thus any environmental degradation would be balanced by the corresponding energy and resource savings which the computers enabled or by the non-usage of other destructive technologies; there was the further consideration that computers did not cause significantly more environmental damage than did other technologies. Some activists argued that CMC use decreased the environmentally damaging effects of other activities, and thus had energy- and resource-saving potential. Energy is saved, for example, because 'it's much more energy efficient for me to email Australia than to send a parcel or go there. There's also video conferencing' (Charlotte Cosserat, CAT). Furthermore, paper usage might be reduced, as information does not need to be posted and the need to print thousands of flyers is reduced[12]. If you compare computer use 'to the pollution of making letters, making stamps, sending a letter and it gets put in a postbox, picked up by a motor vehicle, transported, shuffled around it's much more energy intensive' (Pete, founder and co-ordinator, MO).

Using this justification, activists such as David (Media liaison, NE Green Party[13]) suggested that, by not using other potentially environmentally damaging technologies, his use of computers was to some extent negated, 'I don't have a video, I don't have lots of other things that people have, I don't have a car to compensate for having a computer.' Dave (GSN) used a similar argument but was more cautious of whether such justifications are adequate: 'I like to get on my high horse and say I've not got a car, so everything else that I do pales into insignificance, which is completely untrue but it sort of keeps me happy.'

Furthermore, a few activists argued that, set within the context of other sources of environmental damage, that stemming from use of CMC was not significant enough to be a priority. Jessy (McSpotlight) asserted: 'Computers are such a small part of what you use . . . They are so minuscule compared to light bulbs and cars and travel and washing machines.' Similarly Sarah (MO) affirmed: 'We've got to prioritise. I'm far more worried about farming than I am about new technology like the internet.'

Advancing the argument of having to 'fight fire with fire', interviewees also asserted that having a certain control over CMC and using it to increase their campaigning effectiveness against the technology's own developers and investors (the military and the corporations) were productive: 'It's almost better to use the technology against itself, and that's kind of a statement in itself to say – "I'm using technology, but I'm also destroying technology at the same time." And then to use that paradox is something' (David, NE Green Party). Thus activists have co-opted the technology for their own ends. This control, to an extent, serves to negate the environmental impacts because, unlike many other technologies to which environmentalists object (such as bio-technology), they are able to subvert, and benefit from, its use.

Bob (McSpotlight) argued that environmentalists need to participate in the internet in order to determine how it is used and to help maintain the freedom of the medium from corporate control. Using CMC, Mary (Peace Action[14]) asserted, activists were able to 'have a voice in a place amidst all this materialism and worshipping of technology'. Furthermore, some interviewees attempted to avoid aspects of the technology with which they disagreed by customising PCs to make their use less like that envisaged by the multinationals: 'I'm actually running a form of UNIX on [my PC], which is obviously completely free . . . and then you get people using Macintoshes, and there's plenty using Amigas and Acorns . . . I dislike Microsoft' (Dave, GSN).

Mitigating the environmental effects through re-usage, recycling and renewable power sources

Environmental activists also overcome the apparent contradictions in their use of CMC and their preference for appropriate technology by mitigating the environmentally damaging effects of computer usage. They did this by re-using and recycling components, reducing the energy used by their computers and by using renewable energy sources. Many sought to minimise their consumption of hardware by re-using existing components to construct or upgrade existing machines, or by recycling their disused equipment. For example, *SchNEWS* relied upon reusing old computers: 'A lot of the stuff that we get is recycled in itself. There's no bit of the equipment in there that's been bought fresh, new. All of it is donated or put together from bits of other computers . . . So, in that sense, it's recycled' (Jo Makepeace, *SchNEWS*).

James (EF!) used skips as his source for parts: 'We do go looking in skips, and that is where we found a really good computer recently . . . Skipping is a good environmentally friendly way of getting computers.' Despite the recyclability of their machines, however, they were not always of sufficient standard to accommodate the latest software. Thus McSpotlight had to compromise further between their aims and their environmental qualms:

> There is a bit of division again in McSpotlight between people who think you should keep using the old slow ones [computers] and other people who think we are doing a good service making McSpotlight, and if we can do it in less time and more efficiently then it's better to get a fast new one. (Jessy, McSpotlight)

This process of re-using old machines formed part of an awareness of all of the aspects of using computers that are environmentally damaging, such as power sources, printing inks and paper consumption. Even when new computers were purchased, such as at CAT, attempts were made to keep them in use for as long as possible: 'We've still got 10–year-old Amstrads; we're still running on 386s on some parts of the site . . . We use computers to death' (Paul Trimby, information service co-ordinator, CAT). Even when their equipment came to the end of its useful life, 'we get rid of them appropriately: [we] recycle them' (Sarah Jenkinson, former media officer, CAT).

In addition to using recycled components, many try to reduce their computers' energy use by purchasing Energy Star equipment, by ensuring that machines not in use are switched off, or by using laptops. Laptops require less power than desktops: 'We use a laptop. In one sense, they are less recyclable – the components are much harder to take apart – but they use far less energy' (Charlotte Cosserat, CAT).

Greenpeace, FoE, CAT, Lyminge Forest and MO all used renewable energy sources to help power their computers (and offices) and thus to reduce the environmental impact of technology use. Most of the site at CAT is powered by a combination of water, wind and sun channelled to provide two currents – one for general use and a precision current required for the running of computers. At times, however, load management is required and there have been problems in generating enough electricity to power the computer monitors: 'Monitors are very power-hungry, and that's why we tend to use laptops, because their screens aren't so power-hungry, and [that] does limit, to some extent, the amount we can expand' (Paul Trimby, CAT).

Many at FoE objected to the speed of obsolescence of computers, the pollution produced during their manufacture and the energy required for use. In order to reduce their environmental impact, FoE continued to promote the use of renewable power sources (and more broadly alternative technologies), the use of environmentally designed computers, the recycling and re-use of computers, the switching off of monitor screens and, finally, by advocating the use of open systems and not brand products. When purchasing its computers, FoE took into account an environmental audit of computer technology conducted by the BUND organisation, Germany. FoE's Acer hardware was the most environmentally friendly computer equipment available at the time of purchase. In this way, FoE attempted to mitigate some of the effects of their use of computers by selecting the produce of 'the least environmentally damaging companies that we can, although technical considerations are also important' (Tony Canning, FoE). FoE also publicly criticised the computer industry for its lack of environmental consideration: 'We put out a press release at the time that we bought the computers, which was reported in some of the specialist press attacking the very low standard that there is in computing, for energy efficiency in particular' (Simon Festing, former housing campaigner, FoE).

Furthermore, FoE has campaigned for the recycling of a variety of goods: 'We've got an organisation campaign priority starting next year [1999] on sustainable consumption, and I know that one of the things it's going to focus on is white goods – white electrical goods and PCs' (Susan Pipes, former GIS co-ordinator, FoE). In FoE's London offices, 'we try not to be in the three year throw-away cycle ourselves' (Tony Canning, FoE), and they also donate old equipment to charities and schools. Local groups similarly limited their purchasing of hardware. Birmingham FoE deliberately bought only one computer and its other machines were put together from bits of older machines: 'The machines that we use for the most part are recycled machines anyway, which would have otherwise been scrapped' (David Blake, Birmingham FoE).

In the *Green Home Handbook* FoE advocated buying computers with the Energy Star rating, and switching off monitors and printers when not in use (Sydenham 1996). FoE published *The Green Office Action Plan* (Friends of the Earth 1996), which aims to help businesses to reduce their impact on the environment. Furthermore, FoE tried not to consume too many brand-name software products. They used Windows, but not Microsoft's *Word*, and advocated the use of open system software.

At the Lyminge Forest protest site activists wired-up recycled computers to windmills in order to avoid use of environmentally damaging power sources. Using a wind generator made from 'an old computer hard disc' (Mike, Lyminge Forest), placed on top of a tree house, activists were able to generate 12 volts through a dynamo – 'On a windy day, you charge a battery in twenty four hours, a 36-amp powered battery' (Mike, Lyminge

Forest) – and recharge car batteries. Enough power was generated to run the camp's laptop, power lighting, CB communications, computers, and radio and tunnel ventilation systems (Cramp 1997; Newsome 1997; Nuthall 1997). Those at the camp were also able to use pedal power to provide electricity for a band they hosted, and they used solar power during the summer (Birkett 1997). At times, more power was needed than could be generated in this way however, so non-renewable sources were used: 'In the summer I use solar power to charge up my batteries. During the winter I've either got a windmill . . . or I go to the garage to charge up my batteries' (Merlin, Lyminge Forest).

Those at MO similarly attempted to compensate for the environmental effects by using alternative power sources. This was because they were aware of the paradox: 'Taking the latest communications technology into a field you run into dilemmas: how do you power it? You could use a generator, but at what cost in pollution? You can't complain about fossil fuels and oil slicks whilst filling your jerry can at the local garage' (Anon 1997a). They used wind and solar energy to power the office equipment, producing a 12-volt supply which was stored in two batteries in the van and then processed through an inverter (converting 12v DC to 240v AC) to supply the two laptops. In emergencies, MO used a hand-cranked generator which produced 12v, but had encountered problems with this, as a lot of computers need 16 volts, and on one laptop they 'had to sort of modify the power unit and make it so it's 12 volt . . . but we're sort of getting a good range of 12-volt equipment together' (James, MO). When MO was stationed at Teigngrace there were too many demands being made of the renewable power source, so that 'running the computer and printer used more power than we could get from our equipment' (Anon 1998b). Despite these problems, Pete felt that they had done their best to reduce the environmental impact of the computer: 'It might have polluted the environment in its *construction*, but it's not polluting the environment now, because it's running off a windmill – it's running from an alternative source.'

The consequences of negotiating techno-environmentalism

Interviewees, it has been seen, sought to employ rhetoric or make practical adjustments to the technology to limit the environmental impact of their use of CMC. This was in response to a general awareness of the negative environmental effects of computer manufacture and use and hence the paradox that environmentalists recognise. Only a few interviewees were either unaware of or did not place value upon the environmental implications of using CMC. For some, this utilisation has resulted from their being persuaded by the effectiveness of CMC and by overcoming their reservations about (and resentment towards) technology. CMC use has also re-opened the debate over what constitutes 'alternative technology', to what extent its use can substitute for existing technologies and therefore which technologies may be used with justification.

Whether the impact (or importance) of the interviewed environmentalists' message remains intact in the light of these issues depends upon the intended audience's approval of the compromises made by the interviewees, something which obviously is difficult to capture[15]. What, then, of the implications of such compromises? There are two key research findings and two significant consequences of the ways in which interviewees have negotiated the tensions within techno-environmentalism. First, the interviews have confirmed both the diversity of the movement's composition and also some common threads of understanding and perceptions of technology between groups which are ideologically and organisationally diverse. Second, interviewees' responses demonstrated that they are not anti-technology *per se*, but accept that some compromises have to be made in their attempts to live sustainably in the twentieth century. Nor are they 'anti-progress', many wishing rather to resolve existing problems and help society to progress towards a more sustainable future. Third, the importance of alternative technology (both as an ideal and in practice) has been re-asserted at a time when large sections of the British population were using some form of technology daily. Not only is CMC compared to alternative technology as if to an ideal, but it has been reclassified by some environmentalists in their attempt to fit CMC to their own definition of 'alternative technology'. Fourth, the debates about Luddism have re-emerged. Despite the ideals of alternative technology, some environmentalists have become more accepting of CMC because of the level of control they are able to exert over its use, unlike other technology such as nuclear power.

Diversity and similarities

The sheer variety of ways in which interviewees sought to justify their use of CMC has confirmed the diversities (and incompatibilities) of those within the environmental movement and has re-confirmed that the movement is no monolith. For example, while some advocated pragmatic long-term use of technology, others (often representing more radical tendencies such as Earth First! or direct action advocates) felt able to utilise CMC in only a temporary manner, asserting that they would dispense with it as soon as they were able. Furthermore, while some agonised over what they perceived to be the severe environmental consequences of computer use, others attached no great significance to this damage.

Despite such diversity, however, there were some common threads of understanding about technology between groups which are ideologically and organisationally diverse. These groups, such as FoE and *SchNEWS*, can have opposing aims (reform and radical change, respectively) and seek to organise for this change using differing models (hierarchical and non-hierarchical, respectively). However, participants from both groups sought to justify CMC use with the need to 'fight fire with fire', and both attempted physically to mitigate the environmental effects of the machines.

Campaigning for change, not abandoning technology

I feel that the bottom line is that, like most of our other activities, modern communications technology pollutes, but that it has some positive implications for the environmental movement, and so we should work on making it more environmentally friendly rather than getting rid of it. (Charlotte Cosserat, CAT)

A far more positive outlook towards technology was detected among interviewees than has traditionally been represented in the academic literature (with the exception of Pepper 1996). Not only were interviewees not anti-technology *per se*, or were simply pro-AT, but they dealt with the complexities of modern life, in part, by refusing to automatically abandon the use of high technology. Interviewees sought to use CMC in a positive way to press for social change and also to make it more environmentally friendly – illustrating to others how the technology could be put to constructive use and trying to shape future utilisation of CMC.

Thus the interviewees were resolving the tensions by seeking a compromise solution. This is similar to the way in which, according to Roach, women deal with the masculine nature of CMC. Although interviewees did not approve of the ways in which CMC had been manufactured (or was used by commerce), 'they redesign the game with new rules' (Roach 1995: 138). Environmentalists, just like many women, 'have not adopted the "radical" stance of rejecting participation in computer networks, but have attempted to transform a reality' (Roach 1995: 138) in order to benefit from CMC on their own terms. This suggests that environmentalists are also continuing the traditional role of social movements as producers of knowledge (Eyerman and Jamison 1991). They are often the source of ideas that challenge the processes of the existing societal system. Such ideas are normally articulated by the movement intellectuals, but in this case ideas are expressed in practice by those using the advanced technology. Such activists are leading the way in converting elements of CMC technology in order to reduce environmental degradation and in encouraging the public to use the technology in more radical ways. Consequently the environmental movement is in a position to develop new ways of thinking about computers.

Finally, while encouraging the use of CMC, interviewees also serve as a caution to the public about over-reliance on virtual interaction. As Robins

(1995) has observed, many of the proponents of CMC see cyberspace either as an alternative to society (without the existing social problems) or as a way through which to (re-)create a 'perfect society'. Rheingold's (1994) vision of a new 'social commons' to replace the lost public spaces is a form of virtual communitarianism. This idealisation of community, argues Young (1990), reflects a desire to rid society of difference, asymmetry, antagonism and conflict. In contrast environmentalists reassert the need to remain close to nature, to strike a balance between the virtual and the natural world, to maintain the importance of face-to-face interaction and thus to value and prioritise the protection of the environment as their core concern.

Reclassifying technology to suit definitions of alternative technology

In seeking to resolve the tensions surrounding their use of CMC, interviewees have re-emphasised the importance of alternative technology. Not only is CMC compared to AT as the ideal, but to an extent CMC has been reclassified by some interviewees to suit their definition of AT. This is not necessarily overt but many strands of activists' justifications include references to aspects of AT that can be taken to apply to CMC.

The fundamental ethic of ATs is to be self-sufficient, to be constructed within a local bio-region, by locals often using recycled and inexpensive parts. The production and use of computers are rarely in keeping with such an ethic. Computers tend to be mass produced in factories, often utilising components produced in different parts of the world, for the purpose of profit. However, interviewees have identified certain attributes of CMC which allow it to be equated with AT. The technology is becoming easier to use and cheaper to own, and requires less energy to run. CMC enables free speech, public access and participation, and can also be constructed out of scrap and adapted to run from renewable power sources. In essence, interviewees are able to use rhetoric and practical adjustments to align the technology with a definition of AT.

Controlling the form and use of the technology

A common thread in the interviewees' decision not to abandon CMC technology but to use it in positive ways, and the potential for CMC to be reclassified as a form of AT, is environmental activists' ability to *control* the technology. As Pete (MO) suggested: 'A lot of the media . . . are very controlled in what they say . . . controlled by the advertisers, controlled by the broadcasting standards, and the internet is just open'. This control can be interpreted as the ability to use a potentially environmentally destructive technology to aid environmental campaigning, to impart some of activists' (environmental) values into the technology by physically mitigating some of its environmental consequences or in playing a part in influencing the future design and use of the technology.

Furthermore, the redefinition of CMC as an alternative technology enables a sense of *ownership* over CMC which has not been as readily achieved with other forms of high technology, such as nuclear power or car manufacture. What is unique about CMC is the extent to which interviewees have been able to use the technology against its makers, to physically deconstruct it (either by building computers from scraps, or using renewable power sources) and assert a role in the creation and continually evolving design (by their presence in cyberspace interviewees are part of the virtual community which is shaping its continued existence).

This control is also manifest in the increasing use of open source programs. By freely providing the source of software, anyone is able to copy, use and improve it. This not only curtails the need to purchase expensive corporately produced software, but facilitates innovation in CMC by enabling source code to be written by an infinite number of enthusiasts in a collective project (de Silva 2001). The international open publishing newswire network Indymedia illustrates the outcomes of such collaborations (Meikle 2002). Thus, in contrast to corporate emphasis on copyright and ownership, activists have benefited from adopting a participatory approach and thus subverted the control of the larger corporations.

At this juncture it is opportune to return to environmentalists' views of technology and, in particular, interviewees' relationships with Luddite principles. Neo-Luddites (re-)emerged in the late twentieth century to oppose the computer, among other technologies. They were sceptical of its advantages and preferred the alternatives (Whittikar 1996; Schwarz 1997; Graham 1999). Among these neo-Luddites are several environmentalists, 'many of us have begun, in recent years, to see industry for what it is . . . [to] reject industrial logic and embrace our desires . . . down with all kings but King Ludd' (Anon 1997b: 65). It was Bauerlein (1999) notably who identified Earth First! 'monkeywrenchers' to have been the only members of the new Luddites to have actually put their ideas into practice and to destroy the technology to which they object.

However, as with the original Luddites of the early 1800s, who were not against all technology, but did not want the new weaving looms to destroy their livelihoods, the interviewees were not against technology *per se*, and appear less threatened by it if they have a measure of control over it. Interviewees have managed to negate many of the negative environmental effects of the CMC technology by developing self-built, renewably powered, shared machines, and have thus to an extent subdued some of their neo-Luddite tendencies. By being able to assert control over the technology's production, utilisation and future, the threat that computer technology posed has been reduced.

Continuing to question technology

Environmentalists are using CMC to fight against advancements in other technologies (such as bio-technology), and are thus using one major technological development of the twentieth century against others. Computer manufacture and use also have damaging environmental effects. This has produced a paradox for environmental activists, but one which most are aware of.

In terms of using CMC, a variety of attitudes towards it were displayed. Some interviewees were sceptical of its use, fearing that virtual communication could take precedence over offline interaction. Others, however, adopted CMC, arguing that technology was not intrinsically bad – but that it depended on how it was used. There remains a small neo-Luddite contingent who argue that compared to the environmental and health problems of computers, 'it is quite insignificant whether some individuals find that the values of a technological society – speed, ease, mass information, mass access, and the like – are served and enhanced by such machines' (Sale 1995: 257). However, the majority justified their use of CMC using rhetoric and/or practical measures. Few were anti-technology in general, even those involved in radical campaigning. By paying attention to the paradox and personally resolving it, many felt that the purity of their message remained intact.

The measures employed by environmental activists confirmed the diversity of views among the British environmental movement, but also identified some main tendencies which unified the different groups. Overall, there was a general trend towards resolving the paradox of CMC use by arguing that the 'ends justify the means' and that, wherever possible, attempts should be made to physically reduce the environmental impact of computers. There was a tendency therefore not to abandon high technology wholesale, but rather to utilise what was of benefit to them and attempt to 'redesign the game with new rules' (Roach 1995: 138). By dealing with the paradox of computer use, interviewees also reasserted the importance of the ideals of alternative technology to many within the movement. The modifications to computers that interviewees achieved, together with the verbal rhetoric extolling the advantages of the technology, enabled a redefinition of CMC into one which suited AT's criteria, making the technology less threatening to environmentalists. Finally, the control and ownership that interviewees perceived themselves to have over the technology served to diminish what fears or resentment they may have had towards it. Whether this control will become constrained with time by commercial and state interests' penetration of cyberspace (through commerce and surveillance) will be explored more fully in chapter 6.

Notes

1 The term 'techno-environmentalism' should not be confused with the term 'technological environmentalism' or 'technocentrism' as used by Pepper (1984). Pepper uses the term to refer to the dominant approach to viewing the environment by a society. Such a perspective advocates that humans are able to manipulate and appropriate nature for their own means and that use of high technology is desirable.

2 High technology is rejected by many environmentalists for a number of reasons (Lewis 1992). The dehumanising effects of the production process and the destruction of jobs (and thus of social relations) are identified as a major flaw of advanced technology. The waste, pollution and health effects (through production and consumption, such as allergies to plastics) are genuine problems. Technological developments are also said to enable centralisation of power and to produce more numerous means of social control and surveillance. Many technological developments are seen as an affront to nature. Genetic engineering is taken as an example of humans apparently trying to play God. Finally, Lewis (1992: 124) believes that eco-radicals are anti-science. Science is depicted as the 'progenitor of harmful technologies', and as taking a reductionist, rather than an holistic, view of the world.

3 Earth First! (EF!) is a radical environmental network which first came to prominence in the UK in the early 1990s as being proactive, confrontational and encouraging the destruction of machinery or crops (Seel 1997). EF! eschews any formal structures or memberships, being deliberately non-hierarchical. It is a fluid network and incorporates many individuals who are involved in other campaigns. EF! UK publishes a monthly newsletter called *Earth First! Action Update* and the yearly journal *Do or Die*. EF! also organises twice-yearly gatherings, in winter and summer. There are several EF! web pages, such as the EF! Leeds website (www.leedsef.ukf.net) and pages from South Downs Earth First! (www.eco-action.org) – which contains the action updates and lists of contacts for local groups. Any activists are quoted as participants but are not to be taken as representatives of Earth First!

4 It is now possible to use CMC without directly accessing a computer – through WAP phone technology or digital television. In Australia, Melbourne's Indymedia collective have also developed the PIMP interface which enables users to download audio reports onto Indymedia (an open publishing newswire) websites directly through a phone. For further details see Pickerill (2004).

5 The original Luddites of the early 1800s smashed the mechanical looms that were responsible for their unemployment. However, they were not against the technology *per se*, but were opposed to its inappropriate use and their lack of control over its implementation (Boal 1995; Sale 1995).

6 An online questionnaire was attached to the Save Westwood protest website for the period between January 1998 and May 1999. It was to assess how respondents had found out about the campaign and the website, their involvement in the campaign and their views about using new communication technologies. Over the seventeen-month period that it was online forty-three responses were

received. As there was no visitor counter attached to the website it was not possible to determine what percentage response this represented.

7 There is a large body of literature which critiques CMC, but the majority of this
is not written from an environmental perspective or by environmentalists (see
e.g. Webster and Robins 1986; Boncheck 1995; Stoll 1995).

8 An email-based questionnaire was posted to members of the Green Student
Network in April 1999. Its purpose was to assess similarities and differences
across the group. There were seventeen completed responses to the questionnaire. At the time the email list comprised seventy-six members, so there was a
22 per cent response rate.

9 Reclaim the Streets (RTS) was originally formed in London in 1991 (Anon
1997c). It began with small anti-car actions, and then started the now infamous
Reclaim the Street parties where roads were taken over and traffic stopped for
a day by activists who then held a party on the street, or as in July 1996, the M41
motorway (Jordan 1998). Such actions have inspired replicas world-wide, and
autonomous groups have temporarily adopted the name. Although RTS began
with a focus on transport issues, it was more broadly interested in the political
and economic forces which drive 'car culture'. Subsequently RTS was associated with the anti-capitalist protests in London on 18 June 1999, and May Day
2000. Its website is at www.reclaimthestreets.net

10 (S)hell was a group that undertook direct action against the oil company Shell.
In particular the group occupied Shell's headquarters in London on 4 January
1999.

11 This is because 'I want a society where people actually communicate with each
other directly and have control over their own lives and communities, and
[because] the higher level the technology in a society, the more alienated people
are from each other and from the decision-making process' (Dave Morris,
McSpotlight).

12 However, the paper-free office promised by the use of computers never mate-
rialised, and significant use of paper and printing materials continues despite
electronic storage.

13 The North East Green Party is a faction of the national Green Party. The Green
Party, committed to ecological sustainability and social justice, stands in local,
general and European elections. The North East Green Party seeks to support
the Green Party's aims and also campaign about issues in the local context.
Their website is at www.gn.apc.org/negreens.

14 Peace Action began as a small Newcastle University students' group which
aimed to take informed action for global peace. It used direct action tactics to
protest about unethical arms trading, nuclear power and weapons, and pollution.

15 For example, it could be inferred that CAT advocate that appropriate and measured use of technology is justifiable. Its target group is comprised of individuals of the general public who are intrigued to know how their current standard
of living could be maintained using fewer environmentally damaging technologies. CAT is able to adequately justify its CMC use within the context of its
mission and remit.

3

Inclusivity and changing organisational forms

[T]he constraints to cyberactivism are largely those that hobble other political involvement: commitment, time, money, expertise . . . those who may benefit the most from counterhegemonic uses of the Net may have the least access to it. (Warf and Grimes 1997: 270)

In addition to the paradox surrounding their use of computers, environmentalists face problems in gaining access to CMC. Access is obviously a prerequisite for the use of the technology, but the ways in which activists organise their access can reflect (or contradict) their broader organisational principles.

There is a tendency among British environmental groups to promote the need for participatory democracy. There is an emphasis both on the need for inclusion – of themselves – in the political decision-making process and more broadly on participatory democracy as a model for an open and integrated society. Such models of inclusive, non-hierarchical or consensus decision-making structures are put into operation (or at least attempted) by many groups, including the majority of the case studies in this book. In order to practise according to their ideals, this attitude of inclusiveness should be reflected in environmentalists' use of CMC. Yet many groups have to compromise between their principle of inclusivity and the need for efficiency. Environmentalists at times have to moderate their desire for participation according to the more immediate pressures of meeting campaigning demands.

This chapter examines how environmentalists' attitudes towards inclusion are translated into their use of CMC. By analysis of how they have secured and shared access to the technology it explores the extent to which they are able to practise those ideals or whether their vision has been compromised. It begins by outlining the importance of inclusiveness to environmentalists, and then explores the ways in which environmental activists have secured access to the technologies, how they have tackled any problems encountered and, additionally, whether CMC use has altered organisational forms. Overall, the chapter demonstrates that the interviewees' attitudes, while reflecting a desire for inclusion, lead to practices of exclusion. Participation is often extended only to those individuals already within the movement or to particular movement groups.

The chapter is divided in two. First, the patterns of access are delineated and the ways in which access problems are viewed and tackled by interviewees are explored. The second part is concerned with the effects of organisational form on CMC use, and the effects of CMC on organisational forms.

The importance of inclusion

One of the core aims of many groups in the British environmental movement is to gain representation of their views within the political power structure. Organisations such as FoE attempt to gain access to, and influence, decision-making arenas, while groups such as Earth First! aim to make their voices heard by taking direct action (Friends of the Earth 1990; Rüdig 1995; Doyle and McEachern 1998). Most environmental groups place great emphasis on increasing their (and public) participation in the decision-making process (Lowe and Goyder 1983).

Environmental groups have employed a diverse range of strategies for achieving environmental change (Pepper 1996). These strategies have included alternative approaches to democratic processes (Doherty and de Geus 1996). For some this has involved support for authoritarianism: 'the more democracy is understood to be government *for* the people rather than *by* the people, the more compatible with the objective-driven nature of green thinking it becomes' (Dobson 2000: 122). However, for others (as the case studies will show), promoting more participatory forms of organisation and governance, promoting decentralisation, transparency, openness and inclusion (Paehlke 1998), has been a priority. Support for forms of direct democracy is growing (see Budge 1996). Many, especially anarchists and those involved in DiY Culture, try to put their ideals into practice through their own organisations, which are structurally informal and non-hierarchical, and operationally autonomous at local community level (Rooum 1992; McKay 1998). Importantly, this is to ensure more than just an equitable form of organisation, for 'activists begin to act as if the world they want to live in has come into existence. Prefigurative politics means acting now as you want to act in the future' (Jordan 2002: 73). This is supported by Melucci's assertion that 'the organizational forms of movements are not simply instrumental in their goals, but are goals in themselves' (2000: 95). How this is expressed in practice varies between groups, but will often include attempts at autonomous organisation, consensus decision-making and avoiding top–down leadership.

FoE is slightly at odds with the other cases in this context. Although it claims to strive to facilitate grassroots participation and to attempt to minimise bureaucratic structures, what has been achieved has not been to everyone's satisfaction: 'while looking like "new politics", groups advancing direct democracy through the mobilization of greater citizen involvement in the political process, we would argue that *de facto* there is little in participatory terms which distinguishes them from political parties' (Jordan and Maloney 1997: 187). I explore this point later in the chapter.

This emphasis on inclusion has implications for groups' use of CMC. A desire for participation in political processes may have been one of the stimulants to activists' use of the technology – using CMC to be better able to communicate with politicians and the public. The importance of participatory organisational processes, however, should also be reflected in their attitude to use of the technology. If there is not uniform access to CMC, then the potential to enhance participatory democracy is curtailed. There has been much optimistic rhetoric about the possibilities that greater interaction between citizens and power-holders via CMC might result in new forms of non-mediated democracy (Rheingold 1994; Rushkoff 1994; Gray 1995; Holden and Szerszynski 1999; Dahlberg 2000). Thus the ways in which environmentalists view and overcome access problems is a useful frame within which to examine what environmentalists really mean when they propose participatory models of organisation.

Tackling access problems

To begin exploring how participation is actually practised it is pertinent to examine what access activists have had to CMC and how they have tackled any problems of access. These will now be considered concurrently.

Access to CMC is not so much limited as constrained unevenly across the population (Angell 1992; Haywood 1995; Atton 1996). This confines the contribution CMC can make to increasing participation:

> If the facilities and expertise necessary to gain access to the internet are only accidentally available to grassroots groups (which is often the case), whereas they are structurally available to the institutional forces they face, the use of information technology becomes just another example of structural inequality. (Dordoy and Mellor 2001: 174)

Furthermore, access to more information does not necessarily trigger participation, and more people being able to voice their opinions will not necessarily translate into more participatory forms of organisation (Reid

1999). As Miekle (2002) observes, there is a plethora of forms of interactivity online, but only one form – conversation – actually enables open debate between several participants, which would seem to be the form most likely to result in participatory organisation.

Access to CMC is shaped by several constraining factors: finance, location and office space, technical skills and training, technical specifications and support, gender, class, ethnicity and language. Importantly, access to CMC is about more than access to hardware or software – it is about social agency because it is 'a social practice involving access to physical artefacts, content, skills and social support' (Warschauer 2002, p. 10).

Precursors to using CMC are money to pay for access to the technology and the knowledge of how to use it. These are determined by an individual's location within society. CMC users in Britain are overwhelmingly white and middle class, and this results in a monocultural predominance online (Graham and Aurigi 1997; Lockard 1997; Jordan 1999a). Furthermore, British environmental activism[1] remains dominated by the middle classes (Mattausch 1987 and 1989; Bagguley 1992; Sherkat and Blocker 1993). Critiques of the middle-class radicalism thesis point out that the environmental movement draws on a mixture of classes, and many of those involved in direct action are working class (Bowlby, Bowlby and Lowe 1992; Rüdig 1995). However, the existence of some working-class, or even 'class-less',[2] people in environmental groups does not necessarily unsettle the assertion that the environmental movement is influenced by middle-class *values* or is based upon class politics. In addition to class, the social base of British environmentalism has also been linked to individuals who are tertiary educated, white, young, urbanite and non-religious (Rüdig, Bennie and Franklin 1991; Witherspoon 1994; Tranter 1996). Those in the environmental movement who fit that profile are in a good position to gain access to CMC. This also highlights the exclusivity of part of the movement, which might limit certain groups' ability for outreach, or reflect a lack of desire for inclusivity.

A division can be identified between the ways in which the interviewees have sought to aid their fellow activists (those integrated with the social movement) in overcoming the access problems and the ways in which the interviewees have tried to ensure that their use of CMC was accessible or non-exclusionary (for example, by having low graphical content on their websites so that they are easy and quick to download or by not using language in a potentially offensive manner), for the intended audience (those not integrated into movement networks). While the division between these two contingents is fragile and fuzzy, it serves as a useful theoretical delineation with which to analyse environmentalists' perception of the importance of helping *others* gain access to CMC. The latter is dealt with first, in the sub-section which follows.

The issue of access

Although many of the interviewees encountered difficulties in accessing CMC, they accorded differing levels of importance to the issue of access to the technology. The efforts made by environmentalists to overcome access constraints also reflect their perceptions of the usefulness of CMC, which ranged from those who regarded CMC as accessible only to an elite few (and who therefore saw reliance upon the technology as problematical) to those who considered that access was universal.

Many accepted that the accessibility of CMC was limited and that there were exclusions: 'You're excluding the poor, the off-lined, the people in countries that don't have great internet access' (Gideon, McSpotlight). Without uniform access many raised the concern that debates were occurring online which were not being repeated or were not inclusive of those without CMC access. For GSN, having an email list had eased many of their previous communication difficulties, but it now meant that 'sometimes there's a problem with discussions moving on, leaving certain people behind without them being involved in the formulation of certain ideas and plans' (Tristram, GSN). However, overall, 'It's still more accessible than anything we could have created any other way' (Dave Morris, McSpotlight). Thus even those who accepted that access was limited argued that this should not detract from the technology's utility as a tool for distributing information to those who were online. Others thought that the falling costs of the technology meant that most people would now have access: 'It's getting cheaper and cheaper, and it reaches a point where virtually everyone can get access to it' (Mike Slocombe, co-ordinator, *Urban75*[3]). Susan Pipes (former GIS co-ordinator, FoE) argued: 'It's not that it's just down to those people who've got money . . . You're getting [the] internet in schools and libraries, so people can get access to the information.' James (EF!) also noted that CMC 'makes it more accessible to other groups of people, because it's an easy-to-access form of communication. People with speech impediments, dyslexia, people who lead disorganised lives can find it quite easy to use.' Asked why some people did not use CMC, David (media liaison, NE Green Party) had little sympathy with them:

> I have very limited patience with people who find the internet and things hard to use, I mean it's common sense . . . I think it's an illogical fear of things. I don't think there's any real reason to be worried about it or find it difficult to use the web, any more than it is to use a telephone.

Irrespective of accessibility, however, many environmentalists identified word of mouth as their most important source of information, and felt that those without access to CMC were not to be concerned over missing anything crucial. Given the access restrictions, many activists agreed with Ed

(GSN): 'You have to remember to offer alternatives . . . Always keep going back to older methods to address any excluded people.' At Lyminge Forest, for example, activists valued CMC only as a channel, albeit an important one, through which to distribute, not to gain, information.

Finance: minimising costs, encouraging donations and fundraising

Groups and individuals faced different financial costs for their use of CMC. Financial constraints on the use of CMC by environmental organisations are widespread, but rarely entirely prohibitive. Although such constraints limit the quantity and quality of CMC that organisations are able to provide, there was a general perception that 'the technology has come down so much in price . . . that it's now possible for activists to buy, blag, borrow technology and pay for the service' (Toby, *SchNEWS*). All the groups in the case studies sought to minimise the cost of their CMC use by encouraging donations, fundraising, and using old and existing equipment. Student-based groups, such as GSN or Peace Action, were able to benefit from free CMC provision at most British universities, while FoE, as a large NGO, was able to raise funds to finance use and could afford a leased ISDN line. Moreover, FoE benefited from donations – 'Our web server was donated by Sun [Microsystems]' (Susan Pipes, FoE) – but drew the line at sponsorship in order to preserve its independence: 'If we started endorsing people, we could get everything for free, but we wouldn't do that' (Tony Canning, IT technical and support manager, FoE).

The smaller non-hierarchical direct-action groups (such as *SchNEWS*, Lyminge Forest and McSpotlight) faced the largest financial barriers because many of them had no working budgets: 'We talked about [paying for access] for quite a long time before it happened, because *SchNEWS* was pretty skint' (Chris, *SchNEWS*). At Lyminge Forest, it helped that locals 'provide much of our food and building materials' (Blue 1997: 20) and that money was raised through stalls at festivals. However, donations were irregular and the cost limited CMC use: 'I use the internet café. I get ten minutes [online], but it means I can't do long letters back to people' (Blue, Lyminge Forest).

Although costs were thought by some to be a deterrent to use, both *Squall*[4] and *SchNEWS* moved into producing online to help reduce the costs of producing the paper version of their respective newsletters, and activists at Lyminge Forest saw using CMC as reducing some of their costs. Moreover: 'It also allows us to do a lot more which we couldn't otherwise afford' (John, Lyminge Forest), such as publishing colour pictures.

Cost was a problem for CAT; its proponents struggled to get CMC prioritised for funding. There was concern that the website did not generate revenue and therefore was a drain rather than an asset. This debate was re-ignited when CAT was about to be charged for their previously free ISP and proponents had to convince others that the website was valuable enough to pay for. Furthermore, CMC access was uneven. Each department organised its own ISP and modem connection, which multiplied the fees being paid: 'We are all doing it on separate phone lines, so we are paying separate sets of standing charges and [for] separate sets of phone calls' (Charlotte Cosserat, information officer, CAT). CAT reduced costs by upgrading existing equipment rather than purchasing new machines, but had to pay for much of their hardware: 'We have had some stuff donated to us, but it's generally fairly old technology, and hasn't been compatible with the newer stuff that we've got' (Steve Jones, former ATA co-ordinator, CAT). Costs were further minimised by relying on volunteers to construct and maintain the website.

The Mobile Office minimised the cost of getting computer equipment by collecting bits left over from actions, sharing people's personal possessions, using donations, asking for payment in kind for work and applying for grants. They returned the favours they had received by donating computer equipment to others: 'We've left some computer equipment with the campaign in Teigngrace, in Devon, and some other equipment with the campaign in London' (James, MO). McSpotlight used old computers and relied on people using their own equipment: 'All of the equipment was donated, and everybody worked for free. McSpotlight was initially set up without a single penny being spent' (Anon 1997d: 6).

The majority of the groups had access to free space for their websites[5]. FoE had its own in-house server, reducing costs (and providing them with more control); and some radical groups also had their own servers: 'Myself and some friends . . . have a server . . . permanently on the internet, which is paid for by a little bit of slightly more commercial work, and that then hosts all the stuff we want to do politically. So there is literally no cost involved, except our time' (Chris, (S)hell). *SchNEWS* benefited from a free ISP and free office space (provided by the band The Levellers), and received several donations: 'Both the Macs we've been using for three years were donated to us, as was a lot of the other equipment. We've found it really easy to get hold of equipment for free, because of the reputation, you know – people love us' (Toby, *SchNEWS*).

Some groups moderated use to minimise costs: 'We only go on the web if there's something we specifically need to look for, because it's expensive' (James, MO). Costs were also put in perspective: 'I reckon it is still cheaper to do emails on a mobile phone than it would be to actually send letters' (Pete, founder and co-ordinator, MO).

Location and office space

In addition to financial obstacles, some environmentalists faced physical restrictions in accessing CMC. A lack of communal office space adversely affected certain groups' ability to access CMC. The larger and better-funded organisations, such as FoE, were able to afford workspace and computer access for most staff, including their regional campaign co-ordinators (RCCs). At CAT, overcrowding of the office space was relieved by the construction of a new information centre. Other smaller groups, such as *SchNEWS* and McSpotlight, also had offices. However, for FoE local groups, access problems were compounded by a lack of office space. In his appraisal of FoE computer access, Allen (1996) concluded that access to computers was significantly increased where there was communal office space. Many local groups' email access was only through a computer in one member's home, and this 'led to bottle-necks in the group if information wasn't being passed on, and a burden of responsibility for communicating if it was' (Allen 1996: 12). However, FoE local group members also used CMC to overcome the difficulties of meeting communally: 'We communicate using email – thus we don't really need meetings. The email conference effectively becomes a long protracted meeting . . . it works really well' (Maurice Spurway, Exeter FoE, quoted in Ritchie 1999b: 12).

It is often difficult to run computer equipment in the environments in which protesters operate – 'It's quite impractical to have a desktop computer if you're squatting' (Laptop Mike, RTS). Residents of protest camps, especially those in rural locations, faced significant restrictions in their access to office space. For those at Lyminge, located in a forest, access to the internet was restricted to locations off-site until the final stages of the protest, in 1999, and this was reflected in the difficulties activists had in regularly updating their website. A campaign office was established in a flat in Canterbury for a few months, but this was several miles from the forest camp. Thus editing of the website was stalled: 'It's very difficult to get us all in one place – me, Merlin, laptop, *Dreamweaver* [web design program] and a phone line to plug into . . . It's been slow' (Mike, Lyminge Forest). Later, an activist's home, in Folkestone, was used for access, and by late 1999 Merlin was able to use CMC, via a laptop and mobile phone, from within the forest, powering access from car batteries.

A key innovation was the MO project which made office facilities available to those living on protest sites by taking a van kitted-out with technical equipment to protest sites: 'It's making the facilities open to all sorts of different people, so the idea is to bring these sorts of facilities and the know-how, and all that stuff, to places where they wouldn't normally be available' (Pete, MO). Furthermore, activists at Lyminge Forest and from MO used solar and wind energy to power their laptops, which enabled their computers to be located away from the National Grid. However, physical problems remained in the form of security issues. Kit was lost at each protest, and because 'people don't respect stuff, and so much stuff gets lunched-out on protest offices' (James, EF!). At Lyminge, 'hanging on to the stuff' was difficult (Mike, Lyminge Forest), and this also limited the sharing of equipment. Being on a protest camp also meant that it was harder to physically co-ordinate editing of web pages or to purchase kit: 'I was down at the A30 [a road protest in Devon], I was on site for nine months and a lot of that time is high eviction and stress . . . [the difficulty is in] actually getting . . . to leave site, to be able to go off and get [equipment], a lot of the time' (Pete, MO). In contrast, the majority of participants at GSN had free access to CMC at their universities, but only during term time. Peaks of activity on the discussion list occurred mid-term, and troughed during university vacations, reflecting the importance of location to accessing CMC.

Technical skills, education and training

Despite increasing computer literacy, improved user interfaces and software simplification, skills are still necessary to utilise CMC (Walch 1999). This need for skills can act as a form of exclusion. There were strong skills differentials among the case study groups, and usually only a few individuals in a group had technical knowledge.

While email packages are increasingly simplified, the skills required to write web pages are becoming more complex[6]. Interviewees had acquired the skills with which to use CMC through different paths. The majority were self-taught: 'You definitely don't need the university thing. I think you just need to be a geek when you are teenager' (Chris, (S)hell).

Individuals had reached different levels of ability, and some felt limited by the lack of available training: 'I just sort of blunder my way through it . . . it's really expensive to get lessons' (Andy, GSN). Many groups had a small skills base and responsibility for technical tasks fell upon a limited few, putting such individuals in positions of power within a group. At *SchNEWS* there were only two people who could edit the website, and Toby noted: 'I need to train more people to do it because it's going to fall apart if I don't do that soon.' This fits patterns identified with other technology use, where a 'product champion', with the foresight and the requisite skills, initially encourages technology use, and is consequently responsible for training others (Buchanan 1993). In some cases (such as at Lyminge Forest), the removal of the product champion results in an interlude in CMC use.

Others identified the divide between 'the computer bods' (Sarah, MO) and those less skilled, as producing a tension:

The conflict remains between the technocrats, who know how to do everything and go into their techno-babble in their [e-]mail, and say 'Oh god, its
simple', and then other people who feel that these people are excluding them
from something they want to be in. They want to hear about all these things
but they don't have the knowledge. (Ed, GSN)

Thus those with the skills often bear the responsibility to share them.
Groups made efforts to share their skills and have training sessions. FoE had
extensive training schemes and advised local groups on how to use CMC.
When email was first comprehensively available, Richard Weatherley
(former IT manager) tried to educate FoE staff about it: 'We ran some training courses; I wrote and distributed a user's guide; I ran awareness and discussion sessions at FoE strategy days and conferences; I did presentations;
I briefed the board; I tried to encourage women to use it.' However, even
where formalised training was available, 'people tend to sign up for it and
then don't turn up . . . Turnout is often low' (Tony Canning, FoE).

SchNEWS also arranged training days: 'Usually once a month . . . we
teach basic desk-top publishing, email skills, internet' (Jo Makepeace,
SchNEWS). Toby (*SchNEWS*) also tried to make sure that people were
involved in the website and thus sharing responsibility for it. He was
careful to ensure that others could understand the processes by which he
had constructed the site: 'Whatever you do, think hard about whether
others with less skills than you can take over or join in: skills like WinWord,
typing, scanning are easy, but html coding harder, and CGI scripting pretty
rare' (Toby 1997).

At Lyminge, it was Merlin and John who had computer skills, and they
informally taught Mike and others. People would congregate in the loaned
flat in Canterbury and share computer tips. Later on in the protest, Merlin
would visit Worzel's house and teach him there: 'I've learnt from Merlin
and Mike, here, and another guy called John . . . and we'd just sit around
and chat, and I sort of picked it up that way' (Worzel, Lyminge Forest).

McSpotlight initially drew inspiration from the N5M events,[7] thus benefiting from the skills of the Amsterdam activists – xs 4all: 'They were hosting
it, and they were telling us all these clever techniques they had' (Jessy,
McSpotlight). At McSpotlight those with skills taught those without: 'We
had a big pool of people who wanted to help but didn't know bugger all . . .
It doesn't take five minutes to learn to do basic html, so we soon had lots of
people doing that' (Jessy, McSpotlight). Furthermore, McSpotlight were
able to benefit from a division of labour by attracting a pool of volunteers
with a range of specific skills, so that when they've come across something
they can't do, 'such as graphic design, complicated programming, someone
with those skills has always come along' (Helena, quoted in Anon 1997e).

There is a precedent for skills sharing within the environmental movement, especially in direct action for which workshops are used to impart

skills or individuals learn by example from others. Individuals with specific skills, such as tree climbing or media liaison, are often are willing to
share their expertise and train others. The few highly technically skilled
individuals at the forefront of innovative CMC use also attempted skill
sharing. However, teaching complex computer programming is a time-
consuming and lengthy activity, and it was as much as some could do to
encourage individuals to experiment themselves.

Thus, there remains a dilemma as to whether the aim of particular protests is to include as many participants as possible (alluding to the 'logic of
numbers') or for those already involved to concentrate on becoming technically adept (as Greenpeace does with its specialist teams of activists).
Although these aims can appear to co-exist, resource restrictions often
dictate the prioritising of one or the other. Furthermore, an inclusive
protest often precludes the use of more ingenious actions – which might be
construed as radical and thus would dissuade sections of the public from
participating in the broader protest. Thus it can be hard to reconcile such
specialisation with the desire to incorporate more participants because
online actions become increasingly complicated and thus less accessible to
those without the requisite skills.

Technical specifications and support

Hardware and software problems further hindered activists' CMC use
and, except at FoE, were often left to the individual to solve. Software problems were compounded by many groups' reliance on old machines. Pete
(MO) experienced many hardware compatibility problems when setting
up hybrid systems or using computers from alternative power sources
(Anon 1997f). *SchNEWS* was unable to provide PDF versions of its newsletter online until 1999 because 'the programme that makes PDFs was actually too sophisticated for the ancient machines that we were doing the
SchNEWS on' (Chris, *SchNEWS*).

CAT was constrained by incompatible computer systems. Some staff
were working on Macs while the website was written on a PC: 'I did get
the idea of how to put it on [the website] but in actual fact you struggle to
find the software for a Mac to be able to do that' (Sarah Jenkinson, former
media officer, CAT). CAT experienced additional problems because of the
limited number of telephone lines. Staff had to share the modem line with
the fax machine and creditcard line. Consequently access was only really
possible out of hours: 'You have to go online at 5.30 when people have
clocked off for the day' (Steve Jones, CAT).

FoE employed a full-time IT team, but had difficulty retaining IT per-
sonnel (due to the uncompetitive wages they could offer), and this contributed to problems of co-ordination and communication. Technical support

for regional offices was complicated by distance, but IT staff visited offices annually, used FTP access from head office to check their computer configurations and 'for hardware problems they're on maintenance contracts so we send engineers out' (Tony Canning, FoE). However, the regional FoE offices were still suffering a lack of technical support: 'It's difficult for them to deal with the remote offices. Sometimes things will be down two or three days at a time' (Mike Birkin, south-west RCC, FoE) and they 'could really do with some modern hardware at some point' (David Blake, IT systems support, Birmingham FoE). Local groups received considerably less support due to cost constraints[8], but were offered workshop and training days which included CMC use. Aware of the access problems faced by local groups, FoE ran the West Yorkshire Pilot Project which provided several local groups in West Yorkshire with free CMC access and training (Allen 1996). The project concluded that many of the IT problems faced were not helped by a lack of IT support from head office. Access to the one computer per group became an issue in local groups, and access to a laptop instead failed to overcome the problem because it was invariably still controlled by one person and there was no communal office space within which it could be easily shared.

Diversity

Research on gender and CMC has engaged with the possibilities of 'neutralising' the importance of gender or swapping gender roles while online (Haraway 1990; Stabile 1994; Wakeford 1995; McCormick and Leonard 1996; McRae 1997). Research has also highlighted how women were (though do not necessarily remain) under-utilising CMC compared to men (Jordan 1999a; Escobar 1999; Mastrangelo Gittler 1999). Within the environmental movement there have been eco-feminist critiques of the way in which gender is bypassed as an issue of concern or discrimination (Mies and Shiva 1993; McKay 1998). Meanwhile, there remains a divisive patriarchal factor in activism, exemplified by the masculine culture of protest camps (Groombridge 1996; Walcroft 1998).

Environmentalists can face problems of access to CMC because of their gender or their ethnicity. White males have tended to dominate the use of CMC. Some women had the skills to use CMC proficiently and had key roles in particular groups' technology use. There was, however, a general lack of female involvement in CMC use in the case study groups. This was in contrast to the almost equal representation of both genders in the groups. There was a perception that this was 'because computers have traditionally been a male kind of thing' (Jon Ivar, GSN). In the cases where women *have* played key roles in CMC, they had done so since the first adoption of the technology by the group, for example FoE (in particular,

Susan Pipes) and McSpotlight (Jessy). In other cases, males had dominated CMC use from its inception and became, in effect, its gate keepers. This male dominance could inhibit others becoming involved. To the question 'If a woman came along, would she be able to help on the internet?', Toby (*SchNEWS*) replied: 'It would be seen as unusual, but she could certainly do it . . . I'd really like to hope that she wouldn't be put off by the nature of the people – the guys involved who use computers – the nature of the conversations they have.'

Some groups, such as McSpotlight, 'did try and get in as many different backgrounds as possible . . . We came against the barrier of everyone who was out there tended to be from a similar background, and the networks that we were connected to . . . From the inception there was definitely a distinct lack of different ethnic backgrounds' (Bob, McSpotlight). This reflects the general lack of ethnic diversity in the British environmental movement: 'The racial split is endemic [in] Brighton . . . there hasn't been a lot of outreach work to get more people from ethnic minorities involved' (Jo Makepeace, *SchNEWS*). It was also felt that any gender or ethnic bias was not a result of the attitudes of the environmentalists, as 'everyone involved in McSpotlight is pretty much sort of non-sexist, non-racist, people', but was 'more a by-product of the net than a by-product of McSpotlight in itself . . . There has been a male dominance in computing' (Gideon, McSpotlight).

Few groups sought overtly to balance the gender division in CMC use. At Lyminge Forest, where no women were involved in the website, Mike said that they had asked women whether they wanted to contribute, but that 'not many women want to get involved in the media side of things. They see it as intrusive and they just want to get on with their own things.' Consequently, although women and multiculturalism were identified as lacking in most groups' use of CMC, there were few initiatives to redress the balance. It was argued that women were not interested; or else a woman using technology would be singled out to illustrate that there was no exclusion, when she was really a token. This is also a reflection of discord among some environmentalists about the monoculturalism of the movement (Kala 2000). Thus, there seems little possibility that environmentalists' use of CMC would contribute to a questioning of patriarchal dominance, or the development of an alternative social (and gendered) order, as suggested by Escobar (1999).

Language

Finally, language can constrain CMC access. CMC reinforces the emphasis on use of the written word and prioritises English as the common language (due to its American origins). This can serve to exclude those with other languages and those who are illiterate. In GSN, 77 per cent of questionnaire respondents were native English speakers, but Bulgarian, German, Portuguese and Italian were also represented. McSpotlight was the only group to include other languages (by translating the original McLibel leaflet) and by encouraging and linking to anti-McDonald's websites written in non-English languages. Furthermore, the type of language used can constrain access to newcomers, icons in emails – *and*, a_more, :-), 'do', </sarcastic> – or activists' slang – *fluffy*, *spiky*, *brew crew*, *lunch-outs*, *tat* – can be difficult to interpret. Within a protest setting this may quickly become meaningful to the outsider, but if encountered through CMC alone it can serve as a form of exclusion.

Although some activists were reluctant to use CMC, others felt constrained in their access, and this influenced how they were able to use the technology. Most of the constraining factors were a result of the funding limitations of the interviewees' affiliated groups. Thus FoE was able to afford CMC access, office space, skilled employees and technical support, whereas those at Lyminge Forest suffered from a limited income and the many demands on their existing resources. Among the interviewees there was a general awareness that access to CMC was not uniform and most groups stressed the importance of continued use of other communication channels and information distribution methods. Many of the non-CMC users claimed they did not feel excluded, and some activists highlighted the variety of ways users could achieve easy and free access if they wanted. In this way, most of the interviewees considered that it was up to individuals to secure their own access and that access difficulties should not outweigh the advantages of CMC.

Creating new avenues of access

In addition to acknowledging and attempting to resolve the access problems they faced, activists employed CMC as a way to create new avenues of access to information they wanted to distribute. Accordingly, many tried to ensure that their form of CMC use did not unnecessarily exclude members of the intended audience[9].

Using CMC as a way to provide access

Environmentalists have used CMC as an inexpensive means by which to reach an international audience. In addition, providing information on the internet diverted enquiries from time pressured campaigners and reduced publication costs. Franny Armstrong (One-Off Productions) organised a global screening of the McLibel documentary (which had been excluded from mainstream television) via email, with the film streamed on the web: 'From just one email message, 104 screenings in nineteen countries were held and we estimate that about 8 million people watched the film' (Franny Armstrong, One-Off Productions).

SchNEWS used CMC to reach a new audience. Distribution of the newsletter via email made it accessible to those who might not have socialised in activist circles (and thus not received a hard copy). CMC was also used to retain its audience: 'We lose less people, I think, people [who] move from paper to email then stay with us longer than they would have done if they'd had to send stamps' (Chris, *SchNEWS*). With PDF being used on their website, *SchNEWS* further increased their accessibility by making it possible for web users to directly print off formatted versions of the newsletter. *SchNEWS* also tried to shape people's use of CMC, recommending websites for '*net-diving* rather than net-surfing, so you actually go and dive into particular sites' (Jo Makepeace, *SchNEWS*).

FoE used CMC to provide public access to restricted government environmental data (Pipes 1997). The Chemical Release Inventory (CRI) increased access dramatically: 'Between 1995 and 1996 the Government recorded 797 visits to its regional offices to get CRI information, and we had over 25,000 individual queries to the database . . . So it's a whole magnitude difference of people being able to get this information' (Susan Pipes, FoE).

Finally, CAT used CMC to overcome their spatial access problems. By providing information on a website (including a virtual tour of CAT, information sheets and an online shopping service) and answering information inquiries via email, it was able to get its message out 'to as wide an audience as possible, because not everybody is going to come to mid-Wales . . . People can access us from all over the world, which is marvellous; we've suddenly become an international organisation' (Charlotte Cosserat, CAT). CAT also used CMC to reach a specific audience – the young: '[T]he website is going to be perhaps our main route for attracting newer and younger people into ATA [Alternative Technology Association]' (Jones 1998: 2).

Simplicity of online presence

Most of the case-study groups increased their online accessibility by refraining from using complex graphics or plug-ins on their websites. FoE minimised its use of complex features to enable access by people who were using old browser software or a slow modem: 'In the majority of cases, we try to keep away from using frames just because they can be quite difficult to navigate round, but also it bumps up the technology' (Susan Pipes, FoE). Additionally, because in the early days of CMC use more people had access to email than to websites themselves, some services were limited to email to extend the number of people who could be involved: 'Climate On-line is designed as one way to get into environmental activism, and it is deliberately just an email thing as this makes it far more inclusive' (Charles Linn, former website developer, FoE). Birmingham FoE even built in a facility so that users with slow modems could download the whole site and read it offline: 'I want to be as inclusive as possible' (David Blake, Birmingham FoE).

McSpotlight sought to find a balance between accessibility and innovation.[10] It was 'important for us to try and make the site obviously as interactive and as flash as possible, . . . not to make the core ideas and the core content unobtainable, but to make it as inclusive as possible on every browser, on the slowest machines' (Bob, McSpotlight). Furthermore, McSpotlight sought to reduce the costs for its audience by enabling the site to be downloaded free of charge or viewed as a CD-ROM which enabled 'unlimited use, free of the constraints of continued Net access, line rentals and connection charges' (Atton 2000: 2). Similarly, *SchNEWS* kept its website 'deliberately low tech' (Chris, *SchNEWS*).

Other methods of distribution

Most environmental groups continued to utilise a range of methods of distribution to prevent their use of CMC excluding any potential audience. The Mobile Office sought to ensure that 'nothing goes out on the internet that doesn't [also] go out by word of mouth or by flyer' (James, MO). Other methods included leaflets, publications, street theatre, videos, print-outs of emails and sections from websites. Those at Lyminge 'use as many methods of getting information across as possible, and the internet is one of those tools . . . People aren't always going to get the leaflets and people aren't always gonna find the website, but hopefully between the two you'll get a fair few people [who] will be notified as to what's happening' (Wizard, Lyminge Forest). Others printed emails they received and took them to those without access: 'Whenever I got any emails I'd print [them] out, and take [them] to [protest] site, and let everyone read [them]. I wouldn't just email straight back. I wanted everyone to say what they thought and just talk it out, so everyone was involved with using it' (Rachel, EF!).

FoE was also aware of the risk of exclusion and continued to provide paper-based materials:[11] 'We could get too reliant on electronic forms of communication, and that might actually rule out the possibilities for other people to share the information . . . We have to be very conscious of making sure those people are still kept in the loop through traditional forms of communication such as the post and the telephone' (Chris Crean, west Midlands RCC, FoE). There were, however, more publications, in terms of documents and briefing sheets, available on the web than through the post via the publications department. FoE has also focused campaigns on information which is available only over the internet, such as the CRI and Factory Watch, which could result in exclusions.

Providing the access facilities

While many activists tried to make access to CMC easier for those within the movement, ensuring that their use of CMC did not exclude members of the intended audience, few actively sought to provide the access facilities to CMC, not viewing such provision as part of their role. The exceptions to this were the Mobile Office and CAT. MO provided access to CMC for activists constrained to living on protest sites and hoped this would serve as a model which they encouraged others to replicate. Part of CAT's remit was to provide information, and within that the group included the need to provide access to CMC. Thus, CAT built the Autonomous Environmental Information Centre which housed four public access computers. Although internet access was guided towards specific environmental information (using direct links), it was also possible to access the whole of the internet on these computers.

Changing organisational forms

Access can be mediated by membership to a group and CMC use could alter the functions and structure of an organisation. In groups which strive for non-hierarchical forms of organisation, it is instructive to examine whether CMC is used to strengthen inclusion or contribute to an already uneven balance of power.

Access to resources has historically determined positions of power within groups: 'resources have provided positions of relative power, even in a deprofessionalised and biodegradable network. . . . Throughout EF! (UK)'s existence, groups . . . with a strong resource base have influenced the direction of the network in terms of repertoires, organisation and issue-focus' (Wall 1999a: 88). CMC could serve to reduce the urgency of the requirement for extensive resources and thus contribute to non-hierarchical attempts at organisation: as Klein, for example, has stated (2000a: 396), 'the Net is more than an organizing tool – it has become an organizing model, a blueprint for decentralized but cooperative decision making. It facilitates the process of information sharing to such a degree that many groups can work in concert with one another without the need to achieve monolithic consensus.'

Furthermore, CMC might facilitate the flattening of existing hierarchies and help groups to resist the pressure of formalisation by sustaining decentralised forms of communication (Poster 1997; Walch 1999; Washbourne

1999b). With CMC, all users have the facilities to interact with the information and with each other: 'hierarchy is irrelevant, because everyone has equal access to the network, and everyone is free to communicate with as few or as many people as they like' (Woolley 1992).

Bimber has argued that CMC use facilitates the operation of activist groups without the need for institutional structures. Thus there is 'the possibility of decreasing coherence and stability in interest group politics, as the group process loses some of its dependence on stable public and private institutions' (Bimber 1998: 144). The outcome would be groups that are more fluid and diffuse and networks with an ability to mobilise more quickly. In this scenario it is the informal groups, which tend to be poor in resources, that are liable to benefit most from CMC use.

Yet the potential for CMC use to alter the internal dynamics of groups, such as serving to flatten existing hierarchies, will be reliant on individuals having unconstrained access to the technology. It is to be expected that the uneven patterns of access between and within the case-study groups will be reflected in the way in which CMC has impacted on the groups' organisational forms.

This section has three parts. It begins by illustrating how the innovative use CMC by the interviewees has been encouraged by their non-hierarchical organisational structures, which provided space for them to experiment. Then, I show that CMC has enabled a convergence of groups' communications, easing many groups' internal communication problems and speeding up internal flows. The third section explores a negative consequence of CMC use, in that some nuclei of control have clustered around its use in non-hierarchical groups. These nuclei work against the aims of such groups to organise horizontally. Yet, despite this, CMC use has contributed to such groups' resistance to the pressure to formalise and develop hierarchies. In comparison, the case for CMC use flattening existing hierarchies remains inconclusive.

The freedom to experiment

McSpotlight, Lyminge Forest, *SchNEWS*, the Mobile Office, GSN and CAT attempted non-hierarchical and fluid forms of organisation, and reflected the broader culture of DiY, which supports initiative and individual action. This encouraged individual autonomy, expression and experimentation: 'There's no structure . . . People can do what they want. They can join one camp or they can go and start their own camp . . . There's no leaders, no rules, it's just autonomous. Everyone just gets on with it and it works' (Matt, Lyminge Forest).

Without a hierarchical chain of command, individuals were able quickly to grasp the opportunities they perceived CMC to offer and to make use of them: 'Nobody has overall editorial control, so that's given me the confidence to push ahead with the work I want to do. I've just done it, and I haven't got permission off anybody to do what I've done' (Steve Jones, CAT). Although this structure facilitated novel uses of CMC, it also complicated the decisions about website content: 'You're presenting a group that doesn't have a formal decision-making structure . . . You have to be in touch with the group to be aware of the nuances of what . . . is the – often unspoken – consensus' (Laptop Mike, RTS). Such freedom and the dynamism it engenders are especially useful to environmentalists able to use the technology in creative and novel ways to capture attention. These opportunities are often short lived as internet innovations quickly become standard and thus lose their attraction for mainstream media coverage or as a hook with which to attract a curious public.

FoE has been criticised by less centralised groups, such as EF! (UK) for being too hierarchical. Despite a network of regional campaign co-ordinators and local groups, FoE has been described as more like a 'protest business' rather than a democratic organisation (Jordan and Maloney 1997). A reliance by FoE on passive supporters rather than active members has limited participatory forms of organising. Staff, however, were encouraged to participate in organisational decisions, and Washbourne (1999b) has argued that FoE is less a hierarchy than an 'unbounded social network of the like-minded'. Furthermore, FoE chose to support the notion of direct action, but not to actively take part (Schwarz 1994): 'As FoE has established its authority for rational argument, it has distanced itself from the more militant forms of protest. Though civil disobedience and direct action were contemplated in its early days, it now eschews any illegal or disruptive activities' (Bate 1983: 132). This has differentiated FoE from the DiY and participatory culture of the more radical groups.

Early use of CMC at FoE was undertaken without formal permission. Theoretically, support had to be gained through a series of management approvals, but Richard Weatherly (FoE) ignored the process: 'I would have been chewed out by several management team members.' The eventual need for official funding, and thus for requesting support through FoE's procedures, frustrated those keen to use CMC in innovative ways: 'It didn't have somebody who was high up there, on senior management, really being able to push through that we need investment in this. I'd say it just feels like a year of . . . not being supported to be able to take it forward' (Susan Pipes, FoE). Re-allocating funding in such a large organisation, however, required strategic redistribution of significant resources; and because such decisions had to pass through FoE's hierarchical levels, the adoption of CMC was slowed down. In contrast, groups whose structure has enabled rapid and experimental adoption of CMC have often used the technology in particularly innovative ways, as exemplified by McSpotlight.

Convergence of communications

Internal co-ordination and communication are liable to be facilitated by groups' use of CMC. CMC can help prevent information getting lost or misinterpreted. When campaign offices are located separately from a protest site a split can emerge between the site and office, which could result in communication problems. There was a need for those on-site to be able to communicate their message directly and to receive information quickly, thus 'having the [Mobile] Office on site meant people were informed instantly on what was going on, thus avoiding confusion and lost messages. People on-site were also a lot more informed as to the facts about the campaign' (Anon 1998b).

CAT used CMC to overcome the need to cover the distances between offices on their 7–acre site. Staff used email to communicate internally.[12] 'It's actually easier for me to email them, it's so quick and so cheap for me to send stuff to publications or to education or biology by email' (Charlotte Cosserat, CAT). This system was not perfect, however, and electronic data were still exchanged on floppy discs when large files had to be exchanged.

FoE's website helped stem the flow of queries to campaigners by pre-empting many requests for information. However, some campaigners were flooded with email requests: 'You can end up spending too much of your time responding to emails or deleting emails when you should be campaigning' (Adrian Bebb, real food campaigner, FoE). Although local activists had been encouraged to email campaigners, FoE established a protocol for email use: 'We cannot enter into debate on email. If an issue needs to be discussed, please phone. We will only respond to emails when appropriate, or when requested to acknowledge receipt of an email' (Friends of the Earth 1998a). By incorporating the use of CMC in procedures and policy guidelines FoE limited its full benefit. FoEs intranet, however, did ease information sharing between staff: 'I can access any files – they are all on the same network – and if I want to look in one of the campaign team areas and look at their files I can access them remotely' (Mike Birkin, FoE).

CMC was also used by GSN to ease communication problems. CMC was a cheaper and more frequently used means of communicating with its dispersed participants than the newsletter or gatherings: GSN 'had chronic communication problems, in that people would be in touch within their local area, but as a nation-wide figure it just wasn't together' (Ciaran, former list co-ordinator, GSN). Producing and distributing the newsletter had been time consuming and costly. Using CMC strengthened its ability to communicate at the national level and facilitated a more inclusive form of communication, one which enabled discussion between the whole group at all times, not just between those at the gatherings or within the core cliques. Furthermore, contributors to discussion were not limited to those who

shouted loudest, or were most eloquent, as 'with email there's a great lev-
eller: everyone's got the time. They can spend as much time as they like
thinking about it before they reply' (Andy, GSN). However, many of those
on the GSN email list rarely contributed to discussions (according to questionnaire results), and part of the rationale for establishing regional lists was
that smaller lists might encourage more people to communicate, thus negat-
ing the advantage of GSN being a national list which facilitated national co-
ordination. Although this regionalisation aided the move towards a more
inclusive network, it mitigated against one of the original aims of GSN, the
national co-ordination of students' environmental concerns.

Thus, overall, most of the interviewees felt that CMC had aided the
internal communication flows of their groups and increased the speed of
these flows from pre-CMC states. In cases where a high percentage of participants had access to CMC, its use eased internal communication problems and speeded up internal flows. As a result participants were better
informed and felt more included in the daily operations of a group.
However, in groups where CMC access was uneven, its use resulted in the
exclusion of some participants.

Hierarchies: nuclei, subversion and flattening

In all the case-study groups but FoE, there were attempts to organise in a
non-hierarchical manner. Despite subverting organisational structures,
however, informal or hidden hierarchies developed in some groups. For
example, Cindy Harris of CAT argued that 'in any co-operative there will
very often be invisible, latent hierarchies. I think all you can do is have a
formal structure which explicitly doesn't recognise hierarchies . . . there is
obviously here a hierarchy of people who've been here longest' (quoted in
Harper 1995: 34).

Specific clusters developed around the use of CMC. There were no
chains of command within these clusters, though they did tend to exert
control over use of the technology. These nuclei of control developed in
response primarily to uneven access between participants in a group, but
also as a result of some environmentalists' reluctance to use the technology. These nuclei were often unintentional, and there were some efforts to
prevent their development.

At Lyminge Forest, although 6–8 people were involved in creating and
maintaining the website, there were essentially four key individuals in
control of it – Merlin, Mike, John and Worzel. This was due to access problems, but also because of the group's general disinterest in becoming
involved with the technology. For some, the technology was seen as a dis-
traction from the task at hand: 'I don't think it would matter if it wasn't
there' (Red, Lyminge Forest).

As to whether it was easy for others to become involved in the website there were mixed opinions. Di, who did not use computers, thought that 'all you would have to do is ask and they would let you'. Ben, however, felt inclusion was not encouraged: 'You could if you wanted to, but really Mike and Merlin do it all. When we write leaflets people tend to go round the site asking if anyone wants to help or put stuff on it, but not for the internet.' Merlin refuted this, and claimed that he'd tried to make sure that a range of people were involved: he went 'around asking people specifically for that purpose . . . if I was talking to people I would often offer. If anyone wanted to contribute they could either dial in on the computer or just write something down, and it can be typed up if they don't want to use a computer.' Merlin identified the key problem as motivation – 'It is quite hard to motivate people into actually getting pen to paper' – rather then access issues *per se*. However, although the physical access to the website was controlled by a few key enthusiasts,[13] and while they did appear to try to include others and help them overcome their access problems, clearly not all access issues were resolved.

This tension, between how participants perceived their own and other's practices, reflects the broader contention of this chapter. Often activists felt they were being inclusive, while others perceived themselves as being excluded. In many ways *inclusion* and *exclusion* are relative: 'access exists in gradations, rather than in a bipolar opposition' (Warschauer 2002: 10). However, it also highlights a possible discontinuity between interviewees' intentions and their practices. While it is not possible to arbitrate such opinions on the basis of interviews alone, the fact that there are discrepancies between interviewees' accounts suggests that more could have been done to share access to the website.

At McSpotlight the nucleus influenced what went on the website: 'There is a hierarchy of access privileges to the whole site . . . it goes through a chain of checks and approvals' (Bob, McSpotlight). Some objected to this form of content control:

> The anarchists amongst McSpotlight felt that it was part of the ethos that anybody's opinion is valid, and other people on the team thought that the good thing about McSpotlight was that it had an identity and it had a certain style, it had a certain witty tone to it, and we needed to maintain that . . . It was a sore point and it was never resolved. (Jessy, McSpotlight)

However, the core cluster at McSpotlight initially made key decisions and then faded in importance: 'Once the launch was enacted the core group quickly fell apart, and they're still around but there is no direction or agenda in the same way there was at the beginning. And that's extremely intentional' (Bob, McSpotlight). At *SchNEWS*, while the three key individuals did include others' opinions, they also used their influence to stall ideas with which they disagreed: 'You can't necessarily expect the web team to do . . . things they don't agree with' (Chris, *SchNEWS*). However, over time, the core group has gradually become composed of different individuals, preventing the same people dominating control over the website.

Similar clusters of control developed in the case-study groups around other technologies or tasks because of skill differentials or issues of access, such as the CB radio, or activities like climbing. These nuclei served as a form of oligarchy and were in essence contrary to most of the groups' desire for non-hierarchical organisational forms. On the whole, however, such control was not viewed by participants as constituting any form of exclusion or as being detrimental to the group.

This was most clearly demonstrated at CAT. Thorpe (who instigated the use of CMC) resigned, leaving the responsibility to Martin Donnelly, a volunteer. Thorpe's absence, Martin's (low) status as a volunteer and the informality of much of the staff interaction (facilitated by the organisation's co-operative aims), together with the departmental autonomy, prevented an oligarchy developing around control of the website. In fact, no one took editorial control. Although, technically, Martin made many editorial decisions, and most staff would turn to him when requesting changes to the website, he had not taken on the role of website editor; nor is he perceived by other staff to have done so. He was viewed more as the technician than as the scriptwriter: 'Mostly the text is pulled from the department, saying what they do, and publications about particular technologies, and they just re-format it in html and put it on the web. So there's very little of it written for the actual web itself' (Paul Allen, development director, CAT).

There was, however, a desire at CAT to get more people included in the website. As a result of its growth, CAT had become segmented to the extent that not everyone was able to comment on all matters, as had been possible in the past (Harper 1995). It had an elected management group that included representatives from each of the autonomous departments. The website required inter-departmental co-operation and agreement, but the management system was not designed for such activities, and as a result no one took overall editorial control. Rather than the management team taking on the responsibility, or CMC use triggering an adoption of a less departmentally segmented structure, departments gradually carved out their own sections of the website, over which they took editorial control. Thus, CMC use did not result in an organisational change at CAT, but was used to reinforce the autonomy of each department.

In this way, some groups used CMC to help them resist the development of oligarchies and maintain their non-hierarchical methods. The pressure to formalise – to provide a rigid organisational form able to attract resources, reach a wide audience and present a cohesive image – is felt by many environmental groups (Doyle 2000). Grassroots or direct-action campaigns tend to have a limited existence – either evolving into formal organisations (and thus often a hierarchy) or dissolving, once the action is over. CMC use, however, can ease the resource and communication issues, and can enable groups to sustain and widen their decentralised networks through low-cost and speedy international interaction. This helped networks to retain their fluidity and dynamism, and to evolve according to their changing partici-pants, resisting the pressure to formalise: 'We didn't want it to be formal. We didn't want to be identified as this huge campaign group that was ever-growing and eventually turned into Greenpeace online . . . The whole point is that McSpotlight is there for anyone to take along, and no one person or group of people are responsible for it' (Bob, McSpotlight).

CMC facilitated groups' tapping into an international arena at no extra cost. At McSpotlight email was used to co-ordinate international contribu-tions to the website: 'They were communicated by email pretty much entirely, we never met half the people from around the world that we worked with' (Devin, McSpotlight). CMC also aided activists' visibility through their web presence, even when resources were low or participants few:

> There is a tendency for protest nodes to arise, to gather information, offer spaces and resources for activists, and then either to disappear as the protests conclude or to evolve into other campaigns. Activists employing CMC are able to adapt their resources, to continually transform and re-invent them-selves with a facility only partially available to print media. (Atton 2000: 2)

Thus, CMC helped activists to be involved in multiple projects, maintain-ing campaigns through low-activity periods. For example, McSpotlight is 'not going to be the dynamic and fast-moving innovative website it was when it was first created' (Devin, McSpotlight), but it can remain access-ible, despite there being few individuals still involved. It has become essentially a virtual protest node that requires few resources to continue. Consequently, through the use of CMC, radical grassroots groups are able to achieve more permanence. This diminishes the extent to which large NGOs are crucial as central nodes for resource and information provision, and encourages the decentralisation of the environmental movement.

CMC may also be employed to flatten existing hierarchies (Walch 1999). Those at FoE used CMC to ease communication across the national network (head office, regional offices and local groups), via the intranet and within local groups: 'I used to be writing memos and posting them to Underwood Street staff, maybe sometimes three or four memos a day . . . Now that all just goes via email . . . There's no doubt the volume has increased because it is so easy, but it has also replaced a lot of paper-based communications' (Mike Birkin, FoE). However, many barriers remained to nation-wide communication between local groups. CMC has improved local group communication with head office, but has not been used effectively for inter-group dialogue.

Despite information sharing via campaigns, such as the FoE's Wild Places[14] website – to which local groups would contribute their own information – the importance of the head office was preserved. Most information was still routed via the central office using CMC, which limits its use in strengthening a grassroots network. The hierarchical information flow of the network was maintained rather than CMC being used to bypass formal organisational structures. Decentralising power to the regional level has been aided by a network of regional campaign co-ordinators, but much co-ordination at this level is achieved via the telephone and face-to-face meetings rather than CMC. Furthermore, the construction of FoE's website also serves to maintain its hierarchical structure. The website content is decided upon in the same way as official published information is sanctioned: through a series of stages 'from the campaign team through the public information officers, who invariably re-write it for the mass public. Then, at the end of the line, I am in charge of the layout on the website' (Charles Linn, FoE).

Participatory democracy or elite technology?

Access to CMC varied between the case-study groups according to their resource levels, and between individuals in each group or organisation. There remain 'invisible price tags draped all over the electronic scenery' (Lockard 1997: 220) which were recognised more readily by some interviewees than others. This limited access to CMC, and the possibility that it is consequently an elite medium has implications for future uses of CMC, such as the curtailment of mobilisation possibilities. Such non-uniform access has become manifest as nuclei of control cluster around the technology.

The problems of access to CMC pose a difficult challenge to activists, and one which results in those online having to compromise their ideals:

> [E]ducation activists should be and in many cases are working as hard as possible to correct this problem of access, even though it does seem almost insurmountable. At the same time, contestational forces cannot wait to act until this access problem is corrected. Only in theory can we live by what ought to be; in practice we must work in terms of what is. (CAE 1996: 28)

Cyberspace was initially touted as being free from the bureaucratic and hierarchical tendencies of existing society. However, many problems of access have yet to be resolved, and technology will not solve the fundamental social problem that large numbers of people find it hard to communicate and take decisions together (Barbrook 1995; Tsagarousianou 1998). Far from being an aid to inclusivity, CMC use can prove divisive and can increase marginalisation: 'environmental gains made through this medium will disproportionately reflect the needs of the populations who have access . . . drawing attention to the environmental problems of well-off communities at the expense of those affecting poorer regions' (White 1999).

Environmentalists' attitudes towards inclusion and CMC can be considered from two vantage points. First, it is important to examine the ways in which general access to CMC was secured and access problems tackled – reflecting activists' views on the need to include as many participants as possible in the use of CMC. Second, whether activists' inclusion in the decision-making processes of the group to which they were affiliated was maintained, altered or improved as a result of the use of CMC is significant – reflecting activists' views on the need to operate their own groups using inclusive organising principles.

Principles of participation: between theory and practice

In theory, many environmentalists, and the majority of those interviewed in the case studies, advocate the importance of participatory forms of organisation and the inclusion of a wide population. In practice, framed through analysis of their attitudes to problems of access to CMC, interviewees did not always make attempts to include others. This reflects a tendency within some quarters of the environmental movement to purport to be inclusive, while actually practicing exclusivity. Thus, participation and the need for inclusion were often related only to those individuals already within the movement or particular movement groups (or cliques).

Many environmentalists concentrated effort into exchanging skills, providing office space and helping overcome financial restrictions. However, hardware and software problems, and the lack of female and multicultural involvement, and of the representation of non-English languages have rarely been tackled. Furthermore, most interviewees were of the opinion that it was up to individuals to secure their own access and that access difficulties should not be allowed to obscure the advantages of CMC. This attitude reflects a wider trend in cyberspace, that of 'electronic individualism' (Lockard 1997: 222).

This assertion of individual, not communal, responsibility could also be a reflection of the broader monoculturalism of the British environmental movement. CMC use has intensified many traits that were already visible – its lack of diversity and its class divide. Among the environmentalists in the case-study groups there was a predominance of white, young and tertiary-educated individuals. This is not to say that *no* environmentalist groups are inclusive – as organisations such as CAT invest heavily in attempting to reach a wide audience; but it is to say that some sectors operate as cliques and do little to encourage the participation of others.

This might be explained by a fear that inclusion would dissipate existing solidarities and disperse the network. Furthermore, not all of the interviewees supported moving towards participatory governance of the electorate as a whole; rather, what they wanted was the inclusion in government and/or corporate policy of their particular demands – which could be unrepresentative of the larger population. The ways in which access to CMC was tackled reflect a wider failure in the environmental movement to consider those on the margins and to seek their inclusion.

Overall, there were two key beliefs about access to CMC. First, a belief that it was vital for as many people as possible to have access to CMC was held by some, who, as a result, saw their role to be to encourage others to overcome barriers to access. Such environmentalists aimed to use the technology before it became commercially commodified, and tried to assert a role in shaping its use: thus as many of them as possible would have to gain access and utilise it early on. This was reflected by those interviewees who organised training sessions and repaired old computers for environmental groups.

Second, there were those who believed that access would remain an exclusionary barrier, regardless of efforts to the contrary. Faced with evidence of the lack of uniform access to CMC, some interviewees accepted that they had to compromise their theories of inclusion when it came to practice. This shows a similar pragmatism to that displayed in dealing with the environmentally damaging aspects of computers. In other words, it is not the responsibility of environmentalists to ensure that a democratic society prevails; rather, their priorities have to be in environmental protection. Furthermore, some suggested that although full access is desirable, it is not essential – that activists could illustrate, using small-scale examples of technology use, what would be possible if a more democratic structure of organisation were to be adopted by society. They could use CMC to highlight the inadequacy of the current system of non-participatory decision-making structures, which in turn could encourage others (even those without access to the technology) to critique the system. This viewpoint was reflected by those interviewees, who, rather than encouraging the widening of access, concentrated on using the technology in innovative and tactically productive ways.

The tensions between these two points of view are not easily resolved. The former requires significant effort on the part of activists, consuming time which might otherwise be spent campaigning. However, if the issue of access is not addressed, groups' use of CMC could compound existing, or create new, exclusions. Uncritical CMC use could result in an elite electronic netocracy fracturing any attempts at a heterogenous movement.

Internal organisation structures

Usage of CMC *within* organisations, however, appeared overall to facilitate the inclusion of participants, by easing existing communication problems and reinforcing the use of non-hierarchical organisational forms. Without uniform access, environmentalists are theoretically unable to benefit fully from the potential of CMC. Their online communication networks extend only so far, and others have to be contacted by using traditional methods. This means effort has to be duplicated into using an increased number of distribution channels. However, despite some exclusion (for example, those not online in GSN), CMC had eased previous communication problems and speeded up the flow of information between participants. Moreover, other forms of communication (such as telephones, face-to-face meetings, newsletters) were maintained in most cases, and it appears that more people were included by CMC use than were excluded. Despite the existence of nuclei of control, CMC was used successfully to reinforce resistance against the pressure to formalise and to enable groups to retain their fluidity of structure. Resistance to the pressure to formalise was entrenched in most groups, but CMC was used as an additional decentralising tool.

This analysis of CMC use by activists reflects a broader schism among environmentalists over the ideal of participatory democracy. The debate about how to move towards participatory democracy is one about timing and effectiveness. While many employ the logic of numbers to argue their investiture in decisions, others have mobilised influence through the moral superiority of their argument alone, without the need of popular support. The former requires mass access to CMC, and the latter activists' access to power holders (possibly via their use of CMC).

Tensions exist among activists, not only about how to communicate for environmental change, but who it is that activists ought to communicate with. The problems of accumulating the hardware, software, finance and skills necessary to use CMC have made visible once more the juxtaposition of principle and practice that many environmentalists face. Practising participatory democracy can be a slow and inefficient process. Consensus decision making can be difficult with large groups, and enabling individual responsibility for action can lead to ineffective protest when a cohesive response is required (for example, in blockading) (Klein 2001; Jordan 2002).

The perceived urgency of the environmental crisis tempers activists' ability to be rigorously inclusive. This is demonstrated clearly by the complexity and the time demands of training in internet skills. Often such attempts at skill sharing are sidelined by the more immediate demands of campaigning activities.[15] Furthermore, as illustrated by the nuclei of control around CMC use: 'A broad dispersal of power within an organisation lessens the risks of oligarchic domination but also introduces sources of power which are very difficult to control . . . [and] are not subject to democratic election' (Della Porta and Diani 1999: 162). The techniques used to practise participation can also limit the ability of groups to make the most of their skills and knowledge. Jakubal (2002: 49), in reference to EF!, elaborates on this:

> People use 'good' consensus process to reach a decision that everyone feels positive about . . . But good process in no way guarantees good strategy, especially if most of the participants are inexperienced . . . What makes this scenario doubly tragic is that often there are experienced people involved, but their knowledge isn't considered valuable enough to listen to in any meaningful way . . . Giving everyone equal air time brings the whole group down to the skill level of the least-experienced individual . . . What we've ended up with is an ideology of empowerment that hides a practice of disempowerment.

While sharing skills and operating using participatory methods may be productive in the long run (by widening the movement and establishing alternative democratic practices), to be influential and effective in the immediate term requires the maximising of existing skills and knowledge. This involves a strategic focus on honing activists' abilities and on increasing a group's internal efficiency (such as its communications network). Most groups have concentrated on the latter in respect of their CMC use. Effort has been exerted to help fellow-activists gain access and skills, but this has been tempered by an understanding of the importance of being an effective activist group; hence the prioritising of campaign objectives. Moreover, access has rarely been extended to those outside of existing movement networks, limiting the possibility of new participants.

Their inability to fully adopt inclusionary practices means that groups' adherence to ideals of participatory democracy is more theoretical than real. Most cases attempted political participation (for example, direct action is a direct form of participation) and felt that CMC could aid the mass interactivity required for direct democracy, but only if access issues are more fully resolved. As has been acknowledged since the feminists critique of the 'tyranny of structurelessness' in the 1970s (see Freeman 1970), rarely has a pure participatory form of organisation been practised. Environmental groups have been engaged in a continuing process of experimentation and evolution towards the ideal. Many activists continue attempting participatory forms of organising, despite the limitations, because, '[i]t might even be that dis/organization for all of its often unwieldy forms of co-operation and hidden failures, is important because it makes the future begin' (Jordan 2002: 74). CMC use has brought to the fore once more the tensions of balancing participation with efficiency, and short-term gains with the need to sustain a movement over time and create a future in which activists want to live.

Using these understandings of how groups operate participation in practice, their attempts to use CMC to mobilise participation and network are explored in the next chapter.

Notes

1 The social base of environmental *activism* differs from the social base of environmental *concern*, which reflects a wider cohort of society (Sherkat and Blocker 1993).
2 Increasingly people, especially radical environmentalists, are questioning the relevance of traditional notions of class (Rüdig, Bennie and Franklin 1991; Jordan and Maloney 1997). Lowe and Shaw (1993), in their interview with Sam of the Dongas Tribe, create an image of a classless being: someone who has detached themselves from society to such an extent that she should not be placed within any of society's categories, including that of class.
3 *Urban75* (www.urban75.com) is an online magazine about environmental direct action, rave culture, drugs and football.
4 *Squall* (www.squall.co.uk) was a quarterly magazine catering for the alternative, direct-action market including squatters, travellers and environmentalists. Started in 1992, *Squall* was produced on paper for its first five years, but since June 1998 has used the internet as its primary medium for dissemination.
5 There are several ISPs offering free space to environmental groups; for example, GeoCities, many organisations, such as OneWorld, Association for Progressive Communications (APC) and many universities provide space.
6 Despite the plethora of web design packages available, there is increasingly regular use of languages such as Java, rather than one, simpler, standard of html.
7 N5M (www.dds.nl/~n5m/n5m3) was a conference in Amsterdam about 'tactical media'.
8 Although FoE's original concept of FoEnet included extending its facilities to the local groups this vision was never realised due to an estimated and infeasible expense of £500,000 (Lamb 1996).
9 For *SchNEWS* 'the target audience is, in order of priority, activists, journalists and academics, and then anyone else, so we did keep those people in mind when we actually designed the site' (Toby).
10 For example, for a live debate on the McSpotlight site, the software was kept deliberately simple 'we felt that getting hold of the IRC software often put people off. This runs on just CGI scripts, so anyone with *Netscape 2* or higher can join in' (www.mcspotlight.org/livedebate/help.html).
11 This is also partly because FoE did not want to put too much information on its website and undermine their sources of income from publications or membership.
12 This was despite the fact that 'computers on site aren't networked, it means that

the only way we can send internal emails is by sending them off-site and then coming back on again' (Steve Jones, CAT).

13 Not only in terms of physical access and possessing the skills, but by restricting the number of people who knew the password which enabled the website to be edited.

14 A website with an interactive map illustrating the UK's Sites of Special Scientific Interest and the threats to them. Its aim was to give public access to FoE's unique database and help generate support for the Wildlife Bill.

15 Participatory democracy being a slow process can be advantageous to environmental decision making as environmental problems require deliberation and long-term solutions (Swift 2002). However, this works only if environmental groups are operating in a society that has adopted a form of direct democracy, not one in which representational politicians are funded (and thus influenced) by corporate donations and set a frenetic pace of decision making.

4

Mobilisation, solidarity and network cohesion

The fundamental way that we are going to carry on campaigning is by engaging people on the street and talking to people and putting our message over through local media. The internet just adds another medium through which we can get our campaigning message across. (Chris Crean, West Midlands RCC, FoE)

Mobilising participation is a crucial function of many environmental groups. They aim to mobilise those already within the movement (those already integrated) to join in with the specific environmental activism of their campaign, or to motivate the general public (those who are not integrated) to become involved. The purpose of this mobilisation varies between groups, as do the ways in which they seek to mobilise participants and who they are aiming to mobilise. For example, FoE uses participants as a source of funding, to support their argument (appealing to their strength in numbers) and to encourage environmental awareness. Similarly, activists at Lyminge Forest wanted to attract donations, although their key need was to attract activists to the forest to help them prepare defences.

The need to mobilise participation for environmental activism reflects a broader issue for society, that of how participation in political life can be encouraged (Walters 2002). In chapter 3 the emphasis by many environmental groups on participatory democracy and the difficulties in practising such ideals through their own organisational forms were explored. This chapter continues that theme, but more closely examines how participation in activism (rather than in just CMC use) is encouraged, and the the value of CMC specifically to this endeavour.

While Putnam, Leonardi and Nanetti (1993) have used the social capital concept to argue that increased involvement in social organisations will lead to greater participation by the public in political life more broadly, there is substantial debate about the likelihood of such processes.[1] Putnam *et al.* suggest that individuals will seek to maximise their situation and will learn from experience that collective action leads to increased social capital (positioning within the community and in political life) and tangible benefits – material and economic. Thus that individuals will benefit economically and materially in the long run from participating in social organisations and society will benefit by greater participation of individuals in political life. It remains unclear, however, how radical direct action and other collective political activities – often cast by the media and conservative politicians as destructive of democratic principles and with the potential to result in significant personal cost – could be deemed acts of rational subjects attempting to maximise their position within society. Putnam further fails to show how involvement in mundane volunteer groups such as 'bird-watching societies and soccer clubs leads to a high level of civic engagement, democratic politics and high-quality government performance' (Levi 1996: 47–8).[2]

Such interpretations of social capital theory do attempt to resolve the traditional understandings of the 'dilemma of collective action' that questions why individuals would invest in group activity which might not immediately benefit them, using an economic understanding of rewards received. In contrast, social movement perspectives of participation are centred more on sociopsychological aspects. Thus it examines the triggers of individuals' inclusion into activism – face-to-face interaction (and accompanying friendship networks) and the use of moral shocks. New social movement theorists especially have focused on the personal triggers to collective action. Melucci (2000) has suggested that participation can be concerned primarily with a search for personal identity and the solidarity gained from being part of a group.

These approaches emphasise face-to-face interaction as of primary importance. This ignores both the burgeoning literature on online communities (Willson 2002; Chin and Mittelman 1997) and the possibility of online relations generating new forms of participation. CMC could be used as an additional tool with which to reach a greater variety of individuals and attempt to mobilise their participation in environmental protest. The degree to which groups will employ CMC depends on whether the individuals they wish to marshal are deemed to have access to such technology, and the effectiveness of their existing methods. CMC has the potential to facilitate cross-movement or cross-cultural interaction, enabling the sharing of ideas and perhaps boosting feelings of solidarity. It could also act as a new means by which like-minded individuals could connect to each other (irrespective of spatial distance), help form a (global or local) united consciousness and mobilise participation around a specific issue (Stefanik 1993; Boncheck 1995; Alam 1996; Schwartz 1996 and 1998). CMC could also be a useful vehicle through which to reach the wider public, frame education about environmental issues and encourage people to participate in an interactive debate (Kellner 1998; Walch 1999).

As the nature of protest diversifies to include CMC, and as activists network with each other through new forms of communication, the notion of an environmental *movement* may also change. Furthermore, if relationships could be built between a greater number of individuals and groups through CMC, then there is a possibility that more democratic models could be organised so as to facilitate the environmentalists' goal of participatory democracy. All of these possibilities, however, are reliant upon CMC enabling productive forums for communication and interactivity.

These debates are explored in this chapter through four key sections. I begin by considering how the interviewees have used CMC to mobilise participation. Next, the use of CMC to assist (international) networking and the organisation of environmental activism are detailed. This is followed by an examination of the impediments of using CMC for mobilisation and networking. The final section draws together the implications of CMC use for the interviewees' ability to mobilise participation, and concludes that rather than mobilising new cohorts of participation CMC serves to strengthen existing networks.

Mobilising participation through CMC

CMC has been used by several of the case-study groups to mobilise participation both in support of existing methods and so as to overcome some of the limitations of those methods – such as enabling a wider audience to be reached and at reduced cost. There were five key processes through which the case-study groups attempted (and often succeeded) to mobilise participation. They were using CMC: as a gateway to activism; to raise the profile of their campaign; for mobilising online activism; to stimulate local activism; and in attracting participants to existing protests.

Before this online mobilisation is explored, however, it will be useful to briefly note how groups mobilised participation *without* CMC.

Mobilising participation without CMC

Although environmental groups worked towards different ends, and thus needed to mobilise participation for a variety for activities (such as illegal direct action or legal leafleting), they utilised a similar repertoire of methods to attract recruits. There is a predominant reliance upon distributing requests for mobilisation through existing movement networks. These networks are traditionally accessed using word of mouth, magazines, newsletters and flyers. Those not integrated with such networks are

reached through stalls in high streets and at scheduled events, by publicity through the mainstream media, by leafleting, and sometimes, in the
case of larger organisations, through advertisements. For example, FoE has
traditionally sought to mobilise participation by providing accurate information and encouraging individuals (and their local groups) to act upon
it. This information was disseminated in leaflets, the subscribers' magazine *Earth Matters* and the local group magazine *Change Your World*,
through publicity stunts, via other publications and in press releases.

Those at Lyminge Forest sought to attract participants (and supplies) to
the Forest, raise public concern and generate media coverage. To mobilise
participation activists spread information by word of mouth and in the
underground literature (such as *SchNEWS*[3] and *Earth First! Action Update*),
press releases, leaflets and telephone trees. The activists present at the
Forest had themselves been mobilised through word of mouth,[4] leaflets,
and underground publications.

Mike (Lyminge Forest) identified difficulties in attracting participants to
live in difficult conditions (though, for some, this has become a lifestyle
choice):

> You are going to be dirty, at some point, cold, wet. You are expected to work
> hard. You are relying on other people's charity and your own wiles to get
> what you need . . . How many people in these days of body deodorant and
> fast cars and going out clubbing . . . want to come out and get dirty and wet,
> and possibly cold, and get paid nothing for it?

Gateway to activism

CMC has enabled groups to advertise their location and aims to an international audience. This has provided a gateway to activism for potential participants and a starting point from which they could join. Using the
technology, activists with limited resources can provide more visible and
numerous entry points to activism than used to be possible, and thus have
the potential to mobilise greater numbers. The use of CMC may also hold
particular promise in attracting new participants previously unconnected
with any other activist group. Traditionally, gaining access to protest information involved knowledge of the existence and source of underground
publications, or that information came from personal contacts. Now such
information is more easily located on web pages and may even be occasionally linked to from British news corporations' websites (such as BBC Online).
SchNEWS, McSpotlight, FoE and GSN have utilised CMC for this purpose.

Chris (*SchNEWS*) believed that publishing *SchNEWS* electronically had
attracted a new audience: 'A lot of people that were just looking [online]
casually have started to say, "Hey, this is really good! Can you send me it
every week by email?" We win them over. You can kind of build up a loyal

following.' One of McSpotlight's aims was to stimulate public debate about McDonald's, and McSpotlight's online debating room acted as a route via which more individuals could become involved in the campaign; for example, Gideon (McSpotlight): 'I didn't volunteer, I got invited. I was a regular poster [to the debating room], and they said "Would you like to help out?"' Keogh (1996) noted that, unlike EF! (UK), RTS and FoE, whose websites appeared to preach to the converted or merely offered 'a window into the home of a community, rather than an open door', McSpotlight 'nurtures a like-minded community by arguing a case rather than bludgeoning with rhetoric'. This increases the possibility of non-integrated individuals becoming involved. The site was specifically structured to be accessible and easy to use by the public, using a fresh and innovative design, with site maps, an introductory tour and a search engine to help new users around.

FoE used CMC to extend its traditional membership drive, providing environmental information which it hoped would stimulate concern and, subsequently, action. FoE was able to trade on its reputation and well-known name to attract those curious to their website, but it also advertised its location on flyers. Access to the website was facilitated by having, reportedly, 4,000 links to itself on other sites (Charles Linn, former web developer, FoE). In 1998 the website attracted over 20,000 visitors a week (Friends of the Earth 1998b) and 'is beginning to be considered as a comparable mechanism to print, in terms of numbers, of getting in front of the public' (Charles Linn, FoE). FoE provided a number of entry points through which newcomers could become active. However, the website had yet to serve as an effective vehicle for encouraging membership, though the numbers donating online were increasing.[5]

FoE also provided a window on to several campaigns, using innovative aspects of CMC. For instance, FoE used its website during the A34 Newbury bypass campaign (www.foe.co.uk/action/newbury). It incorporated a clickable map of the proposed bypass with hypertext links to descriptions and photographs of the areas threatened (Schofield 1995). There was also an online petition against the bypass for people to sign. Launched in June of 1996, the Java Virtual Car (www.foe.co.uk/car) was a fun interactive guide to the environmental impacts of motoring. The user was able to make sounds by beeping the horn or patting the dog, sit at the wheel and look under the car's bonnet. Each action produced information about the environmentally damaging effects of cars.

The GSN email list could also act as a gateway. Email simplifies the process of first getting involved in activism, especially if networks are fluid and changing:

> I get quite a lot of emails from people all over the place saying they want to get involved . . . It's easier than when you've got old publications, like, with

a PO Box address and you don't get a reply, and you don't know whether
that's because they haven't bothered to reply or because they've moved. At
least with an email you know you're in contact with somebody. (Andy, GSN)

Although two-thirds of participants were introduced to GSN through face-
to-face contact, around 25 per cent were introduced through a website
(though not necessarily the GSN site, as the email list is advertised on other
sites).[6] Thus CMC may well have provided an important entry point to
activism for these individuals.

In these ways CMC and, in particular, websites offer potential participants a gateway into activism, one which may have been harder to locate
prior to the use of the technology. It is at this stage difficult, however, to
guage how many actually became mobilised through the provision of such
information. The low number of those who joined FoE online indicates the
limitations of the website as a conduit for increasing membership.

Raising group profiles

Using CMC to raise the profile of their campaign, activists were able to
indirectly aid their attempts at mobilisation. CMC was used as an additional form of advertising, one which 'tripled *SchNEWS'* subscription'
(Chris, *SchNEWS*). More significantly, however, their often novel use of the
technology triggered media attention. National newspaper articles, and
sections of television programmes were devoted to the use of CMC at
Lyminge Forest and McSpotlight (see Nuthall 1997; Ineson 1999).

Online activism

Not all the case-study groups attempted to mobilise participation in activities unrelated to CMC use, such as attending a protest in the street; many
tried to stimulate participation in activism undertaken online. FoE's
Climate Change online campaign, launched in August 1997, was an email
network of individuals who, at the command of FoE, sent out personal
emails to world leaders attending the UN Climate Change Summit in
Kyoto, urging them to protect the environment. It is difficult to judge what
contributions online campaigns such as Climate Change have made to
FoE's political lobbying capabilities, but the response was disappointing
for campaigners: 'We should get 50,000 people involved in theory, but we
have got 2,000 so far. But a lot of these are very active . . . when we ask them
to do something about 85 per cent of them do it, which I think is really
quite a high percentage' (Charles Linn, FoE). Although FoE was the only
case-study organisation specifically to encourage the use of CMC as a
medium through which to take action, there are other groups which do
(see chapter 5).

The results of a supporter survey undertaken by FoE in November 1997[7] further illustrated that despite 18 per cent of FoE supporters using the internet or email on a daily basis and there appearing to be a strong level of 'active' support (with 60 per cent of supporters having sent off a campaigning postcard and 46 per cent a letter), only 3 per cent have sent an email as part of an FoE campaign (Friends of the Earth 1998c).

Decentralisation: stimulating local action

A key way of mobilising participation was through the distribution of information to stimulate the co-ordination of local activists. Using an international medium, McSpotlight, FoE and GSN sought to provide information which was relevant to local populations so that they could use such knowledge in their area. McSpotlight's website contained practical advice on how to lobby against multinationals, as well as links to local groups. It included versions of the original defamatory leaflets, translated into twenty languages to print off and hand out, and 'loads of campaigning materials for campaigning in traditional ways – placards, slogans and posters, and all sorts of other stuff that people could take off the internet and take back into the real world' (Devin, McSpotlight). The website also reported what actions had occurred and supplied ideas for future actions such as subvertisements of McDonald's' adverts. Email was also used for information dispersal: 'The global McLibel list server now has 3,800 people subscribing to it' (Dave Morris, McSpotlight).

FoE facilitated local participation through the provision of local data, and encouraged local groups to get connected and to use CMC for coordination. Although FoE had often emphasised the local mobilising of participation, many of its campaigns had been run nationally using national data. Websites such as Wild Places and Factory Watch[8] enabled data to be provided at a macro scale, a task that had previously been prohibited by cost.

The Wild Places campaign was specifically aimed at encouraging local action to save Britain's biodiversity and expand support for a UK Wildlife Bill. The website (www.foe.co.uk/wildplaces) aimed to empower people by making accessible information about sites of special scientific interest (SSSIs) and the threats to them (Juniper 1997). On the website the user is able to create a map of their local SSSIs by entering their postcode; they can search for a particular SSSI or update the website themselves with information. FoE was also able to gather new information from locals who interacted with the website information: 'For Wild Places we've asked people to write in and tell us what's happening to their local SSSIs, and we've have fourteen instances that we've actually been able to verify, or correct; that's new bits of information over the web' (Susan Pipes, former GIS co-ordinator, FoE). Providing such information over the internet made local information accessible to people in a way that could not be served by other methods: 'We did a report on SSSIs, and it was two inches thick and we gave it away to twelve people, and then we put the same information on the web . . . In the first six months we had 7,000 – what we calculate as – different people coming to look at the website' (Susan Pipes). Placing databases of information on the website has enabled groups to generate their own locally specific data. Local groups have benefited from greater access to such information, which in turn is likely to have helped mobilise them to launch local campaigns.

FoE relied upon its regional groups to undertake local activism, and used CMC to encourage them. It did this by providing contact details and links to the websites of the local groups on the FoE website, thus advertising its existence to potential members. FoE also used CMC to communicate with local groups, thus enabling those groups to receive information quickly, as opposed to through the bi-monthly newsletter. Birmingham FoE felt itself becoming increasingly co-ordinated in its campaign approach as a result of the regular information it received through email from the national FoE and other groups. However, not all local groups chose to utilise CMC. Although Chris Packham (former co-ordinator of Newcastle FoE) received a lot of information from his RCC via email, he preferred to communicate by telephone and in person:[9] 'Unless people meet face-to-face they won't know what is going on really.'

FoE also used email for its campaign networks, which are issue specific networks for members of local groups. FoE UK benefits by translating national campaigns into local contexts and giving national targets local relevance. Local groups benefit by having a channel through which they are able to interact with campaign teams at national FoE.

Through the West Yorkshire Pilot Project FoE attempted to facilitate the development of a decentralised network of local activists to take action locally and nationally using CMC. Email was used as a tool for organising campaigns, exchanging news, disseminating drafted and re-drafted reports, requesting help and for an electronic fax facility for contacting the local press. The main benefit that CMC was perceived to have, however, was on perceptions of a West Yorkshire group identity, which in turn mobilised members to support campaigns (Allen 1996). In addition, Mike Birkin (south-west RCC, FoE) was developing a south-west regional website on which local groups' activities would be regularly updated, facilitating co-ordination of regional action.

FoE also initiated an information campaign about the risks of genetic engineering, and this stimulated local action (www.foe.co.uk/camps/foodbio). On the website FoE included the map grid references of all UK genetic engineering test sites. Although it may not have been explicitly FoE's aim, direct action groups used the information to locate test sites and destroy the crops, and the action was so effective that FoE was accused of giving direct action protestors too much information.

Through GSN participants would attempt to mobilise each other by posting requests for help with protests or campaigns. Keith (GSN) thought this information acted as a trigger: 'Exchanging information can extend to organising actions, in that you'll get a couple of people who'll want to organise a coach from an area of the country up to some event somewhere else, and that should spark things off. It's a catalyst anyway.'

For many participants GSN was not the first place they had heard about particular actions – word of mouth was their source – but the email network did provide more details about such actions. This potential to mobilise was also reflected in the topics of discussion. The most talked about topics[10] were 'local group actions, meetings and gatherings', indicating that participants were keen to actively mobilise.

As GSN participants can be involved in campaigns and groups in addition to GSN's, it is difficult to determine the extent to which it is GSN that has mobilised these activities. Three-quarters of the GSN questionnaire respondents take part in demonstrations and a quarter have lived on protest camps, which suggests that the network includes a number of very active environmentalists.[11] The experiences and beliefs of these individuals are likely to contribute to the usefulness of GSN as a space within which to exchange skills and to mobilise: 'The amount of people is not so important, but it's the people who happened to be on it . . . those people were the people that were prepared to go to actions, go to demos, were publicising' (Toby, GSN).

Attracting participants to offline protests

Actually stimulating participation in existing protest (rather than the creation of local action) is likely to be one of the most difficult aspects of mobilisation because of the additional barrier of distance. At Lyminge Forest CMC was used in addition to the traditional methods of mobilisation to attract participants to the Forest. Although activists were attempting to reach a wide audience and to encourage general support, they were also trying to reach those already within, or sympathetic to, the movement as they were the people most likely to become involved. This could have been achieved through the existing network ties and communication structures, but CMC was used because it is faster than newsletters and able to reach a wider audience than word of mouth: 'It helps a lot having the website because you are just reaching people, people who are like-minded and doing the same kind of thing . . . Basically, they are activists' (Blue, Lyminge Forest).

It is likely that potential participants would hear about the protest through several of the existing channels. Furthermore, even if individuals had heard about the protest only through CMC before they visited the Forest, they may have already been integrated into movement networks. Of those on-site, few had heard of the website before they had arrived in the forest. While some questioned its usefulness, arguing that word of mouth was the main way of getting information out, others, such as Merlin, argued that the internet had been a useful mobilising tool: 'I know of quite a lot of people who visited the Forest because they had heard about it over the internet.' Jani (Lyminge Forest) cited email discussion lists as another source of information for many who had subsequently visited the Forest, as well as triggering her own involvement: 'I wouldn't have been involved in any [protest] if it wasn't for the net . . . I was on an email discussion group and [an activist] actually emailed that group, UKPagan, and said that there was a protest at Lyminge.'

Web pages acted as a form of confirmation of the protest and Blue (Lyminge Forest) noted: 'I know people were using the information on the internet because people were using the maps [to locate the protest] which were really useful. It saves having to do mail-outs by post.' Email was frequently used to spread eviction alerts and thus to act as a back up to the existing telephone tree: '[If] there was an eviction imminent . . . you could phone all round the country and . . . at least half the people you phoned wouldn't be in . . . You use email, and then it gets around and it snowballs – it's not just the people that read it, but they'll pass the message on' (Worzel).

The demographics and opinions of those who viewed the Lyminge Forest website can also be used to infer what potential the website had for participant mobilisation. The website readership can be inferred from the questionnaire results.[12] The demographics of this readership[13] reflect those traditionally likely to become involved in environmental activism – predominantly young university-educated individuals, with commitments which provided free time (such as full-time education), with 72 per cent of them based in Britain (thus making travel to the protest site feasible for many).

The majority (86 per cent) of respondents claimed to be very interested in environmental issues, and many actively took part in a variety of environmental activities, with 32 per cent taking part in direct actions. It is also significant that 41 per cent of respondents *first* heard about the protest at Lyminge Forest via the internet. Of other sources, word of mouth accounted for the second highest percentage of 17, more than learned of it through local news or magazines. Thus, word of mouth (through protest networks, or those living locally to the protest) continues to play an important role in the spread of information about protests. Of those respondents who initially discovered the protest through the internet, 60 per cent found the website by following a link from another page, and 28 per cent by specifically searching for it. This re-affirms the importance of advertising one's website and obtaining links to other sites, and it supports the notion that there are online networks linking together the various autonomous environmental protests, so that once one protest link is discovered it is easy to get information on others.

The 23 per cent of the total respondents who had contributed to the campaign had undertaken a range of activities: 18 per cent visited the site, 13 per cent supplied food, and 8 per cent had donated money. Of the 77 per cent of respondents who had not contributed to the campaign, 43 per cent expressed an interest in visiting the site, with 19 per cent interested in living on-site. Although it is not possible to determine whether any of these respondents did in fact contribute to the campaign in these ways, a significant potential for action was illustrated; and there appears to be potential also for online actions, enabling website readers to bypass some of the physical restrictions (such as distance, time, money, commitments) which might have been seen as prohibitive of their involvement previously. The respondents' demographics and beliefs (47 per cent agreed with taking direct action) are suggestive that many have the time and motivation to participate in a protest such as Lyminge Forest; in other words, that the website is being read by an appropriate audience.

Lyminge Forest provides the only example through which participants were mobilised by CMC to actually attend an existing protest. Moreover, its success and the demographics of its website readership hint at a pattern which might be replicated elsewhere. Bob, of McSpotlight, said of his experiences at a demonstration in London that 'a few of the people there weren't online, but obviously it went out from there: the people online were the nodes and it went out to the tree', illustrating how online information was fed out to those not online, mobilising a range of participants.

Although there is evidence that CMC does have a mobilising role, it remains difficult to discern its exact significance in generating individuals' involvement in particular protests and campaigns. It is also the case that the majority of those interviewed had either become involved without the use of CMC, or that CMC had (by their admission) played only a peripheral role in their engagement.

Modifying relationships: global linkages, accelerated interactions and new coalitions

Email has been an absolute revolution in terms of communication. It is *the* method of communication among environmentalists and other social activists world-wide and it can make an awful lot of difference to who can be an activist, how well connected you are, how quickly you can react to events. (Devin, McSpotlight)

In addition to mobilisation, CMC has been used by the interviewees to facilitate networking and to boost solidarity among activists. Using CMC as a networking tool, they were able to share solutions and ideas and draw strength from each others' support, interact more quickly, and mobilise some assemblage of international participation in their campaigns. Overall, CMC increased the efficiency and strength of existing network linkages and enabled new connections.

Drawing strength from (international) linkages

CMC has been used by activists to create, or reinforce existing, linkages with other groups – both nationally and internationally. A key benefit of using CMC was the boost to morale received from communicating with other activists: 'It's good to know that people are doing other stuff similar to you elsewhere, and it's good getting support because it's not just five of you versus the great motorway monster. There's lots of people all over the place all doing it and all having varying degrees of success' (Dave, GSN).

The news of others' successes served to encourage the interviewees to continue in their campaigns and as a source of solidarity with activists, even if they were in disparate locations. McSpotlight and Lyminge Forest used CMC to generate international support.[14] Interest from abroad resulted in visitors to Lyminge from Canada, Germany and Poland: 'I think from an international point of view we get a lot more connections . . . During last summer a lot of the visitors were saying, "Hey, we looked at the website", and these tended to be European' (Mike, Lyminge Forest).

This interaction correlates with Warf and Grimes' assertion that using the internet to establish links between struggles internationally may boost the morale of the protesters and 'reduce activists' feelings of isolation' (1997: 268). Even when visitors do not materialise from these interactions, 'it is encouraging to see other people from the other side of the world doing a similar sort of thing' (Merlin, Lyminge Forest). This was particularly important for places of protest where few individuals were actively involved, such as small FoE local groups: 'That can be quite an isolating experience, so just being able to be in contact with this whole network of people round the country doing something like you must be really supportive' (Susan Pipes, FoE). Such interaction enabled the interviewees to feel that they were part of something bigger than their own campaign.

CMC use also facilitated communication between groups which or individuals who were physically or ideologically distant from each other. CAT used its website to overcome physical distance, attracting an international audience: 'Requests for pages from the CAT site have come from all corners of the earth – from Iceland to New Zealand, Mexico to Hungary, Jamaica to the Philippines' (Anon 1998c: 4). GSN participants were able to bypass the problems of distance in order to connect with like-minded individuals: 'Having access to at least an email dialogue with so many million people around the world, you end up with twenty or thirty that you can actually get something together, which wouldn't really happen in Brighton' (Andy, GSN).

At FoE, despite efforts (by RCCs and the West Yorkshire Pilot Project) to encourage local groups to develop networks between each other, there were limited examples of success. FoE's use of CMC has, however, enhanced the relationship between local groups and head office by facilitating better exchange of data through sites such as Wild Places. This site enabled local groups to update head office quickly with their situations – making FoE overall a more responsive and informed organisation. Consequently, local groups have gradually taken on a greater role within the FoE UK network, though this is not entirely due to the use of CMC, being part of a shift in the organisation as a whole (Washbourne 1999b).

McSpotlight also facilitated the international connection of like-minded individuals who had been campaigning against McDonald's in their own country. It served as a point of amalgamation for all the information individuals had been collating and it drew together activists from a range of movement backgrounds, further facilitating cross-movement and international interaction: 'It's making protest movements feel like they are international . . . It's really being felt within activist circles that we are part of a global movement against capitalism and neo-liberalism, and it's enabled boundaries to be crossed over' (Devin, McSpotlight).

Thus CMC eases interaction between groups which and individuals who might be ideologically distinct. This is most evident for FoE which used CMC to interact with some of its critics – especially radical direct-action protesters. The provision of the GM test field locations on its website enabled direct-action protesters to locate the crops to destroy. FoE is officially opposed to the use of such illegal action, but was able to indirectly help radical activists achieve their goals. A further example of the use of CMC by FoE to communicate with other organisations was the development of the URGENT (the Urban Regeneration and Greenfield Environment NeTwork) website set up by Simon Festing (former housing campaigner, FoE). It was a separate autonomous site from FoE and had information from a variety of different organisations, including direct-action groups: 'It's basically about a spirit of co-operation, because one of the lessons we learned from the anti-road movement was . . . [that] Friends of the Earth . . . needs to co-operate with other groups, and it needs to be seen to be doing that in a way which is not pushing our weight around' (Simon Festing, FoE).

Furthermore, the anonymity of CMC has enabled small protests and groups that may not normally meet to discuss issues to be picked up more quickly by the bigger organisations because of postings on email lists which both receive:

> It's helped information sharing between groups. I mean it's quite easy now for example for Earth First! to find out what Friends of the Earth is doing, there's not this kind of secrecy and problems of thinking 'What the hell are they up to?' . . . It's helped internal co-ordination in the environmental movement. (David, media liaison, NE Green Party)

Sharing solutions and exchanging ideas

CMC has been a valuable part of the process of interacting with new contacts and in increasing the interaction between individuals who are already acquainted. These relationships facilitate the use of alternative tactics or solutions, and broaden the range of individual opinions represented in environmental movement debates.

The facilitation of communication between distant entities made it easier for individuals or groups to encounter alternative practices and ideas, which could aid their own problem solving:

> By using the internet you can see that other people have the same sorts of problems and then have completely radically different ways of solving them . . . It's made people able to interact more with people in other countries and get hold of more information and probably introduce new ideas, more cross-fertilisation of ideas. (Rebecca, Newcastle Community Green Festival[15])

It also highlighted other causes for concern: 'You pick up on other peoples' experiences, like social injustice and Third World debt' (Dave, GSN). This interaction 'enabled me to communicate with a large number of people, and with a wider spectrum of the environmental fraternity . . . it's given me a wider view of the world' (Ed, GSN).

These processes of learning from other movements and groups have always existed, and are not reliant on the use of CMC, but the technology has reduced the cost and increased the speed of these interactions – contributing to a potential increase in exchanges. This cross-fertilisation of ideas was also an indirect result of using CMC. Those at Lyminge Forest attracted international visitors to their protest partly by having a website. Activists on-site shared their skills and learned from the visitors, continuing cross-cultural interaction.

In addition to increasing encounters between previously unassociated individuals, with whom to share ideas and skills, CMC use strengthened communication channels between individuals already associated. Participants of GSN were particularly enthused about the regular contact with associates and the potential to extend the number of those involved which CMC afforded: 'It's more in speed of information and low-cost information to the people who are involved in a group and building up a kind of periphery to that group as well' (Tristram, GSN). CMC created 'more regular forums for prolonged debate which has made me more thoughtful and a more skilled strategist and communicator' (Richard, GSN).

This debate was not only one between disparate individuals: it was possible at any time and between any activists. For Zoe, GSN was a connection into a space where like-minded individuals were continually engaged in debate: 'Its changed the time basis of it to some degree. It's not that you can only go and be an environmentalist *here*, at *that* meeting, at *that* action, with *those* people: now it's anytime that I am in my office, on my computer. I can just go and say some stuff or find out some stuff.' Thus, CMC has contributed towards the opening up of opportunities for interaction with other environmentalists – overcoming previous temporal and spatial constraints. McSpotlight also sought to encourage online debate through its 'debating room', which at its peak received 100 contributors a day from a variety of international environmentalists[16]. The specific usefulness of such online debate, however, is hard to determine. While linkages can quite easily be made using CMC, the value of debating forums is dependent not only on how they are designed (in terms of the extent of interactivity) but on the aim of the debate and its participants. In many forums it is to be doubted whether real dialogue or discussion occurs over CMC: 'In Usenet political discussions, people talk past one another, when they are not verbally attacking each other. The emphasis is not problem solving, but *discussion dominance*' (Davis 1999: 177, italics added). Thus for such debate to be productive it required commitment from participants to focus on constructive exchanges. This issue is dealt with in more detail in the section which follows.

The consequences of these opportunities for increased (online) debate are twofold. First, CMC has enabled individuals' ideas to be distributed more freely and more quickly consumed within the environmental movement. Its relative anonymity, interactivity and ability to transcend physical space meant that increased numbers of activists were able to contribute to debates and put forward ideas. Consequently, for those online the possibility of a more participatory model of involvement in formulating environmental activism develops, given the evident difficulties of having constructive debate via CMC.

Second, CMC enabled in-depth communication about tactics between a wider range of individuals prior to an event. Such interaction may have meant that more individuals were willing to undertake actions, perhaps developing their own autonomous actions, because they themselves had taken a part and thus had a personal investment in the organisation of the event.

Accelerated interactions at a lower cost

One of the greatest advantages of CMC is the speed at which interaction can occur across vast distances. This rapidity enables improved networking, response times and ease of information gathering. These features were to prove useful in co-ordinating global protests, such as J18, where the rapidity of interaction across vast distances facilitated networking, the calling for participation and the building of the momentum of actions. Using CMC, news of international actions could also be spread quickly via email: 'If there is something in Nigeria or the United States, you can find out about it very, very quickly and communicate in real time with people' (Ian Willmore, media unit, FoE).

In addition to existing methods, CMC contributed to the task of keeping environmentalists up-to-date about events: 'It is one way of keeping supporters regularly informed about key news from the campaign' (Dave Morris, McSpotlight). It was particularly important for those collating newsletters: 'We would not have the degree of international coverage [without CMC] and – because of the price of phonecalls – national coverage because of the speed and the sheer amount of stuff that people can send us from round the country' (Toby, *SchNEWS*).

CMC was a particularly quick way of informing people about forthcoming actions, and thus increased the response rate of some of the interviewees to national calls for action: '[At] GSN I was finding out immediately about stuff going on round the country, which I would have found out about *after* they had happened, normally, and although I didn't go to many things I was kept much more on the ball [about] the momentum of things' (Mary, Peace Action).

This ability to put out calls for participation, right up to the final days prior to an action, enabled activists to maximise one of their greatest assets on a larger scale – spontaneity. Email was purported to be more useful to activists than websites in enabling fast international communications. While websites played a valuable role by providing a noticeboard on which to post issues, email was fast and accessible to more individuals. Email was used 'as a sort of update and alert-type medium, but also for just discussing issues and planning strategies, and planning events and actions. The web we tend to use . . . just as a place to put information for the general public, [and is] not really used as much for a networking tool' (Devin, McSpotlight). An added virtue of email was that 'it goes direct to the person; you haven't got to persuade them to go to your website' (Jessy, McSpotlight). Jessy remarked also on the utility of the forwarding feature, which extended the reach of email-posted information.

Global solidarity

The relatively low cost of interaction via CMC and the speed of communication exchange convinced some of the interviewees of their greater ability to act at an international level. Environmentalists were able to provide solidarity for international struggles as well as to become involved themselves in such campaigns. Furthermore, McSpotlight's high-profile success served as a blueprint, triggering replicas for other campaigns worldwide.

In addition to this support and exchange of ideas, CMC has been used to help co-ordinate global protests. As 'activism's going more global . . . it's the cheapest, fastest way of getting information between the countries' (Jo Makepeace, *SchNEWS*). Tristram (GSN) claimed that CMC enabled small anarchist groups to co-ordinate global protests, whereas previously only the larger lobbying organisations would have had the money and contacts necessary:

> I can imagine how, if you're Oxfam, you could co-ordinate something globally without the internet, but if you're Reclaim the Streets or Zapatistas, that is not really an option in the same way. Although it is expensive and it does disenfranchise some people who can't afford computers, in other ways it is quite democratic, and it does allow people to contact large numbers of people for relatively small costs. So I think June 18 probably wouldn't have happened without internet technology.

J18's scale was global. International actions were organised simultaneously, and this would have been significantly harder, slower and more expensive to network and achieve without CMC. Despite the organisation of some global protests such as J18, the protests against the WTO in November 1999 and other actions in Gothenburg, Prague and Genoa, international interactions were more often than not used to assert the importance of specific place-based campaigns. This use of CMC reflects what Washbourne (1999a) terms 'translocalism' – using technology to reach an international audience and mobilise a global consciousness, while simultaneously reasserting the importance of the local action. This was also exemplified at Lyminge Forest where an international audience was contacted in order to affirm the importance of a small forest in Kent.

Overall, the interviewees suggested that CMC use has contributed to modifying existing relationships with other British environmental groups and international activists. Many of the networks were already in existence, although new connections were also being made, and through these relationships some of the interviewees felt more able to undertake international action.

Impediments to the usefulness of CMC

There were significant impediments to the use of CMC in mobilising participation and in developing new global linkages: in particular, there were access and security problems, a resistance to reach out to a new audience, a trend towards 'desktop' activism, a lack of ties fostered in certain contexts by online participation and a reliance upon non-CMC interactions and networks. This poverty of online engagements has significant implications for the possibility of creating conditions in online environments that are conducive to encouraging participation in a productive form (rather than endless or divisive discussion).

Access and security

The effective of CMC to mobilise participation is dependent on access, which, as we have seen, is unevenly distributed. Furthermore, even those with access were sometimes restricted in how often they could use CMC, which reduced the usefulness of the technology, especially for advertising forthcoming actions. At Lyminge Forest, one of the main problems identified by the website designers was their inability to update the website regularly. Mike felt that if it had been more dynamic and interactive, users would have spent more time at the website and perhaps have been intrigued enough to get involved in the campaign. As it was, the website did not form a focus for camp information, and thus was perhaps less useful for mobilisation than it might have been. In addition to access problems, some interviewees were concerned about the lack of security when encouraging or co-ordinating actions using CMC. As chapter 6 will show, some activists sought to limit the kind of information they posted online, impeding the usefulness of CMC for mobilisation.

A diffuse audience

Information transmitted via alternative media tends initially to reach only the audience to which it is directed. By posting information to a website, however, a wide and diffuse readership is immediately reached. Even email messages are forwarded to multiple discussion lists, and membership of these lists is often not moderated. Thus mobilising via CMC engages with a diffuse audience – an audience which may not be immediately sympathetic to the environmental cause. Some felt that the audience could become so diversified that it would prevent any cohesion arising from online interactions, with all communication becoming lost to debate rather than contributing to the organising of action. Richard was concerned that GSN did not have a sufficiently strong student-specific agenda as its identity had been diluted by the mixed participants of the list and thus the topics of discussion diversified. The risk of trying to co-ordinate actions using such a diverse list is that consensus will never be reached: disagreements arise which seem never to end and can dominate the list. Though this holds potential for a wider range of individuals to be mobilised, some of the interviewees did not want to engage with this wider (and sometimes hostile) audience. Dave (GSN) used to take part in the newsgroup uk.environment: 'I gave up on it thinking, well, there's no point, I'll never convert these people to my point of view. I'm wasting time arguing with them [when] I could be doing something useful.'

In this way CMC can paradoxically also contribute to a narrowing, not a broadening, of the audience with which one engages: 'The danger with things that you do through email groups is that you are only preaching to the converted' (Tristram, GSN). This is because 'the attraction of much of the internet is, in fact, in finding a like-minded virtual community' (Perry and Leigh Vanderklein 1996: 359). This is to the detriment of interacting with new audiences. This was confirmed by Jim (1999: 8), who argued that online environmentalists

> apparently labour under the illusion that, having clicked on 'send', their thoughts have been widely disseminated to activists interested in the topic(s) under discussion. They haven't. They've been circulated only within a very small bubble of the educationally and financially privileged floating in the internet ghetto.

Furthermore, although email distribution lists which posted national news about environmental activism enabled more individuals to be kept up to date, there were also complaints that lists such as ALLSORTS (run by RTS) became dominated by southern events, primarily in London, indicating a difficulty in maintaining the national lists which are still relevant to a wide audience.

A reduction in activity

While interaction through CMC *has* resulted in some offline activism, several environmentalists maintained that using CMC has meant that they are now paradoxically 'less active in real life' (Lyminge Forest questionnaire respondent no. 20). In this way David (NE Green Party) argued CMC enabled a false feeling of activism: 'It's probably made me less of an activist. It's so easy to find out what's going on that you feel involved even if you're not actually doing anything.' Other interviewees found that the sheer amount of information they received via CMC, and the international nature of much of it, could work to reduce empowerment, curtailing the impulse to take action: 'It's a massive list these days, dozens of articles every day, and I don't have time to keep up with them all . . . And it's quite scary, some of the things you find out . . . and it's got to the stage where I think: I'm so powerless I don't have time to do this' (Dave, GSN). The value of reducing activism to an online presence was also criticised by Froehling (1997: 304), who juxtaposed it with the actual needs of those for whom the campaign was undertaken: 'In Chiapas, people are daily hurt by the conflict, through lack of resources and mistreatment, resulting in injury and death. Displace war into cyberpsace, and these details retreat.'

The poverty of online engagements

A key hindrance to the use of CMC to mobilise participation was the poverty of online engagements. Interpersonal relations can be difficult via email, and online involvement can be transitory. Personal interaction online is often based on 'thin' understandings of identity, and commitment to online transactions can prove to be limited (Kolko and Reid 1998). Some of the interviewees felt that interpersonal relationships via email were hard to develop without visual or auditory interaction. Merlin (Lyminge Forest) was concerned about the 'friends' he had made online, though this did not prevent him continuing to communicate with them: 'You can't get to know someone through communication in cyberspace because with email you don't even get to hear their voice . . . I've had friends that I've only met through cyberspace, not met in real life, and it's a bit worrying in a way because you don't know what they're like really.' Andy (GSN) found that the technology encumbered his ability to build up a relationship with someone: 'It's like they're disposable people. You can just sort of go "Oh well, I haven't got time for that lot there", and you just delete them.' The risk of being disposable hinders feelings of solidarity developing between individuals interacting on email lists. In this way people can concentrate more on having instrumental relationships that provide self-gratification, but with little consideration for the consequence for the online 'other' (Schofield Clark 1998; Willson 2002).

This lack of commitment reflects not only a lack of investment in online relationships, but also a lack of trust in reciprocation. Crucially, this undermines a key component of mobilisation. Both the economic and the sociopsychological model of participation stress the necessity of trust to further political activism (Walters 2002). The emphasis that Putnam (2001) places on physical involvement suggests he is cautious of online possibilities, which may not foster trusting relationships, but might actually contribute to the further alienation of individuals from their communities.

Andy (GSN) found that people had few qualms about posting harsh criticisms online which could put people off contributing to some lists: 'They all lay into you really badly . . . I think you are more likely to get criticism over email: people might not say anything to your face'. This confirms Hartley's predictions (1999) that people online would behave in a less orderly manner and be more inclined to be rude, abusive and antisocial.

This lack of concern for others' opinions returns us to an earlier point about the value of online debating forums and discussions. If online discussion becomes dominated by the individual's desire to speak rather than to listen, to achieve personal goals rather than to work collaboratively, then there are few mechanisms available with which to refocus the purpose of the forum. Many email discussion lists have been abandoned due to excessive off-topic or divisive postings. CMC is, in many ways, not well suited to collective projects. As Meikle (2002) affirms, online activism is often akin to speech – not always reasoned and often unfinished and ongoing. In this context it can be extremely hard to delimit such conversations or ever reach enough consensus to move forward with decisions or coordination.

Furthermore, many email contacts are temporary: 'Very often you get an internet address or an email address, and you email it, and it bounces back and it's gone' (Rachel, EF!). Moreover, although online activism helped individuals located elsewhere to take part in the action, it also enabled them to contribute without engaging in the movement, a form of spectatorship. Charles Linn (FoE) found that it was difficult to build up a relationship between those engaged in online actions due to a lack of information about them, and this affected decisions about which online actions it was possible to mobilise: 'We need to look at how to get people involved online. We also need to look at how to store data of people's interests efficiently. Email addresses alone are not really enough. We need more information.' Without the fostering of friendships or solidarity their involvement is more likely to be transitory because it lacks the long-term commitment necessary to achieve many of the environmentalists' goals. Thus online interaction has reduced the importance of distance, but it has also reduced the necessity to commit. Finally, the fundamental differences between disparate groups are not overcome just by using CMC. Although CMC has eased the processes of communicating between groups, and the possibility of finding some common ground, it did not mean activists would necessarily form real bonds of friendship.

Reliance upon non-CMC interaction and networks

Despite the use of CMC, traditional methods of mobilisation were maintained and CMC used only as 'a contribution but not a replacement of traditional campaigning' (Devin, McSpotlight). This was because many doubted (perhaps with due reason) the effectiveness of CMC alone to trigger mobilisation. Most interviewees cited word of mouth as the source of most of their information concerning environmental activism, and friendships and face-to-face contact as the main triggers to their initial involvement. Ben (Lyminge Forest) kept up to date 'through the underground press mainly and word of mouth. Now I am on camp, it is purely by word of mouth. When I leave site I try and pick up *SchNEWS* or something, but most of the time I hear about things from people.' Such experiences reflected the view of others that 'social change will only come when people create mass face-to-face movements and make decisions that way and the more people focus on technology – in fact, the more alienated they are going to become from their communities and their immediate environment' (Dave Morris, McSpotlight).

In this way *SchNEWS* used CMC to reach a wider audience, but maintained its existing audience by using traditional methods of distribution. Similarly, the anti-McDonald's campaign had been in existence for ten years prior to McSpotlight's inception, and for that time means other than CMC had been used to distribute the information. Dave Morris (McSpotlight) counselled: 'You can over-exaggerate: a website doesn't replace direct distribution of information to the public, and in this country alone 3 million leaflets were handed out during the case direct to the public.'

The limitations of reliance on CMC were illustrated by GSN's loose organisational form, which was hard to maintain due to the regular turnover of students at universities. CMC helped ensure GSN's continuation, in that 'the mailing list seems to keep a few people together' (Keith, GSN); however, the network gradually became reduced to a virtual existence (as newsletters and gatherings became unnecessary channels for communication). Without these traditional methods of organisation it became increasingly difficult to attract new students to the network as there were few signposts left of its existence.

However, face-to-face contact was rarely relied upon by activists as the sole source of information, just as CMC might not be regarded as a totally reliable source of information: 'People don't treat emails quite as seriously as they treat something if it's printed . . . Any lunatic can send out thousands of emails telling everybody something's going to happen, but it doesn't mean that they've got a competency to organise it' (Tristram, GSN). For some, it was the combination of using CMC and word of mouth which was aiding support for actions and campaigns: 'Information gets lost when you just use word of mouth' (Mary, Peace Action).

Most individuals will respond only to information which they receive through a reputable source; thus, trusting the source is vital to mobilisation. This has traditionally been assured through word-of-mouth networks or inclusion within reputable newsletters. Thus activists draw upon the solidarity created by the movement networks to ensure mobilisation and the distribution of accurate information. The anonymity offered (and utilised by many environmentalists) by CMC is counterproductive to this need for trust and solidarity (Breslow 1997). Overall, word of mouth appears to be the key way in which solidarity and cohesiveness were maintained.

Strengthening the ties that bind

Groups employed CMC in a variety of ways to mobilise participation: using it as a gateway to activism, to raise the profile of their campaign, mobilising online activism, stimulating local activism and attracting participants to existing protests. The results of such efforts, however, were hard to discern because of the use of multiple methods to attract participants and were to some extent mitigated by impediments to the usefulness of CMC, such as the poverty of online engagements. CMC, however, has been used by the interviewees to reinforce the strength of existing network ties through the modification of relationships between activists on an international scale, helping the interaction of ideas and skills, enabling greater debate between larger numbers of individuals and diverse groups, and increasing the speed at which communications could take place.

Mobilising integrated individuals

Most cases did to some extent attempt to mobilise non-integrated individuals using the moral shock tactic; for example, through FoE's Factory Watch, and McSpotlight's website information about McDonald's. Significantly, though, many used CMC to reach those sympathetic to and those already within environmental networks. As illustrated by activists at Lyminge Forest, it is possible, via CMC and without face-to-face contact, to mobilise those who are already integrated with the movement (or who are in similar movements). CMC is simply a quicker, cheaper and more global method of utilising these networks, and it has strengthened those existing network ties by easing the passage of communication between dispersed individuals (also see Norris 2001, who asserts that online resources are most effectively used by those who are already active offline).

In all cases, although a wider audience not previously linked into the networks was contacted via CMC, there was no evidence that participation resulted, only that it was easier for such individuals to obtain the information. However, information alone, except in occasional examples of moral shock, is unlikely to trigger mobilisation. FoE has been able to create a virtual linking of individuals who will act electronically when requested to do so (through, for example, the Climate Change campaign), but they did not attract as many participants as they had hoped and the potential for offline collective action seems limited.

Such patterns suggest that the value of CMC varies according to the types of resource that organisations are attempting to mobilise (Diani 2001). Organisations such as FoE that are mobilising mainly professional resources using CMC are able to create virtual communities, but this does not affect mobilisation potential. In contrast, those mobilising mainly participatory resources, such as the activists at Lyminge Forest, rely more upon face-to-face interaction, and so CMC results in virtual extensions that maintain the importance of the existing network ties. Thus the importance of non-CMC methods was re-emphasised.

Sustaining networks, not building them

While the potential to mobilise using CMC alone appears limited, its use *has* facilitated the speed of the information flow within the network, and it has enabled this network to widen without extra costs: 'Word of mouth and phone calls are still there, but [CMC is] creating a stronger network, both in this country and internationally' (Jo Makepeace, *SchNEWS*). In addition, CMC use has enabled new possibilities for co-ordination across theoretical and tactical divisions both within the environmental movement and between social movements. This increases the ability of activists to network on a global scale and for wider social movements to emerge out of such coalitions. Although the mobilising of a truly global environmental movement has yet to happen, and though problems of having productive discussions online remain, CMC has strengthened the existing networks, which had been reliant on word of mouth communication, by providing an additional (international) communication channel.

In this way, CMC has also provided some sort of permanence to these networks. Although email addresses can change and websites become out of date, it was noted by several interviewees that email was an easier way of keeping in touch with activists who had no permanent home: 'If you are moving around a lot you can have a Hotmail mailbox on the web, [and] you can read it from anywhere, from anybody's computer . . . It's cheaper than having a mobile or a pager' (Chris, (S)hell). At Lyminge Forest, contact was maintained with protesters once they had left the site through email, as Worzel (Lyminge Forest) commented near the end of the campaign: 'Most of the serious protesters have moved on, but keep in touch with us by email and the internet.' Similarly, email has provided permanence to GSN, which, without it, might have dissolved years earlier, as fewer people took on the responsibility of organising the gatherings and distributing hard-copy newsletters.

This ability to use CMC to network internationally holds greater potential than the possibilities of mobilising participation online. This network 'allows the movement to be diverse and coordinated at the same time, to engage in a continuing debate, and yet not be paralysed by it, since each one of its nodes can reconfigure a network of its affinities and objectives, with partial overlappings and multiple connections' (Castells 2001: 142).

One of the possible consequences of this increased interconnectivity is a decentralisation of the movement – as and when the need for large resource-rich environmental organisations diminishes and the smaller grassroots groups establish a greater presence using CMC. This would also appease those interviewees who criticised the bureaucracy of large NGOs and stressed that the 'real engine of the environmental movement in Britain is grassroots – it is individuals and small local[ly] based organisations' (Steve Jones, former ATA co-ordinator, CAT). This decentralisation would enable a more heterogeneous movement to emerge as wider influences are included through the smaller groups or linkages are made informally between individuals – because involvement in the environmental movement would not require membership of a large and homogenising organisation. This emphasis on a growth in transnational environmental networks also points towards the possibility of a global civil society, or at least a more effective public sphere.

CMC also reduces the need to have large budgets to co-ordinate global actions. If activists are able to secure internet access, they can use CMC to strengthen their existing non-hierarchical networks, operate using decentralised co-operation, and mobilise quickly and cheaply those within the movement. However, most of the case-study groups, far from organising global protests, were more concerned with asserting the importance of the local and promoting activism on a local scale. Furthermore, for the time being, large organisations are valuable for their ability to launch big public information campaigns, fight court cases and to lobby Parliament.

At present CMC has been used to augment the many media already employed and environmentalists have transferred much of their information on to the new media, using email networks in much the same manner as they utilised word of mouth and networks of telephone trees. While this does not negate the importance of CMC – which is enhancing movement cohesiveness, the ability to co-ordinate campaigns and to produce better-informed activism does suggest that there remains plenty of potential to develop more innovative forms of interaction.

Although CMC seems unlikely to mobilise new participants for the environmental movement, it serves to strengthen the ties that bind the movement together. This is despite the limitations of online communication. Productive discussion is feasible in small email discussion lists or those where there is a strong commitment to a collaborative goal and a respect for fellow participants.[17] CMC is used to help *sustain* movement networks, not build them, and consequently the movement is liable to grow in its ability to work together, or at least have a closer understanding of each other's activities and ideas.

In these ways CMC use has informed understandings of participant mobilisation – demonstrating principally that face-to-face interaction remains of paramount importance, and that other possibilities are continually being tried out. Analysis of CMC use reiterates that information provision alone is unlikely to lead to action (even through the use of moral shocks), and that the *depth* of social engagement is crucial (exemplified through the poverty of much online interaction). These findings have implications not just for environmental groups but for public participation as such in political life. In addition to its role in mobilising participation, CMC offers significant potential to develop new online tactics and new forms of alternative media. These contributions are discussed in chapter 5.

Notes

1   Putnam (2001) does, however, foresee government as a less hierarchical structure that is responsive to the demands of its civil society, and the voluntary associations as practising self-governance, which is in line with many environmental groups' desires for participatory democracy.
2   Putnam also ignores the negative features of associational activities such as criminal gangs and whether 'rival groups in society may exhibit high levels of social capital *within* groups but low social capital *between* them' (Mohan and Mohan 2002: 195).
3   Several interviewees confirmed that they had first heard about the campaign through *SchNEWS*.
4   Wizard (Lyminge Forest) commented: 'There's pretty much an underground network, [and] once you get into it there's people you know . . . and they'll say, "Oh, I'm just off to somewhere else. Do you want to come along?" and [you] get to another site that way . . . Sort of a big family, really, it's sort of a bit of a tribe.'
5   Between April 1998 and April 1999, 207 new people joined over the internet (Charles Linn, FoE).
6   According to questionnaire results, 35 per cent of respondents had heard about GSN by word of mouth, 29 per cent through a local environmental group, 24 per cent through a website and 12 per cent through a magazine or newsletter.
7   The survey was sent to 11,700 supporters as an insert of the November 1997 edition of *Earth Matters*; it had a response rate of 18 per cent.
8   Factory Watch was an interactive map of polluting factories with a capacity to rank local factories according to a range of pollutant measures.
9   This was in contrast to previous use of CMC by Newcastle FoE, which in 1997 had a website that included meeting times, copies of past newsletters and press

releases, campaigning information and a membership form to print off and post. It also included the facility to send a fax directly protesting against the Business on the Moor scheme by Newcastle United.

10 Based on analysis and categorisation of postings to GSN throughout the research period.

11 An email-based questionnaire was posted to members of GSN in April 1999. There were seventeen completed responses to the questionnaire. At the time the email list comprised seventy-six members, so the response rate was 22 per cent.

12 Although the website questionnaire respondents represented only a (self-selecting) fraction of visitors to the site, and despite the lack of other statistics with which to determine the number of site visitors (there was no counter on the site and access statistics were not available), the results do provide an impression of the website readership, although there are clearly some limitations to the data available.

13 This readership was also divided between male (44 per cent) and female (56 per cent). There was a broad spread of ages represented, with a dominance of 16–20 year-olds. Two-thirds of respondents were educated to university level (with 14 per cent to secondary-school level and 9 per cent to alternative levels), and 43 per cent were still in full time education; few were unemployed and there were almost as many in self-employment as in full-time employment.

14 The Lyminge Forest website had an international readership – 72 per cent of the questionnaire respondents were from Britain, 8 per cent from the USA, 5 per cent from Germany, and the rest equally divided between France, Canada, New Zealand, Australia and Ireland.

15 The Community Green Festival was an annual spring event in Newcastle-upon-Tyne. A coalition of groups came together and organised the free festival, which includes bands, stalls, a temporary eco-village and workshops.

16 Unlike those at GSN, the discussions were moderated, though exclusions were limited: 'There's very strict guidelines as to what is moderated out'(Bob, McSpotlight).

17 The functioning of open discussion lists of the Indymedia network is just one example where significant attempts have been made to preserve the usefulness of the list. Specific procedures have evolved whereby consensus decisions are made by participants via email (see Pickerill (2004) for further discussion).

5

Electronic tactics
and digital alternative media

One of the key potential uses of CMC, in addition to its use for mobilisation and co-ordination of activism, is as a tool of protest in itself. CMC could be used for more than the distribution of information, notably as a tool with which to lobby adversaries, undertake 'hacktivism' or as a conduit for alternative media.

Environmental activists have utilised diverse tactics in the attempt to assert their influence upon the decision-making process and society. Such tactics have included lobbying politicians, using the judicial system, manipulating the media, encouraging local participation and taking direct action (Jordan and Maloney 1997; Doyle and MacEachern 1998). Groups have placed differing emphasis on the use of these tactics, whether singly or in combination. For example, Earth First! advocates non-violent direct action (NVDA) and Friends of the Earth UK has used a mixture of all these tactics (Lamb 1996; Doherty 1998).

Direct-action protesters use a variety of methods to publicise their cause or in an attempt to prevent environmental destruction taking place: on-site protest camps, barricades and blockades, tunnels, tripods, air-walkways between trees, tree houses, lock-ons,[1] office occupations, street parties and genetic crop destruction (Seel 1997; Doherty 1998 and 1999a; Evans 1998). Underlying all such endeavours is an emphasis on non-violence, a 'manufactured vulnerability'[2] and carnivalesque performance. Protests such as the Reclaim the Streets events are as much about protest as about dramaturgy, celebration and revelry, creating a spectacle of alternative ways of being (Szerszynski 1998; Chesters 2000b).

Arquilla and Ronfeldt (1998) have conceptualised the growing use by political actors of CMC as being part of a 'social netwar'. They describe how actors can use CMC to target important nodes in networks (such as governments or multinationals) with a strength beyond their numerical capacity and initiate information campaigns, or 'hacktivism', to highlight their causes. In response, they argue that CMC facilitates those who organise non-hierarchically, and thus in order to be prepared for information warfare they urge governments to adapt to such a style of organisation themselves.

To explore this further the chapter is composed broadly of three parts. It begins with an examination of the use online tactics for environmental activism and the reticence to engage in such use. The second section considers the use of CMC as a substitute for the mainstream media on which people have relied, and hence for the production of digital alternative media (DAM). Concurrent to the use of any tactics, environmentalists usually consider the ways in which they will publicise their actions prior to and after the event. CMC has enabled new forms of media to be subject to experimentation. Furthermore, alternative media production is 'not just a precursor to activism, it is activism – writing is action' (Meikle 2002: 97), and thus needs to be examined in analysing tactics. The chapter concludes by exploring whether these changes in online tactics and alternative media production enable environmental activists to be more effective in achieving their aims and targeting their adversaries.

Online tactics of protest

CMC has been used to extend existing tactics into the realm of cyberspace and in developing new forms of action. Forms of cyberactivism include the use of CMC to trigger campaigns and co-ordinate action, to distribute tactical information, in email petitions and for direct lobbying (Harasim 1993; Myers 1994; Schwartz 1996; Walch 1999). In contrast to hacking, cyberactivism tends not to be treated as illegal or as particularly disruptive to other CMC users. The effectiveness of CMC to facilitate activists in achieving their goals in this way, however, remains debatable.

All the case-study groups except CAT used CMC as one of their tools for environmental protest. CAT was not concerned with lobbying or protesting, but concentrated on practicable environmental solutions (Jenkins 1995). There were five key ways in which the interviewees used CMC as a tactical tool: lobbying using email or online fax facilities; broadcasting live video, photographs or text direct from offline protests; creating unofficial websites; and using hacktivism and electronic civil disobedience; and, finally, they considered their online presence to be a form of political symbolism. Critiques of each are undertaken in the next section.

A symbolic online presence

The use of CMC by environmentalists to display information which counters opponents' opinions is in itself a tactical use of the technology. Thus those at Lyminge Forest aimed to update their website regularly, 'that way it looks active and more threatening to Rank [their opponents]' (Mike, Lyminge Forest). Thus the technology was used to signal the environmentalists' potential to mobilise, as a symbol of resistance. The interviewees used their online presence as a form of threat to opponents as much as an actual illustration of what they were doing. For example, *SchNEWS* felt itself to 'have a very live online presence' (Jo Makepeace, *SchNEWS*) which contributed to its image as dynamically empowered. The debate forums on sites such as McSpotlight's and *Urban75* also served to warn adversaries that they, too, had voices.

This online presence was used to aggravate opponents and simultaneously to attract participants. CMC was used as a symbol of strength, and as a source of other inspiring symbols – a space where the drama of past actions could be displayed and replayed. Activists were able to create images of themselves in a form over which they had control. In this way the performance and fun elements of protest have also been extended to the use of CMC. Websites such as *Urban75*'s incorporated direct-action news with games, McSpotlight included videos and cartoons, and CAT had a virtual tour.

By using CMC to create a visible and vibrant image of environmental activism, some of the interviewees were asserting that the technology should remain free from regulation and control: 'There was a freedom on the internet that had to be maintained, and if we were gonna be in any way a small part in maintaining that and furthering the argument, then excellent' (Bob, McSpotlight). CMC was an additional space that environmentalists were attempting to subvert by imposing on it their own cultural values. In this way some interviewees saw their use of CMC as part of setting a precedent for its use in the future: 'If you're part of the process that sets the precedent about how the internet is used, then that's how the internet gets used, and if you're not in there at the beginning, then . . . you've got no complaints about how the internet develops' (Bob, McSpotlight). McSpotlight sought to serve as an example to other activists of the value of using CMC. Environmental activists' innovative use of CMC has thus helped determine how its potential is viewed.

Furthermore, by squashing the stereotype of environmentalists as being anti-technology, activists hoped they would be taken more seriously: 'By showing the public that we can use technology and exploit it in an "intelligent" way, we challenge the stereotyped image of protesters as disorganised drop-outs' (Lyminge Forest questionnaire respondent no. 26). By using CMC to illustrate how the activists at Lyminge lived, Matt hoped that inaccurate assumptions about the protesters might be dispelled: 'Putting it on a website sees us in a more acceptable light. It's no longer underground subversive eco-warriors, it's, like, everyday environmentalists having tea with the local parish.'

Environmentalists' use of CMC is therefore symbolic. They have crushed the stereotype of being anti-technology, and they have used CMC in their own way, rejecting the commercialisation of the technology with their own forms of organisation and decision-making structures. In this way the means merges with the message. Environmentalists have used CMC to symbolise their resistance, as a potent symbol of their vibrancy and their allegiances, and have thus attempted to legitimise their activism.

Electronic lobbying

Several groups utilised CMC as a medium through which they could lobby. Email tended to be used in the same way as letters or faxes had previously been employed, either for personal requests or as part of mass petitions. FoE used CMC to aid its political lobbying, both directly (using email to contact MPs) and indirectly (to co-ordinate and network with other organisations). Political lobbying by individuals was facilitated by draft letters which users could download from the website. Individuals were also encouraged to print off a copy of a postcard from the website called 'Climate Catastrophe' bearing a cartoon of Tony Blair, and manually post it to the House of Commons.

FoE encouraged individual members to use email to lobby politicians with their views. For example, web viewers of the Wild Woods campaign were urged to email Finnish and Swedish ministers. This use of email to non-British politicians took advantage of an important attribute of email, in that to email internationally was no more expensive than emailing locally, facilitating international lobbying: 'I think if the government of Nigeria suddenly got 30,000 emails from all over the world, it is clear to them that there is a degree of international concern about what they are doing' (Mike Birkin, south-west RCC, FoE).

FoE also used its website to post information (and encourage lobbying) in attempts to trigger political responses. FoE launched the Chemical Release Inventory (CRI) and Factory Watch to increase the pressure for a Community Right to Know Act. Launched in 1995, the CRI enabled visitors to enter their postcode and produce a map of polluting factories for their area using government (Environment Agency [EA]) data (Schofield 1995): 'Before we developed the CRI the data [were] like a telephone directory and totally incomprehensible' (Charles Linn, former web developer, FoE).

FoE's use of a mapping interface on to a complex data set over the internet was innovative and a landmark in providing access to environmental information (Pipes 1997). FoE was able to criticise the EA's argument, that it was impracticable to provide such data in a low-cost and easily accessible manner, by doing it themselves over the internet. This stimulated the EA to improve its web provision of data (see chapter 6).

After the success of the CRI, Factory Watch was launched in 1999. This was essentially an improved and significantly updated version of the CRI, with new data and increased interactivity such as the ability to create one's own Filthy Factory league tables and search the database by chemicals, health hazards, industrial processes, companies and areas. The 'Take Action' page again encouraged the reader to lobby local MPs to support a new parliamentary Bill drafted by FoE. Here FoE was clearly attempting to utilise public support for their political lobbying. The launch of the Factory Watch campaign triggered an increase by 500 per cent in people accessing the website and stimulated a response from the EA, which a week later launched its list of top ten polluters (Nuthall 1999).

On GSN's site, several electronic fax actions (where faxes are sent from websites) have been encouraged. For example, a request was made to join the campaign to mass-fax John Prescott (Labour minister for the Environment and Transport) about the proposed second runway development at Manchester Airport, in 1997. Keith (GSN) admitted to using email to lobby – 'I email the occasional government' – and Ciaran (GSN) believed that CMC was 'expanding lobbying power, in that you can get more people to act quickly by email rather than having to get in touch with them by other means'.

Similarly, McSpotlight invited visitors to pressure McDonald's 'We found and published their email addresses, which they did not make public. We also wrote a new version of their "comment" form so that people could send their opinions to them' (McSpotlight volunteer). In all, several groups used CMC to lobby. Using email is perhaps easier (and cheaper) than writing and printing a formal letter, and thus greater numbers of people may have been inclined to take part. However, the effects of (and participation in) online lobbying were difficult to discern, and some critics have suggested that they are ineffectual.

Live web broadcasts during offline actions

Several of the interviewees had advocated using CMC as a medium through which to provide a live feed of photographs or sound from offline actions (using mobile phone links, portable computers and digital cameras). Such live broadcasts were used during the occupation of Shell's HQ in London on 4 January 1999. Using a digital camera, a laptop and a mobile phone, environmentalists were able to publish live pictures and text over the internet direct to the public. Despite being barricaded inside the offices of Shell-Mex House, without power or phone lines, the activists were able to broadcast their occupation and message to the world and its media.

In this way the activists were able to generate their own media which attracted significant attention: 'The site received 10,230 hits on January 4 alone' (Anon 1999c: 127): 'The live internet link from the occupied Shell HQ was our way of getting our message across without the traditional media, which always have their own agenda' (McSpotlight volunteer). Not only was this live, but the use of photographs provided 'a certain amount of credibility to what you are saying . . . By having photos people just are that much happier to believe what they read' (Chris, (S)hell). It was also hoped that potential activists would be inspired by seeing the action live. This use of CMC attracted its own mainstream media attention, though the coverage of the issues remained limited: 'The *Guardian*'s piece on the action focused entirely on the website' (Anon 1999c: 127). Online coverage also provided a form of protection:

> When you are dealing with a big, nasty company – security guards, espe-cially, rather than the police – the fact that you've got a camera isn't always good enough, because they can confiscate the film, but the fact that it's already been broadcast means they have to behave – and [behave] in a legal sense and in an activists' safety sense. (Chris, (S)hell)

Furthermore, the activists combined the occupation and live broadcast with a website similar to that of Shell: 'We went live on the internet with a site which closely resembled Shell's own. We were both using our own media and subverting theirs' (Anon 1999c: 127). Since then, live streaming has been employed during several actions. During the J18 action, continuous video was streamed to the internet, and this was repeated during the protests against the WTO in Seattle (Chesters 2000a; Wilkin 2000). More recently, rather than live streaming, the trend has been to upload short video clips or MP3 audio files of actions. This has the advantage over live streaming of being available online for longer and easily downloadable for copy.

Unofficial websites and subvertising

Another form of online tactic used by the interviewees was to hijack, or produce their own versions of, official (company) websites. McSpotlight developed a guided tour of the McDonald's website, pointing out inaccu-racies and untruths. It used frames to mix the two websites and 'to hijack the McDonald's website and deconstruct it' (Devin, McSpotlight). Similarly, Chris ((S)hell) registered domain names which were similar to some company names, and then posted up counter-information on them. This attracted visitors trying to find the official sites, to the annoyance of the respective companies or associations:

> The British Field Sports Society (whose aim is to promote fox hunting) . . . they got a website called BFS.org so we registered BFS.com . . . the number of people that came there by mistake and were enraged, but you know that's great campaigning because you are getting an interested audience, targeting well. (Chris, (S)hell)

Corporate Watch applied a similar tactic when it launched its website
(www.gm-info.org.uk), which contained information about GMOs and
tended to be negative about the biotechnology in use. The URL was similar
to the government's website (www.gm-info.gov.uk) which advertised the
benefits of GMOs (Vidal 2000a). This mocking of official versions of websites was extended to the World Trade Organisation. The www.wtoo.org
site was a spoof of the official WTO website. The site had been subtly
adjusted using the *reamweaver* software developed by RTMark. This software enabled the easy copying and altering of websites. The tactic of 'sub-
vertising' was also transferred online – moving the physical alteration
of billboards from the street, through CMC, to hit brands online via
their websites. Thus in addition to using the medium to distribute anti-
corporation sentiment, CMC was used to proliferate *agitprop*, offering a
different version of truth.

Hacktivism and electronic civil disobedience

'Hacktivism' refers to the combining of activism with the hacking of computer systems. Hacking, once the preserve of the apolitical computer enthu-
siast, is becoming politicised (Wray 1998a; Taylor 2001). Although debate
continues over what practically constitutes 'hacktivism', uncontested
examples of it include virtual sit-ins and denial-of-service attacks, email
bombing, website hacking, computer viruses, the disruption of databases
and computer break-ins (Denning 1999). It tends to refer to actions which
are aimed at disrupting the normal operations of the target. Hacktivism
enables activists to develop new forms of protest against their corporate
adversaries. It is necessary to move the protest inside, from off the streets,
as 'nothing of value to the power elite can be found on the streets' (CAE
1996: 11). Thus, traditional civil disobedience becomes 'electronic civil disobedience' (ECD), taking traditional street action into cyberspace (CAE
1996; Wray 1998a and 1998b).

The Critical Arts Ensemble (CAE), which produced a seminal work
(1996) proposing the use of ECD, has suggested that there were two pre-
requisites to the practice of ECD – skills and cellular organisation, both of
which exist in the environmental movement. CAE (1996) argued that there
was an unbridgeable schism between a computer hacker and a political
activist, and that hacking skills were essential to undertake political ECD.
Many forms of online activism do require a certain amount of skill, and the
skills required to perform basic ECD are gradually being disseminated and
simplified.[3] There has been a process of mutual education and sharing of
ideas between digital artists, hackers and political activists. CAE (1996)
also argued that ECD will be operated most effectively through small anarchist cells, rather than by larger bureaucratic political organisations. This

is because ECD requires secrecy, speed and consensus, all of which can be hindered in centralised political organisations. Such autonomous cells are much in evidence among direct-action campaigners.

Although both of these criteria have been met, there is only limited evidence of the use of hacktivist tactics by British environmentalists. The most popular ECD tactic advocated was the virtual sit-in *FloodNet* software program. Designed by the USA based Electronic Disturbance Theater, it enabled activists to flood a target website and prevent any genuine requests for information being answered, thus impairing the operations of the target company – a virtual sit-in at a website (Wray 1998a). Several of the interviewees expressed interest in participating in such actions: 'I might be interested, if somebody said we could cripple Microsoft's operations for a day by doing this. We can make a point, because we will lose them some money' (Tristram, GSN). Members of GSN were also encouraged to take part in an EDT-led virtual sit-in of Mexican financial websites in 1998. This form of virtual sit-in was further used in the J18 and N30 protests. In April 2000 the British electrohippies' collective operated a client-side distributed denial-of-service attack on specific companies believed to be harming the environment (DJNZ 2000). Importantly for those who were advocating participatory forms of action, client-side distributed denial-of-service (DDOS) attacks utilised the idea of *FloodNet*, but, rather than mounting attacks from one computer, the action relied on the participation of large numbers of people using different machines, and was thus democratically based (DJNZ 2000).

The effectiveness of such tactics, however, are open to doubt: 'If you kept doing it forever, then they'd just arrest you, because it becomes harassment. So it's great for an action, but it's not a sustainable way of keeping stockmarkets shut' (Chris, (S)hell). Furthermore, few of the targeted sites were actually made inaccessible to other users. Rather, its power lay in its use as a form of spectacle and in the media attention it garnered (which often focused on the process rather than cause). CAE was disappointed with this emphasis on the spectacle created by ECD, rather than seeing it as an effective tactic, and has reiterated its call for underground, less public, ECD to be practised (CAE 2001).

Another example of ECD is the email 'bomb'. This bombards a victim with thousands of messages at once to jam the recipient's email box, preventing legitimate email getting through. There were uses during the Kosovo conflict, the protests against the WTO in Seattle, and during J18 all the directors of Freshfields (an international law firm which services global construction companies) became subscribed to thousands of email lists, which consequently crashed their email system (Denning 1999; Chesters 2000a).

Hacktivists also use computer viruses and 'worms' to damage computer systems. A worm spreads on its own, while a virus attaches itself to files or code and is spread by the moving of these elements (Denning 1999). No known examples of such tactics have, however, ever been ascribed to environmental activists. Hackers have often targeted the computer networks of organisations or governments by hacking webpages, 'breaking into' the computers or redirecting web browsers, and recently such attacks appear to have been motivated by overt political considerations rather than by the more technical aims of the traditional hacker. For example, a British hacker broke into and placed anti-nuclear messages on over 300 websites in July 1998 and the Kaotik Team defaced forty-five Indonesian websites in support of East Timor's fight for independence (Glave 1998; Paquin 1998; Wray 1998a; Vranesevich 1999).

Another form of hacktivism to have been encouraged is the physical tampering with computers. *EF! Action Update* (Anon 1999d) contained details on how to crash computers during office occupations – such as reformatting and repartitioning hard drives and deleting files. Chris ((S)hell) commented: 'I've heard people talking about going to actions with a disk with a virus on. That's the lowest level, but that's the same thing – it's just more physical, less electronic. Simply unplugging a computer is hacking physically.'

Significantly, not all such online actions were operated by hackers but by political activists with enhanced technical ability. Despite these examples, however, Chris ((S)hell) voiced the concern that hacking was difficult to achieve successfully: 'It's not as easy as they make out. There are not that many [who] are that good, actually, and most big hacks that happen are more to do with having someone on the inside – or luck.' Indeed, code makers tend to have the edge over code breakers. Hacking could also be quite destructive, and this raised the issue as to 'whether or not that was non-violent, because bringing down a computer system could conceivably disable fire alarms, could conceivably stop people getting wage cheques and have their houses repossessed. It could do a lot of damage . . . Being destructive like that isn't necessarily very effective' (Chris, (S)hell).

Furthermore, after claims that environmentalists had hacked City of London computers during the May Day 2000 demonstrations, RTS retorted that hacking would not benefit its cause. Thus there was discord as to what constituted peaceful and productive online tactics, and what were the more destructive forms of electronic hacking. Moreover, there were no validated examples of the more extreme aspects of hacktivism being practised by environmental activists, though because hacking is illegal it can be hard to contact the individuals involved. Although some of the interviewees advocated the use of ECD, and some had experimented with it as a tactic, few of the case-study groups had adopted such strategies. For example: 'People suggested that kind of thing, but McSpotlight as a group didn't encourage it' (Devin, McSpotlight).

Reticence to employ online tactics

The use of such tactics has raised debates among activists as to what is non-violent and justifiable protest, and whether online tactics constitute direct action or ineffectual 'desk top' activism. Activists' concerns include: online actions being ineffectual and causing unnecessary disruption; not knowing the technical possibilities or being limited by them; and having other priorities.

A key objection to the use of online tactics such as ECD was that they infringed upon (the often unspoken) netiquette of CMC use. Such actions were deemed to damage the functioning of the internet – such as clogging or diminishing bandwidth: 'The internet is largely built on trust that people won't deliberately cause problems. So we wouldn't want to break that. I think the IT people are worried about that, in reference to the electronic activism we are trying to encourage' (Charles Linn, FoE).

This hesitancy to breach netiquette also reflected the doubts of many of the interviewees over the extent to which online tactics were effective, or that, conversely, they would be so effective that they would prove disruptive for *all* CMC users. For example, the email to fax service enabled by CMC was encouraged by GSN participants in order to flood an adversary's fax machine, but others on the list suggested that it would just crash the system. Thus some online actions were regarded as unnecessarily disruptive of the internet's infrastructure and as ultimately tarnishing the activists' message: 'I think it was a bit of a policy . . . to not do irritating things, not try to bomb McDonald's server so that it closed down . . . We wanted to be seen as a library, taking the high moral ground' (Jessy, McSpotlight).

Online attacks by environmentalists were seen by some as tantamount to blackmail rather than as encouraging positive change in the interests of the environment: 'It is important to keep channels of communication open, and it is better to create an avenue for the organised expression of many views through a sustainable medium than to make the bridge collapse in the rush' (Richard, GSN).

Critiques of ECD often centred upon the claim that it is an undemocratic form of protest, whereby other people's free speech is limited by a few activists effectively closing down targeted websites. This was a contradiction of activists' calls for personal freedom. Others felt that the consequences of such actions needed to be more fully explored in terms of law suits or crackdowns on activists' internet usage. There were also some criticisms of the lack of communication to the public about why certain actions had been taken. These critiques are similar to arguments against the use of direct action, which can become violent and is about asserting the will of a few (though many claim they are acting on *behalf* of society) over that of others. The electrohippies' collective tried to overcome this criticism by developing software which relied on the involvement of a large number of individuals in order to be effective, thus making it to an extent democratically accountable (and illustrative of people power), but which did not unduly damage the internet's infrastructure (DJNZ 2000).

This accountability and the greater openness about the actions, however, also seemed to curtail their effectiveness (CAE 2001). As illustrated with ECD, public online actions often remained spectacles because they were relatively easy to counter (Meikle 2002). In all, it was rarely possible to judge whether online actions were effective. Examples of hacking were seldom publicised: 'Banks, corporations and other institutions often quietly cover-up breaches of their security so as to not create panic in their customers or provoke a wave of copycat offences' (Anon 1999e). Although some of the interviewees took part in lobbying via email, they questioned whether they were even being read: 'I don't think they are very effective. I have emailed Bill Clinton a few times, but . . . it's very easy to just run through and delete the things [you don't recognise] and . . . to filter [them] out' (Tristram, GSN). Few had received responses from electronic lobbying: 'I don't think they [the recipients] treat it as important' (Mary, Peace Action). However, FoE's use of CMC to provide interactive access to data did stimulate the EA to update its own use of CMC and also to launch its list of the ten top polluters, and the GMO campaign was so effective that it led FoE to be accused of giving direct action protestors too much information and was reported in the national press.

Some interviewees suggested that use of online tactics was limited by activists' ignorance of what was technically possible. Tony Canning (IT technical and support manager, FoE) thought that the responsibility lay with IT departments to encourage online tactics: 'We would like to take the use of the net further on the campaign side as there is more you can do with it. But really it is up to us to say what is possible and then [to] push for it. The campaigns' people don't necessarily know what is possible with the technology.' Conversely, rather than lack of knowledge, Devin (McSpotlight) implied that innovative use of CMC was limited by a plateau in the development of internet technology: 'I think the internet will develop new technologies when the bandwidth becomes available, and new innovations will happen, but I think where we are at the moment there is nothing particularly new or sexy there to be exploited.' In that sense the potential of the technology was still largely under debate.

A key factor in the use of online tactics, however, was campaign priorities. The priority of each campaign or group was to achieve its goal in the most effective manner. The role of CMC at Lyminge Forest was confined to that of an additional means of communication, rather than a tool for the deployment of online tactics, though not because of a lack of ideas, but because the activists had other priorities. They had only limited time and resources, and their preference was to build physical defences to prevent their eviction and the development of the Forest. That those in control of the website were living onsite full time probably contributed to this emphasis on physical participation rather than the development of online actions. The most important aspects of the campaign were the 'people here in the woods, building defences and getting media attention – to be quite honest the website isn't that important to the campaign . . . It is useful, but it is not that fundamental. I think it is more important that people are here and building defences' (Merlin, Lyminge Forest). In a different context, however, hacktivism could be the more effective tactic:

> Debates about hacktivism tend to focus upon whether direct political action is a non-sequitor if it takes place in virtual environments. In contrast, I would argue that it is hacktivists' imaginative re-engineering of the technological code contained within the Internet that actually enables them to engage more successfully with the more abstract capitalists' code that paradoxically has most effect upon the so-called 'real world'. (Taylor 2001: 125)

In the street and online: combining electronic tactics with physical protest

The interviewees had not wholeheartedly embraced the use of online tactics, and part of the reason is a desire to root all protest in offline experience: 'Where cyberspace meets other flows of reality is where its potential lies . . . Left by itself, cyberspace connects people in only a limited way and provides only an illusion of participation' (Froehling 1997: 304–5). Environmentalists are campaigning to protect the earth and its inhabitants, and thus, despite activists' ingenious and extensive use of CMC, the importance of physical protest and existing techniques has been maintained.

Rather than shifting activism into the realm of virtual space, bypassing the importance of location, environmentalists assert the value of their particular localities and their need for protection. Local struggles are linked with other local struggles, so that, although one is able to 'take global action locally' (Campbell-Jones 1998: 9) in this era of globalisation, the importance of the local and non-virtual is reasserted.

Furthermore, the interviewees gave no sign of abandoning their use of existing techniques of protest. In most cases CMC was used as an additional tool of protest or during the mobilising and co-ordinating of events, which then took place offline. Interviewees wanted to ensure that there were links from their use of CMC to their old ways of protest. With regard to McSpotlight, Atton (2000: 2) writes: 'The grounding of the site's content in actual struggle is emphasised by the foregrounding of campaign information and leaflets and the assumed requirement for these to be available in print for distribution at protest sites, on demonstrations, in high streets.'

The interviewees felt it crucial to combine online with offline tactics in order to be effective. It is this merger of online tactics with existing methods which holds most potential for increasing the impact of environmentalists' actions. Focusing solely on the technological facets of action would result in losing a great deal of the symbolic, 'media-friendly' and empowering aspects of protest, and online activism holds few of the personal benefits gained from offline activism such as solidarity ties and friendship. Furthermore, the apparent invisibility of online actions poses problems for activists, who have traditionally relied on representation in the media for their publicity. Consequently, environmental activists have incorporated CMC into their repertoire of action, but have maintained the importance of physical protest, be it in the street or on adversaries' premises.

Walch (1999) has identified a growing gap between 'e-activists' and those involved in more traditional forms of protest – a division between those with the technology and those without. In the environmental movement there are signs of this segregation, but the technology has also been taken to the sites of protest – with laptops at Lyminge Forest, and live internet feed from global actions. This attempt at balance illustrates an ability to overcome the schism: be neither a 'hacker' nor an 'activist' only, and use diversity productively to create new identities.

Moreover, this ability to combine CMC actions with other forms of protest has facilitated the tactic of 'swarming' an opponent.[4] Swarming techniques involve simultaneously utilising a variety of tactics to hit a target from multiple directions (Chesters 2000a). Activists have used their technical computer skills in combination with traditional forms of protest to produce a wide array of techniques that can be utilised simultaneously against an adversary. This use of CMC has facilitated the trend towards 'organised spontaneity' (Scott and Street 2001: 41) in protests – whereby affinity groups decide their own courses of action but join with others in concentrating on a particular target. Affinity groups can communicate prior to an action and then each will undertake its own tactics – such as an office occupation, a banner drop, and leafleting, all occurring at the same time that another group is bombarding a company with emails or operating a virtual sit-in at its website.

Despite this potential, however, and evidence of the swarming of opponents combining street-level actions with online tactics during J18, the organisation of large-scale attacks, co-ordinating a variety of groups to take alternative actions, can be problematical. Using CMC to facilitate the co-ordination of several groups for one action can result in the integration of several different tactics and an increasing number of participants. The roles of CMC in the co-ordination could be vital, enabling disparate groups to communicate across distance and ideology with the mutual aim of disturbance to a target. However, without the discipline and the hierarchical chain of command of military units, the co-ordination of several groups can be problematical. It can be difficult to achieve consensus of heterogenous groups as individuals choose to disagree with other groups' choice of tactics, creating dismay for some activists and ultimately dissipating the potential of the action. For example, while some protesters may approve of an office occupation, they may not agree with the use of online tactics.

Furthermore, while environmentalists do have varying degrees of access to CMC, they are unlikely to be able to afford the extensive communication equipment advocated by Castells for military-level swarming. Castells (2001: 161–2) argues that this form of warfare 'is entirely dependent on robust, secure communications able to maintain constant connection between the nodes of an all-channel network', a 'combination of satellite transmission and mobile computer networking'. Activists, on the other hand, can utilise a more basic form of swarming to take targets by surprise, and, as Meikle (2002: 120) suggests, to exploit 'the small cracks that appear in the mediascape through the rapid evolution of technology and catch-up process of regulatory policy'.Thus the challenge for activists is not to match a military-inspired notion of networked warfare, but to benefit from the networking and co-ordination opportunities of CMC and integrate novel online tactics with the familiar (and thus more identifiable and solidarity building) tactics practised at street level. Furthermore, part of the challenge is to use the sometimes apparent chaos and spontaneity of actions to their advantage.

Overall, the use of online tactics by the interviewees suggests that environmentalists' use of CMC constitutes an appendage to, rather than a fundamental shift in, their repertoire of action. The interviewees had appropriated CMC in the manner they had seen fit, rather than using it as others had done before them. This in itself is innovative and contrasts with corporate use of CMC, but in general the interviewees had simply transferred their existing methods to CMC and had not challenged their basic approaches to protest.

Digital alternative media

Environmentalists have traditionally produced a variety of media. Their media were termed 'alternative' because they were considering concepts and policies which differed from mainstream thought and were often used to publicise actions which attempted to change aspects of society (Atton 1996). Alternative media include magazines, booklets, flyers, leaflets, videos, and radio broadcasts, often produced by co-operatively organised volunteer groups (Holloway 1998). In contrast, the mainstream media are typified by the 'corporate ownership of newspapers, television and other media outlets' (Warf and Grimes 1997: 260) and in reflecting the dominant views of society: 'It is believed that mainstream media exclude in principle radical and oppositional ideas, that when such perspectives appear they are negatively framed, or limited in scope, and that oppositional groups must therefore create their own media and forms of communication' (Kellner 1999: 103).

This section explores how the development of a variety of digital alternative media (DAM) might alter the relationship between activists and the mainstream media – traditionally, the important conduits for post-action publicity. Environmentalists' use of CMC as a means for the construction and publication of a DAM had facilitated the interviewees' distribution of material direct to the public (maintaining editorial control) without the need for diffusion through the mainstream media – using CMC as a form of media substitution (Walch 1999; Atton 2000; Lovink 2000). This modifies activists' relationships with (and need for) the mainstream media. Some environmental actions have had to rely on representation in mainstream media in order to publicise their cause. That reliance had in turn influenced their choice of tactics, in that stunts had to be designed and timed to attract media attention. The use of CMC could radically alter this search for media representation by enabling self-representation to a wide audience (Myers 1994; Lovink 1998; Doherty 1999b). Furthermore, CMC use could lower the costs of production, speed up distribution and reach an international audience, transforming the modes of (digital) alternative media. Thus the processes of the construction, format and distribution of the alternative media are altered. These altered processes are now examined in more detail in order to explore changing representations online, reduction in production procedure, new forms of production and the environmentalists' continued relationship with mainstream media.

Direct and detailed representation

CMC decreases environmentalists' reliance upon mainstream media representations and enables 'direct' self-representation to the wider public. This enables them to distribute detailed information about their cause and to do so quickly. Although environmentalists have always produced their own (alternative) media, these often have had limited circulation which reached only specific cohorts of the population (Atton 2000). In order to distribute their message to a wider public, environmentalists have traditionally had to utilise the mainstream media, but consequently have not been in control of what was reported.

By using CMC, many of the interviewees argued, they were now able to directly control the content, image and message they wished to portray: it 'allows us to get exactly what we want to say to the public. We write what we want, and it isn't edited or changed by anyone' (Mike, Lyminge Forest). Interviewees were able to bypass traditional power structures to publish their often unorthodox material: CMC 'allows us to be published without having to go through organised interest groups and power structures who may not like what we want to say or what we do' (John, Lyminge Forest). In addition to being able to publish their basic message, interviewees used CMC as a forum to provide content-rich detailed information (which was not being supplied through the mainstream media): 'Absolute mountains of information were being dug up about McDonald's . . . and this was just sitting in box files and not being [accessed] by anyone . . . The internet seemed the perfect medium to do that' (Devin, McSpotlight).

Thus DAM became 'all about content' (Bob, McSpotlight), about providing the public with all the information about the issues so that they could judge for themselves (George 1999). Despite the Lyminge Forest website being limited in the content it contained – 'It's very visual, but it needs a bit of substance' (Mike, Lyminge Forest) – it was still hoped that it would be used by the public to inform themselves.[5] The website enabled the Lyminge activists to distribute their version of what they were doing (including photographic evidence of the situation) rather than having a distorted (and often uninformed) version disseminated via the mainstream media.

Websites that host activists' viewpoints about campaigns serve also as spaces through which the groups become represented. Thus, the RTS website has come to represent the 'nearest there is to an official line' (Laptop Mike, RTS) from the loosely organised group. However, the mainstream media have used activists' websites as sources for groups' opinions on, or reactions to events.

Previously, the alternative media were confined to their specific audiences, but online, access is available to all (equipped with CMC), which means that it is 'more accessible to different people' (Sarah, MO). This access would, it was hoped, stimulate an understanding of what the activists were trying to do: 'Everyone can find out about the environmental movement . . . Before the internet and websites a lot of people were a lot more ignorant than they are now' (Matt, Lyminge Forest). Not all the interviewees were quite as optimistic that a broader audience was being reached by using CMC. James (EF!) was unsure that creating webpages was worth 'putting [the] effort into them, as they may only be accessed by a small number of people'.

In addition to their ability to represent their own ideas and situation, interviewees could do so quickly, often faster than had been possible via magazines or newsletters. CMC was quicker than receiving the hard copy: 'We get a hell of a lot of info in on email, and we get it quicker than receiving *SchNEWS* or *EF! Action Update*, so we just read it off the computer'

(James, EF!). On the J18 protest activists were able to post up news almost immediately. Video footage from the scene was online within twenty minutes of being filmed and text updates were added from participants, contributed by mobile phone from the scene. During the May Day 2000 demonstrations at Parliament Square, in London, computer terminals were set up in the street, so that participants could give accounts of the events direct from the scene. Furthermore, CMC could be used as a medium to promote more actions. In the past magazines had been limited to promoting actions planned a long time in advance because of the time it took to print and distribute the copies. CMC is able to inform an audience at short notice of impending protests.

Reducing the onus of production

Producing alternative media can be a time-consuming and costly task. CMC was used to reduce some of these pressures. Traditionally, there were several roles (and stages) involved in the production of such media – such as journalist, editor, printer and distributor. With the advent of CMC, these roles can be merged. Although the material still needs to be written, edited and posted online, the task of printing is removed and that of distribution greatly reduced. Thus a single individual can take on all tasks more easily. The result is the proliferation of media outlets, or the ability of an individual to dominate a publication. An example of this is *Urban75*, which is essentially run by Mike Slocombe, where CMC 'means that one person like me can maintain a huge site'. It also enables international co-operation on the production of a newsletter. For *EF! Action Update*, 'all the archives were done in Holland, [and] that distance just isn't a problem anymore, you simply email the stuff' (James, EF!).

Furthermore, in dealing with traditional media the most confident of the activist group often becomes the spokesperson because he or she was willing to talk to the media. Using CMC, however, the quieter individuals can interact with the media (formulating press statements or giving email interviews) or produce alternative media. Thus the role of media spokesperson can be taken on by a variety of individuals.

Using CMC also reduced some of the costs of production of alternative media – especially in terms of the skills and time required. Some interviewees found the costs involved to be considerably less than those of producing hard copies: 'It seems like all the other media are really expensive to produce and get into, and this wasn't: it just costs the price of a local short phonecall to put pages up' (Andy, GSN). This has particularly benefited smaller groups which suffered from a lack of resources. It has meant also that activists were not restricted to producing just one newsletter, but could produce multiple sites, 'because it's not like you are wasting paper by printing a separate newsletter' (Chris, (S)hell).

In terms of skills, Hamilton (2000: 3) asserts that 'internet-driven alternative media still require professionalised skills of composition, coding, and software operation'. However, some of the interviewees deemed the skills necessary to use CMC less problematical than learning how to use other media: 'To make a good video is quite a skilled thing, but to build a simple website is not a skilled thing: if you can write text, you can publish it, and that's it' (Steve Jones, former ATA co-ordinator, CAT).

Finally, *Squall* switched from being a paper-based publication to a predominantly online magazine to reduce costs and labour intensity. This was crucial when the labour were all unpaid volunteers, thus easing the burden on what was often a limited pool: 'There's only four or five people doing it . . . Putting out stuff on a website is less labour intensive . . . If you've got the text you can just chop it in, and away you go . . . It's less tricky and fiddly than producing a fifty-odd page magazine' (Ben, *Squall*). Such online magazines were also easier to update, as new editions were not required: 'With a magazine you have to bring a new issue out every month . . . with a website you just augment what's already there, so it just grows and grows and grows . . . You can update it by the minute' (Mike Slocombe, co-ordinator, *Urban75*).

A crucial aspect of alternative media production is the collection of content, and CMC was used by the interviewees to facilitate this researching of material – from fellow activists, experts and opponents. In the construction of the 2000 *EF! Action Update* the Newcastle-based editorial collective received most of its stories through CMC,[6] although some hard-copy letters were still sent to them. Email was also used to source articles for the EF! journal *Do or Die:* 'Most of the articles are from people who we have contacted through email' (Michael, EF!).

Email was also used to communicate directly with experts: 'You can ask people for their advice and opinions and examples of best practice from all round the country' (Dave, GSN). FoE was able to keep abreast of developments in government: 'We follow what's happening in Parliament very closely . . . *Hansard* on the internet' (Adrian Bebb, real food campaigner, FoE). Finally, CMC was used as a source of information about opponents: Mary (Peace Action) said that CMC was used 'to find out information about bad companies, as this information is harder to get hold of by any other means'.

Diversifying the formats of publication

CMC offers new possibilities for representing information and reaching an audience, but it can also trigger information overload and allow readers to become lost amongst the quantity of material. CMC is a multimedia environment that enables a variety of formats of publication. McSpotlight included video clips and an audio-guided tour of its website. Using these different (and innovative) formats, interviewees hoped new audiences would be reached:

> If you present an argument using a different format in a way that isn't just ranting and shouting . . . people actually read . . . They'll sit [and read] because it [is] so unusual . . . A lot are just playing games . . . but a lot of people drift through the other sections and hopefully learn something on the way . . . The web's an interesting medium, it's informal by its nature, so I think for that reason people are a bit more relaxed when they read it and people are more likely to read stuff than, perhaps, if it was handed to them on a leaflet. (Mike Slocombe, *Urban75*)

This informality of being online has meant that the boundary between a publication and communication has been transgressed. While specific DAM magazines exist, such as *Urban75* and *Squall*, email lists (such as GSN's) also act as a source of alternative media, at the same time as providing a space where one can interact with like-minded individuals and share information.

Likewise, some websites have become online campaign resource nodes, which provide space for groups to present themselves and their material. These retain a similar role to paper-based newsletters, though they are able to contain more information and be updated more frequently[7]. These online campaign resource nodes have several features which distinguish them from similar hard-copy formats. Sites such as McSpotlight and *Urban75* are not produced as editions, but are constantly updated. They are never complete entities, but are continuously evolving. Thus the point of publication has become a continuous moment of flux: 'That kind of archive is really important, a kind of living history' (Jo Makepeace, *SchNEWS*).

This continued building of a website enables a more permanent access to past editions, and thus a more permanent access point to alternative media. Such electronic storage of information is also searchable, and this amassing of publications contributes to activists' sense of a successful past, learning from failures, and gaining a sense of solidarity from others' actions which might stimulate future activism. For example, McSpotlight remained online after the McLibel trial and after many of the associated actions had happened. Many of its original authors have dispersed and yet it continues to be an online campaign node, 'a focus for a protest without a geographical or temporal centre' (Atton 2000: 2).

This plethora of online sources and formats has resulted in some of the interviewees feeling overloaded by the information: 'There's so much out there, but it's very time consuming looking for it' (Worzel, Lyminge Forest). Although lists such as GSN's act as sources of alternative media, they can also become clogged by too much information: 'People have unsubscribed from the email list because the volume has been too high, and attempts to set up a low-volume announcement list have not been successful' (Jon Ivar, GSN).

Thus while there has been a diversification of formats and a variety of sources of DAM, which have potentially made the information more accessible to a wider audience, clarity can sometimes be lost among the wealth of information. Some alternative media have realised this, and *SchNEWS* continues to act as an information filter, preventing readers from information overload: 'It's the same size every week. It's once a week, and I'm aware of the responsibility . . . for not overdoing it on our [email] list' (Toby, *SchNEWS*).

Maintaining the importance of the mainstream media

Despite the uses of CMC as a forum for alternative media, most cases still used mainstream media, and actually sought to attract its attention through the use of CMC. Although activists could control the distribution of their own version of events through CMC, the interviewees were aware that the public would still employ the mainstream media to inform their opinion: 'It is a physical war and it is also a media war. A lot of it is based on public perception . . . We have to fight the media war especially' (Mike, Lyminge Forest).

Furthermore, use of the mainstream media was never purely to distribute information; it was also to marshal support for environmentalists' demands and to generate pressure on politicians. CMC is unlikely to have the same effect as a damning headline in a national paper in forcing the government to react. FoE retained its aim of attracting media attention through traditional stunts, but also used CMC innovatively (such as the CRI) to capture the attention of the media:

> It's a bit of a game, you've got to come up with some sort of stunt . . . It's almost the equivalent on the internet. But the media won't come unless they can get good photographs. A good photograph could be graphics from the website, but you've got to provide something for them to call it a big story to get the message out. (Tony Canning, FoE)

Additionally, all press releases were automatically posted online, and this was the most heavily accessed area on the website. Similarly, at Lyminge Forest, 'media attention has been something that the internet has attracted because all the media like to do stories of people using high-technology in the woods' (Merlin, Lyminge Forest). McSpotlight provided an angle by which the mainstream media could comment about the McLibel trial. Furthermore, despite criticising the media, McSpotlight

delights in citing those media in its own publicity. This ambivalence, coupled
with the mass media's own fascination with the form and use of the site (over
and above its content) complexify the site's characterisation of 'alternative
media', particularly in terms of its processes and its relation to the mass
media. (Atton 2000: 2)

Similarly, CMC was used to bypass the need to attract mainstream
media attention during the occupation of Shell's HQ by posting information direct to a website. However, this innovative use of technology actually attracted mainstream media coverage and was welcomed by some of
the activists (who were criticised by others for valuing this mainstream
coverage) (Anon 1999c). With time, however, the mere fact that environmentalists are using CMC is no longer news.

Rather than make their employment of CMC into a news story, the interviewees sought to interact with the mainstream media through CMC. This
enabled them to provide the information they thought relevant – content,
not just a photo opportunity – direct to journalists. Journalists were
directed towards information on websites to provide them with all the
details: 'When the press ring up, instead of giving them the whole story
and spending hours on end speaking to [them], we can just direct them
easily to the internet' (Tim, HSA[8]). It was thus hoped that journalists would
be better informed and write more sympathetic copy. During the J18
protest, the anonymity gained by activists through email facilitated their
ability to communicate their message direct to the mainstream press. They
were able to use temporary email addresses and give media interviews
from geographically distant locations without risk of discovery.

CMC was also used to speed up interaction between activists and the
media: 'Without the internet, we wouldn't be able to manipulate the press
as much as we do, because you need to have quick communications with
them. We were always trying to do that before. It was just [that] we didn't
have the resources or the money' (Albert, MO). Despite this, faxing was still
deemed the most efficient way of distributing press releases and attracting
journalists' attention, as 'most news organisations still give priority to hard
copies . . . Basically they need it in front of them on a piece of paper, and
they're actually quite slow to use the internet' (Ian Willmore, media unit,
FoE). However, CMC was still 'useful for keeping in touch with people we
already know, particularly in print, who would look at their email and read
something for us in the normal course' (Ian Willmore, FoE).

Changing forms of alternative media

The development of a DAM using CMC has enabled environmentalists to
have ownership over the representation of their cause and actions and so
reduce the onus of production. The use of CMC has enabled new formats

of publication to be experimented with and for a number of them to be presented from one place (such as video, games, text and images all on one website).

These changes, however, have contributed towards a plethora of online publications – what some have described as a 'data smog' (Shenk 1997). Alternative media are no longer *alternative* in their form. This has now become normalised, as compared to other uses of CMC, and there are no confines to what constitutes *a publication*, and there are no longer boundaries to its readership. The once-distinctive processes of alternative media production – non-hierarchical and participatory forms of organisation – are 'now normalised in internet practice' (Atton 2000: 3). This has implications for motivating a specific readership into action. The only constant between print and CMC versions of alternative media is content which comes from offline experience. Similar to many interviewees' objections to using online tactics, their production of DAM has remained grounded in offline protest events.

Moreover, despite these advances in alternative media, the importance of the mainstream media was maintained. CMC has not been used just as a form of media substitution. This reflects a realisation that the mainstream media yield power in society, and this combination of approaches is exactly what Kellner (1999) advocates as part of the development of a radical democratic technopolitics.

Direct targeting

Environmentalists have used CMC to facilitate their mobilisation and co-ordination, their tactics and production of alternative media. This use of CMC enables environmentalists to reach their target more accurately – both in terms of hurting their opponents and exposing their views to an audience. Online tactics enable environmentalists to use a wider variety of methods to swarm an adversary or to compromise a company's computer system, increasing their chances of making an impact. The use of CMC for the production and dissemination of alternative media also enables environmentalists to target their audience more accurately, reducing the need to rely on mediation by the mainstream media, and speeding up the process of distribution to an international audience.

Although the need for wooing the mainstream media was maintained for environmentalists, its importance was reduced, which in turn affected the type of tactic they employed. Environmentalists who had previously used tactics designed to attract mainstream media attention are now freer to choose tactics which might damage their opponents in more direct ways, but which would not attract attention and could then be published via CMC to fellow-activists to inspire copy-cat actions.

A key problematic for the use of any tactic is in measuring its effective-ness. Effectiveness can be determined by the response of the target, via the extent of mainstream coverage or by the empowerment experienced by those taking part. Using CMC has thus facilitated activists' ability to react against their opponents (using online tactics) and simultaneously to bypass them by creating their own space of resistance and forms of com-munication through CMC. However, the use of tactics and the role of alter-native media are not always to target an opponent, but rather to stimulate the population into critiquing society. Effectiveness can thus be measured by whether 'the practice of critique *itself* becomes widespread and accepted, signalling critique as a major social activity' (Hamilton 2000: 3). Thus although the use of CMC could dramatically alter the ways in which environmentalists operate, activists who may remain small in number might be more effective in reaching their goals by continuing to encourage critique and for the population to empower themselves, rather than con-centrating on targeting opponents.

Such use of CMC has contributed to a shifting of power between groups within the British environmental movement. CMC reduces the necessity to have large resources at one's disposal in order to organise large actions or undertake damaging online tactics. Thus CMC is facilitating the rise of smaller grassroots groups (as opposed to the traditionally dominant large NGOs) which are able to use CMC to be effective in their tactics and media.

Despite this potential, however, much of it remains just that – potential. There was a general reticence among environmentalists to adopt online tactics and a desire to root tactics and alternative media to offline experi-ence. This urge to combine CMC with existing practices, and the fact that only limited examples of new practices are being developed, prevent such CMC use being categorised as triggering a fundamental shift in environ-mentalists' repertoire of action. The importance of traditional techniques was maintained.

Activists' reluctance to make full use of online activities has restricted their ability to benefit from some opportunities offered by the technology. However, their attitude also serves to reinforce underlying assumptions within the environmental movement that offline activities are their primary focus. Thus, rather than immersing themselves in a virtual world, and becoming dislocated from local affairs, environmentalists have retained a commitment to offline politics – thus signalling to society the primary importance of the protection of the environment on earth, above and beyond all other actions and affairs.

Chapter 6 explores the final component of environmentalists' use of CMC dealt with in this book: the impact of surveillance.

Notes

1 A 'lock-on' is when an activist deliberately locks himself or herself to something to prevent being moved.

2 Doherty (1999a) has used the term 'manufactured vulnerability' to refer to the way in which environmentalists deliberately put themselves in danger, for example by hanging in trees or locking-on to concrete in a road, in order to call the authorities' bluff, frustrate and delay eviction.

3 Information about how to participate in ECD is available from several websites, activist workshops and activist publications. For example, the EF! Publication *Do or Die*, no. 8 (1999), contained a resource list of references about hacktivism.

4 This use of the term 'swarming' differs from the way it has been employed by Arquilla and Ronfeldt (2000) and by Castells (2001). In their work it applies to military contexts to refer to highly trained units operating autonomously with significant weaponry at their disposal. In relation to activists, a broader approach is taken to represent autonomous units co-ordinating simultaneous non-violent tactics as part of a strategy of civil disobedience.

5 The most popular sections of the site (according to questionnaire respondents) were 'what we are doing' and 'what's going on'; thus people were more interested in what was happening and the alternative news than they were in the general background to the campaign.

6 The majority were gleaned from environmental activism email distribution lists. A by-product of this process was that after the advent of CMC much of the content of *EF!Action Update* (except for the middle sections of the newsletter, which were often original feature pieces) had already been available/delivered to those environmentalists who were online. Although the newsletter served to collate all the information into a useful focal reference point, its necessity was reduced for those online activists who had previously read it as a source of information.

7 Despite these innovations in the format of online publications, hard-copy production continued and 'it hasn't replaced that at all' (Dave, Cornerstone Resource Centre).

8 The Hunt Saboteurs' Association (www.huntsabs.org.uk) is a direct-action anti-hunting (fox, stag, mink and hare) group that organises the disruption of hunts. It is a national organisation, has over 140 local hunt-saboteur groups and produces a quarterly magazine.

6

Online surveillance and counter-strategies

Computerised electronic surveillance has ushered in a whole new phase of domination. (Kovel 1983: 77)

The threat of surveillance has led many environmentalists to fear that CMC is another temporary, rather than a long-standing, space for resistance. Fear of a totalitarian or corporate state, a dictatorial presence which limits any space within which resistance can develop, has led to activists zealously guarding what liberties they have and constantly searching for new tools with which to widen them.

Environmentalists' activities have been monitored and recorded for years by law enforcement agencies and, in some cases, public relations firms and corporations. Strategies have also been employed to counter environmentalists' efforts and successes, hence the term 'counter-strategy'. These include widening state legislation to exclude their activities and companies seeking to disperse criticism by distributing 'greenwash' (Rowell 1996 and 1999; Beder 1997). Environmentalists may fear that CMC could amplify the power of the state and corporate forces to use such tactics, but they also seek to use CMC as a route by which to avoid some of these threats (Castells 1997a). CMC is a medium through which environmentalists could assert their politics, but it is also a contested terrain (Breslow 1997). As companies stake their claim to cyberspace, they are able to assert influence over its regulation and the practice of ISPs and to use CMC as a tool through which to disseminate their corporate message.

The use of surveillance and repression affects the tactics used by environmentalists, and the forms of surveillance and counter-strategy determine in part the operations of environmental groups. This chapter examines environmental activists' perceptions of, and reactions to, online surveillance and counter-strategy, and the implications these threats have for CMC as a space for activism. The relative lack of CMC legislation has created an avenue through which environmentalists currently can maintain some secrecy. However, most interviewees viewed CMC as being essentially a public domain, which therefore was not secure. Consequently, considerable care was taken in what was posted online and it was necessary for environmentalists to encrypt their email communication. Such actions restrict the usefulness of CMC for communication and preserve face-to-face (or at least word of mouth) dialogue as the safer form of transmission.

The chapter begins with an examination of environmental activists' perceptions of the surveillance of their activities and the counter-strategies adopted (and of where they perceive the source of this threat to be). Second, the way in which these perceptions inform and affect their use of CMC are considered, detailing tactics which the interviewees have employed to negotiate surveillance. Third, the responses of the state and corporate bodies to environmentalists' CMC use are outlined. The online surveillance and its associated counter-strategies form an additional dynamic to the tensions between the threats and opportunities of CMC use for environmentalists. Consequently, in the final section, the impact of these tensions upon the perception of CMC as a new space for activism is considered.

Perceiving a threat?

The activities of many of the participants of the British environmental movement have drawn the attention of the British police force and the intelligence agencies (such as MI5 and Special Branch), as well as public relations firms, for a number of years (O'Hara 1994; Bennetto 1998; Wall 1999a).[1] This has taken the form of phone tapping, infiltration, photographing actions and building up a database of prime suspects (Campbell 1981; O'Hara 1994; Lodge 1999).[2]

Protests events are often monitored using video cameras which can digitally map faces and identify the activists (Anon 1997h; Ball 1997; Lodge 1999). Members of *SchNEWS* had been monitored: 'Sussex police once tried to ban our meetings by leaning on the landlord in a local pub . . . Several people have been approached to provide information for cash . . . We are followed around and photographed, and filmed and filed, just about every week' (*Justice?* 1998: n.p.).

In addition, many British environmental groups, such as Greenpeace and FoE, have been infiltrated (Murray 1993). The British intelligence agencies have the power to tap the telephone conversations of suspects, and mobile phones enable police to determine the physical location of the phone user (Campbell 1981; Barnett 2000). Attempts have been made to create a national database of personal details of activists, compile profiles and share such data on the Europe-wide computerised database the Schengen Information System (Elliott and Campbell 1996; Lodge 1999).

The surveillance of environmentalists has extended to their use of CMC. There is only sketchy research available that considers the ways in which CMC is monitored. This surveillance could take many forms: monitoring of the content of emails and websites; observing who talks to whom; the seizing of computers to scrutinise their hard drives; and the interlinking of databases nationally or internationally to provide personal profiles of 'key' activists.

The interviewees perceived the threats (and the sources) of surveillance and counter-strategy through CMC in different ways. Although heavily influenced by the attitude of their affiliated group and the extent of the illegality of their actions, these perceptions were often very personal and represented their individual fears or paranoia. There are several divergent understandings of the threat of surveillance. The most widely held belief among the interviewees was that CMC constitutes communicating through a public domain, and only a handful viewed CMC as a medium in which they could be anonymous, remain inconspicuous or be beyond censorship. The range of these beliefs is outlined below – from viewing CMC as a secure space to believing that all communication is monitored.

Insignificant, anonymous and beyond censorship

In contrast to the offline threats which the interviewees recognised, a handful felt CMC offered a 'safe haven'. Some interviewees also felt that they were too insignificant for police authority attention: 'I don't believe I'm sufficiently important for the police to be interested in listening in to my conversations . . . Activists aren't very powerful and aren't very important at the moment' (Tristram, GSN). Thus it was deemed that the police would pay little attention to information on CMC: 'They are not going to get a massive police presence out just because we put a message out saying we are going to march through Brighton town centre tomorrow, campaigning' (Keith, GSN).

Few interviewees proposed that CMC enabled them to remain entirely anonymous, though some suggested that the technology made it *easier* to retain anonymity compared with other methods of organisation: GSN questionnaire respondent no. 10 said that CMC relieved their 'paranoia about having snail mail monitored by the police'. Some of the interviewees mooted the idea that CMC censorship was impossible and that activists therefore were able to distribute information without interference: 'You can get stuff out there without it being tampered with' (Pete, founder and co-ordinator, MO) and receive 'personal accounts completely unedited/censored from the frontline' (e.g. Ogoniland, or Chiapas) (GSN questionnaire respondent no. 12).

Communicating through a public domain

Despite this optimism, the majority were more cautious and considered CMC a public domain rather than a space for secure interaction. Thus interaction via CMC was deemed as public as a mailed postcard, and activists were urged 'not to write anything down that you wouldn't post to your local nick' (Dave, Cornerstone Resource Centre[3]). Furthermore, GSN 'works on the basis that people do realise that by sending stuff to the list it is going into the public domain' (Ciaran, former list co-ordinator, GSN).

Due to CMC's public nature, many of the interviewees expected leakage from information distributed via the medium. However, they counselled that the benefits of the publicity offered by CMC outweighed the inevitable loss of secrecy: 'You are going to have to lose a degree of privacy if you want to get information out to enough people' (Keith, GSN).

Some groups, however, have sought to benefit specifically from the public nature of CMC, by using it as a medium through which to bypass obstructers who have invoked legal restrictions on what can be published. FoE placed its banned mahogany advert on its web page. It was able to do this because 'the law is a little cloudy over the issue of whether you can put banned advertisements on the internet' (Charles Linn, FoE). The use of CMC by McSpotlight was also a direct result of McDonald's attempts to censor the distribution of the McLibel leaflets:

> Because McDonald's is such a litigious company, no radio show, no TV programme or paper is ever going to print anything about them in this country ... It seemed like the logical thing to do to put it on a medium where it couldn't be censored and where it could be accessed worldwide. (Devin, McSpotlight)

McSpotlight played on the inability of companies to censor CMC, and deliberately circumvented McDonald's legal action against London Greenpeace. In this way McSpotlight was able to use CMC to publish 'millions upon millions of critical words, clips of the films that McDonald's thought it had suppressed, extracts of the banned play, every malicious cartoon and article that had ever appeared, all the information supposedly taken out of circulation by previous trials' (Vidal 1996: 12.).

All communication channels are monitored except word of mouth

If CMC is essentially a public domain, and if online activities are monitored, many interviewees were as cautious of CMC as they were of other vulnerable communication channels (such as the telephone, citizen-band radios, letters and faxes), and they valued word of mouth as the safest form of communication.

Although dates and meeting points for actions were posted via CMC, the finer details were distributed only through word of mouth: 'It's got the potential to be intercepted in the same way as anything – the phone or mail. The most secure means of communication is still word of mouth . . . anything that you want totally kept secret is best not . . . done on the computer' (Pete, MO). In this way CMC was used as a pointer towards other (safer) forms of communication and treated with a scepticism similar to that shown to other technology, such as the telephone: 'We use phones all the time, but we wouldn't say particular things that are incriminating – and that definitely goes for emails' (Blue, Lyminge Forest). Devin (McSpotlight) reasoned: 'In the same way as I will talk about some things on the phone and won't talk about other things on the phone, I talk about some things on email and I won't talk about other things on email.'

If CMC is in the public domain and word of mouth the only secure form of communication, then any interaction via CMC could unwittingly give additional intelligence to environmentalists' adversaries. Opponents can view environmental websites and join email networks to monitor discussions: 'It has also made it 100 times easier for those who are trying to stop us *to* stop us, by giving away all our plans in advance' (Tony Canning, IT technical and support manager, FoE).

The information gathered by surveillance can relate to planned actions; and 'there is also a certain amount of profiling of you that can be built up on the internet very easily by matching groups of people who email each other and building up pictures of who is connected to whom' (Devin, McSpotlight). Moreover, because CMC is text-based and communications are often archived, the possibility increases of such communications being used as evidence of illegality: 'Emails are written down; [they] can get forwarded, [and they're] quite often stored somewhere. If there was some sort of trouble during a direct action, then it would be possible for people to get access to your computer, [and] they might be able get a record of what you were going to do' (Tristram, GSN).

Experiences of counter-strategy

In addition to the interviewees' perceptions of surveillance, several had actually *experienced* it. The content of emails has been used to inform intelligence services. As activists gathered to set up a rave, they found that their intentions had been pre-empted by the police: 'They found it from the internet. They'd managed to find the hidden room [on the website], pulled out where the map was, and they were there ready and waiting for us' (Albert, MO). Furthermore, emails sent by Mark Brown were used against him in a court case relating to the organising of the anti-capitalism protest on 18 June 1999: 'His involvement was said to have been revealed in a vast number of emails found on his home computer by police' (Anon 2000a).

Two instances of ISPs deciding to terminate the activists' use of CMC were known. In both cases the ISP was the university's own server, not a commercial entity. RTS and EF! used to host their websites on the Westminster University server. However, in July 1998 a sensationalised story appeared in the *Mail on Sunday* drawing attention to the fact that 'much of the information about these eco-attacks [against genetic crops] comes from items posted anonymously on a computer website at Westminster University' (Paterson and Lewis 1998). The EF! and RTS activists were informed that they had to remove their sites, despite the fact that 'there has been no suggestion that their content breaks any law' (Holderness 1998). In addition, Oxford University attempted to withdraw a GSN member's use of his email account for using a signature which was a possible incitement to break the law, but which the GSN member interpreted as a 'blatant anti-green/radical bias . . . it seems part of [Oxford University's] message says that I cannot use university IT services for campaigning' (posted to GSN).

Opponents who objected to the content of activists' websites also attempted to shut them down. GreenNet had a couple of cases of companies requesting the removal of sites, both of which it declined. After the (S)hell action on 4 January 1999 at Shell's HQ, in London, when photos of the office occupation were displayed on a website simultaneously with the action, Shell 'phoned up and did some sabre rattling. They said they wanted [the photos] taken off immediately' (Chris, (S)hell). (S)hell resisted, however, arguing that there was nothing illegal about the website. In other cases, interviewees' computers were searched: 'Greenpeace did get a raid at one point when the police came and copied everything off their computer network' (Tony Canning, FoE). Furthermore, the Hunt Saboteurs' Association (HSA) has received several offensive messages via email since the launching of its website. In response HSA posted those messages on its website in unedited form, along with the source email address, which triggered apologies from several posters.

A temporary freedom?

If CMC is monitored and interviewees are experiencing counter-actions online, then perhaps use of CMC for environmental politics has a limited time frame. A few interviewees suggested that CMC provided only a temporary space for environmentalists' use, one which would eventually be restricted by legislation or developed into a corporate medium: 'The whole internet legal thing is obviously constantly evolving . . . It's a case of the law playing catch-up, then, I suppose . . . in which case you might go back to fly-posting things on walls all over again' (Dave, GSN).

Several interviewees feared that legislation was gradually catching up with CMC and beginning to curtail the freedom of the technology: 'I think legislation is going to be more bad than good, because it will stop people having a viewpoint and trying out new thoughts or ideas on the internet' (Kirsty Sunderland, information volunteer, CAT). Existing copyright and intellectual property laws are being extended into CMC. However, many still felt that legislation would not be enforceable: 'I think people [will] continue just to use it, and to break those laws and internet laws which are very difficult to enforce because it's round so many countries' (Rachel, Earth First!).

In addition to concern over specific internet legislation, there were fears that adversaries (state and corporate) were applying increasing pressure on ISPs to discontinue hosting environmental CMC email lists and other websites of which they disapproved: 'pressures are being applied to commercial servers, recently exemplified by the long list of "unsuitable" newsgroups recently sent out to all UK servers by the Police' (*Urban75* 1996).

There were those who felt that academic institutions were not the most suitable places to host radical websites (despite their provision free of charge): 'All it takes is for somebody high up to have vested interests . . . You just need to look at Imperial [College], whose rector is a director of Shell' (from an email to GSN). Several interviewees voiced concern that CMC was gradually being taken over by such corporate interests – both in controlling the means of access and in dominating CMC's content. As CMC developed, some interviewees feared control of the technology and servers necessary to access CMC would become dominated by corporate interests: 'The only strength the internet has is as an international communication network. The second it's under control it's lost that, and it just becomes just another media medium' (Albert, MO). Thus it effectively becomes a mirror-image of offline mainstream media.

This convergence of the corporate interest and the technology would enable users to access it more easily (for example, via innovations developed to corner a market, such as accessing email through digital television), but would simultaneously reduce the space for subversion: 'The future of it is still under debate, and it's probably going to end up being controlled by corporations' (David, media liaison, NE Green Party).

As content becomes dominated by commercialism, activism is pushed to the edges of the medium and filtered out by ISP portal-guided channels of surfing. Thus, Mike (Lyminge Forest) sought to encourage use of CMC which not did play to the corporate rules: 'If you have information, you should put it up on the internet, make sure it is free, sod copyright. So much information isn't shared.' What is not excluded can also be assimilated. For example, *Urban75* had 'just turned down a large corporate on the basis of them being dodgy . . . it would have been a lot of money . . . but it's not worth it'(Mike Slocombe, co-ordinator). Such an offer tallies with Cleaver's experience of receiving 'lucrative proposals to sell-out by funnelling our information to corporate inventors' (1995: 12).

Despite these threats of CMC becoming a corporate medium, Bob (McSpotlight) remained optimistic:

> There was a feeling that . . . it could be a bad tool and that we were fooling ourselves to think we could play with the big boys and that we knew it was the remit of corporations, etc., and that we were gonna be lost on this superhighway of adverts and for sale signs . . . I think even now the sceptics have turned round and said it is a very powerful tool and it's up to how you use it. (Bob, McSpotlight)

Laptop Mike (RTS) similarly suggested that although 'there is an unresolved question about the internet as a whole, about the extent of corporate control . . . all attempts to impose editorial policy are leaky'. James (Earth First!) suggested that activists might simply retreat from corporate occupied (cyber)spaces and form spaces free from infringement, in much the same way as some environmentalists have developed semi-autonomous communities.

CMC is becoming torn between two diverging visions – the internet without a centralised authority with many-to-many communication, and the internet dominated by large monolithic information providers and the imposition of old-style mass-media values. Many interviewees feared that the latter would gain dominance.

Adapting CMC use to overcome the perceived threats

> We do not yet know how sophisticated state monitoring of our electronic networks is, if it exists at all. At this time, the police seem to be playing 'catch up', but we should not assume that they will be so naïve in the future. Further attention must be paid to the use of secure web and email services controlled by ourselves, and to the use of strong encryption software for increased security. (Amusing Pseudonym website 1999)

There has been little research investigating the ways in which environmentalists seek to subvert surveillance. However, activists have employed security measures and sought to prevent legislation of CMC. Environmentalists have argued that electronic activism is essential in order to maintain the right to protest, challenge the influence of e-commerce and reinforce the importance of CMC remaining free from legislative and corporate control (Drew 1995; CAE 1996): 'If the state and corporations cannot tolerate dissent in cyberspace, then they will have a widespread, and legitimate, backlash from those already using the media for this purpose before the advent of e-commerce' (DJNZ 2000: 10). However, unlike the US-based Electronic Frontier Foundation which sought to prevent censorship of CMC and the UK-based Cyber-Rights and Cyber-Liberties organisation, no specifically environmental groups have been set up to protect CMC (Jordan 1999a).

In 1994 O'Hara claimed that environmentalists were not very good at security. By the late 1990s, as illustrated by those interviewed in researching this book, there was an awareness of the many security problems posed by the use of CMC for environmental activism. Despite this recognition, however, few employed specific measures to prevent online surveillance and fewer still took actions to avoid the imposition of legislation upon CMC use or the commodification of cyberspace.

This section details the ways in which the perceived threats informed and affected interviewees' CMC use and what tactics they employed to curtail surveillance and counter-strategy. It explores whether interviewees adjusted their campaign strategies to take account of the online surveillance they understood to be in operation, or whether interviewees sought to adjust the technology to protect the security of their information flows.

Restricting what was posted and discussed online

The simplest measure to ensure security online is to restrict what is posted there. There was a boundary to interviewees' use of CMC, a cut-off point where planning and discussion of actions were moved offline for security reasons. There was, however, disagreement over this cut-off point among those within the environmental movement, thus creating tensions over the extent to which planning should be secret and how much online surveillance was actually occurring. In order to standardise some form of approach, FoE issued a warning on the Campaign Network email discussion lists: 'Avoid discussing sensitive campaign material with the group, especially any future strategies, tactics, or actions, as there is no guarantee that the discussion group is secure' (Ritchie 1999a).

Material that was posted on campaign websites was also vetted for security reasons. At Lyminge Forest, a 'lot of [our] defences we wouldn't put on it, for obvious reasons: we don't want the tunnels being on a website where anyone can get information' (Matt, Lyminge Forest).[4] Although remaining anonymous online requires some diligence, some of the interviewees thought it worth the effort: 'You just have to make sure that you only ever log on from a cyber-café or at university – there are plenty of dead university accounts that you can just borrow, and then as long as you never actually use your real name you are just a computer out there somewhere' (Chris, (S)hell). Ed (GSN) noted the problems of using a university email account where your name and university affiliation are clearly displayed in the address. Instead, he proposed that activists should use less identifiable accounts, such as

> Hotmail: I can see that as a way for people to send whatever messages they want without worrying whether it's being traced. Perhaps they can trace what computer it came from, or what area, but its not the same as when you email somebody and they know which university you are writing from and they've got all your details.

Because of the contentious nature of the issues and the possibility of litigation, the authors of the McSpotlight website tried to remain anonymous (although some names have since become synonymous with the site): 'A lot of people wanted to work on it but didn't want their names involved, ever, and were quite nervous about sending emails and [whether it] was ... being tapped' (Jessy, McSpotlight). In addition, the core group (who established the site) was disbanded: 'We felt that if the core group was kept going it was a target' (Bob, McSpotlight) and thus 'even if their [McDonald's] legal action was successful, it would not help them in their attempts to silence McSpotlight since no individual or group of individuals are central to the running of the site' (Anon 1997d: 9).

Protecting what was posted and discussed online

Rather than limit online discussions some sought to protect their online networks from surveillance and counter-strategy. FoE installed a 'firewall' to protect its internal computer network. This prevented hacking and known spammer emails coming into FoE: 'It contains a lot of internal information, which we would obviously not like the general public seeing – internal documents, current campaign priorities, and staff information. It has information about what FoE is planning for the future' (Tony Canning, FoE). Other cases had not employed so robust a security system, though some activists had tried to encourage awareness of the need for computer security. For example, at an Earth First! summer gathering computer security was the focus of a workshop which explained how to encrypt a PC hard drive to prevent police access, in the event of its seizure.

Anonymity works against the need for trust in action organisation, and thus there were times when names had to be used. A few interviewees used encryption, especially *Pretty Good Privacy* (PGP): 'You can use email and *PGP* and things to send private messages to one another without the worry of anyone ever finding out' (Merlin, Lyminge Forest). There was limited use of encryption, however, and it was not failsafe: 'The weird thing with encryption is that by the very fact of sending encrypted mail it draws attention to you' (Chris, (S)hell). Even if it goes undetected it takes only a small mistake to render the security defunct: 'Even if you use encryption, you may still get things on your computer that, for example, read the letters before you encrypt them or while you encrypt them. It's really hard to make it secure, even if you use things like *PGP*' (Michael, Earth First!). Furthermore, few knew how to use *PGP*; for example, Mary (Peace Action) considered her 'powers of encrypting [to be] well below their [opponents'] powers of de-encrypting'. If activists had been able to use *PGP*, however, they would have been using what is generally regarded as uncrackable encryption.

Additional security measures employed to protect what was posted and discussed online included activists running their own servers, using foreign hosts and establishing mirror sites. FoE, *SchNEWS* (and (S)hell) had direct control over their servers. McSpotlight used a foreign host for its website, xs 4all – based in Amsterdam, 'where the libel laws are the most agreeable' (Devin, McSpotlight). Furthermore, McSpotlight set up several mirrors to its site which were located all over the world. These mirrors meant that if one site were removed or shut down, the others would still remain for the public to access. Part of this back-up plan was the distribution of the McSpotlight kit, a text-only version of the McSpotlight site, 'so if McSpotlight was going to be stopped, we could send out an emergency, everybody could take a copy quickly and there would be copies all over the world' (Jessy, McSpotlight). These security measures freed McSpotlight from localised counter-strategy measures:

> If McDonald's had said this server in this country is causing us offence, we want it shut down, and a judge had said yes, then the servers round the rest of the world could still be accessed in the country that it was found to be offensive in. So it makes McSpotlight a moving target and the leaflet a moving target. It's much harder to shut down. (Gideon, McSpotlight)

Despite the variety of ways in which CMC information was protected by some of the interviewees, the majority did not employ them: 'Most people are probably a lot more excited about being able to email each other than they are about worrying about encryption and security' (Tony Canning, FoE).

Using CMC to maintain the freedom to protest

CMC has also been used as an avenue through which to maintain the freedom to protest. To vent their objections to specific corporations' operations some environmentalists have used CMC as a medium through which to 'brand-bash', McSpotlight being a prime example. By being public about its anti-corporation views, McSpotlight was benefiting from the public nature of CMC, curtailing McDonald's options for response: 'We were all quite ready for them to sue, but they couldn't . . . We were so throwing the gauntlet down and taunting them that it would have been so stupid to' (Jessy, McSpotlight). As was seen in chapter 5, websites were also used to mock official corporate sites such as the World Trade Organisation. These sites offered alternative non-corporate versions of the way things were. The activists very existence on the internet was an attempt to counteract the corporate greenwash.

Environmentalists have been also among the objectors to recent changes in CMC legislation. There has been a plethora of articles condemning the imposition of the Regulation of Investigatory Powers (RIP) Act which have appeared in the alternative media, most of which have called for the total abandonment of the legislation (see Anon 2000b; Anon 2000c; Anon 2000d). The Act enabled police to gain easy access to all ISP records. Of the ISPs sympathetic to environmental activism, GreenNet spoke out against the Act and worked to try either to table amendments to the Bill or to get it withdrawn in its entirety (Anon 2000e). Many environmental critics also included advice on how to avoid the repercussions of the RIP Act.[5] There has been a similar response to the Prevention of Terrorism Act, which although not specifically related to CMC could still have a significant impact upon the environmentalists' activities. Furthermore, on 4 March 2000, there was a demonstration at Menwith Hill (the US spy base in Yorkshire). Many of those present took part to voice their objection to online surveillance and interference in CMC (namely the ECHELON[6] project). In addition to such demonstrations, some activists called for laws impinging on their activities to be ignored. On GSN, a participant implored: 'Don't be scared off by the thought police. Make all your emails illegal by putting in reports of your favourite actions' (posted to GSN).

In addition to these attempts to subvert surveillance, environmentalists were able to use CMC to monitor some of the activities of their opponents. Chris ((S)hell) used the logs from his website to determine who had visited and read the site. This method was used after the office occupation at Shell's HQ (4 January 1999) to determine what effect the action had on its target: 'We had more hits than ever and mostly from Shell employees. It was really gratifying to see that they were all actually taking an interest in having a look ... Word obviously got round the industry, because the second biggest major source of people looking was Texaco' (Chris, (S)hell). Moreover, the technique of tracing CMC use to its source was used on the N30 email discussion list to uncover the identity of a suspected corporate protagonist.

State counter-responses

As environmentalists have used CMC to target particular opponents, state and corporate adversaries have begun to take the threat from online activism seriously and to employ multifarious tactics to disperse any danger they have perceived. The State seeks to accommodate, appropriate and repress different aspects of the environmental movement, aiming to prevent the more radical aspects of environmental protest from operating effectively while legitimising more moderate components.

Creating or modifying legislation

The British Government has passed several pieces of legislation which have directly or indirectly restricted environmentalists' rights to protest. The 1994 Criminal Justice Act effectively outlawed many environmentalists' activities which were previously legal (Collin and Godfrey 1997). The 1996 Security Services Act redefined 'serious crime' to include 'conduct by a large number of persons in pursuit of a common purpose' (Lodge 1999), which could easily apply to environmental action. Many activists' tactics were deemed terrorist under changes to the Prevention of Terrorism Act 2000 and subsequent anti-terrorism legislation passed in the aftermath of the 11 September attacks in the US (Ford 1998; Norton-Taylor 1999; Wadham 1999). Legislation has also been imposed heavy-handedly to discourage other activists – environmentalists have been charged with conspiracy and have faced heavy bail conditions (Rowell 1996).

Despite technical difficulties in restricting who can use CMC because of its basic nature as a dispersed network, those in the British legal system have argued that CMC will be treated no differently from any other existing medium (Batchelor 1995). Legislation is being passed which allows for cases of libel, defamation and copyright infringement to be served against text written on web pages and within emails (Engel 1997a; Tang 1997). An ISP can be sued for what it has allowed to be published under the UK Defamation Act 1996 once it has been made aware of its existence (Middleton 1997; Martinson 2000). Consequently ISPs were adding restrictions into contracts with their customers which obliged their users not to break the law, thus relieving the ISP of any criminal liability. However, the imposition of such laws is restricted by the difficulty in defining what constitutes 'publication' in CMC, in identifying the publisher and in jurisdictional problems (Smith 1996; Carey 1997; Middleton 1997). Finally, the British Government is also seeking to prevent the use of anonymous remailer programs which allow a CMC user to disguise her or his identity (Bowden and Akdeniz 1999).

Monitoring CMC use and using information for intelligence

Police authorities have used online material to inform their intelligence. In the past, environmental activists, such as those involved in Reclaim the Streets, have had their houses raided, and their computers and disks seized (Chesworth and Johnson 1997; Lodge 1999). Furthermore, 'every day hundreds of thousands of faxes, telexes, electronic messages and phone calls are scrutinised, sorted, selected and analysed' by the Key Word Recognition System (Riviere 1999).[7] The RIP Act gave significant powers to the State for CMC surveillance (Sommer 2000). As a result UK ISPs are obliged (if requested) to install a remote-controlled black box which relays all data passing through their networks directly to the Government Technical Assistance Centre (GTAC) (Clarke 2000a; Greenslade 2000). This would enable traffic analysis of emails as well as websites and discussion groups visited (Doward 2000; Kite 2000). Thus, the State would be able to access 'a person's "clickstream" – the virtual record of his or her train of thought' (Bowden 2000: 26).

A unit of the Special Branch at New Scotland Yard, London, monitors environmental activists, including their internet use.[8] Detective Constable Steve Edwards, of the Open Source Intelligence Unit (OSINT), Metropolitan Police, confirmed that the

> Metropolitan Police has been researching the use of the internet and other online services for some time now, and we have known that the WWW was being used by radical groups and those intent on causing obstruction and disruption for the purpose of organising and publicising their activities . My job in OSINT is to use the internet (and other services) to provide operational and strategic intelligence in certain specialist areas.

Commander Judy Davies, City of London Police, confirmed that the police unit undertook surveillance of environmentalists' websites (*Newsnight*, BBC2, 29 November 1999). In addition to the use of online information for intelligence, the City of London Police posted on the City of London Police website seventy photographs of activists taken during the J18 actions. Observers were invited to inform the police if they had any information about the activists' locations. It was claimed by a *Times* reporter that eight arrests were made after their images had been displayed on the web page (Anon 1999f). This use of CMC by the police was unprecedented. Although they have previously utilised the mainstream media by releasing photofits of suspects and running television programmes, such as *Crimewatch*, posting photographs on a website enabled them to reach a different audience and effectively utilise the same technology as the activists. Furthermore, no mention was made of the specific crimes the suspects had apparently committed.

Overhauling their way of distributing information

Many components of the State have a duty to react to environmentalists' concerns. The Environment Agency is one such statutory organisation and is the official regulating body in charge of protecting Britain's environment. The EA has come in for criticism from FoE for not providing enough of its information free to the public and in an easily accessible form. In 1995 FoE used a set of EA data about emissions of polluting substances from industrial processes and produced the CRI on the FoE website. As a result the EA was further criticised and pressured to respond by producing similar interactive maps of their datasets.

The EA does not perceive itself to be in conflict with environmental activists; rather, it sees itself to be fundamentally working towards the same goals, but using differing tactics. The CRI, however, created tensions both between environmental groups and the EA and within the EA (as how to respond). The EA was restricted in its ability to put environmental information on the internet by data-set suitability, problems of updating data, and cost. The data-sets were not all easily accessible electronically, and many were in differing formats. The data-sets also had different levels of accuracy and quality. Once online, the data-sets would have to be updated regularly in order to be accurate (as an official body, the EA could not be seen to be using out-of-date data), which in itself is a huge task. Finally, because the data-sets are so large (and expanding), the cost of putting them online is huge and continuous, and needs to be prioritised by those at a high level within the organisation. Consequently, the EA has found that it's

> much easier for someone else to take one of our data-sets and put it on . . . their website because they can do it as a one-off, whereas as soon as we put it on we have to manage it and update it every day, week, month or whatever. (Paul Deane, internet manager, EA)

In response to the criticisms of its data provision online the EA has expended time and money on sorting its data problems to provide local level data, using a program for converging its data-sets. The EA is also attempting 'more interactive ways of doing things rather than just posting information on web sites' (Paul Deane, EA) as 'we are trying to react to public and non-governmental body pressure to include that interactivity' (Richard Saull, data manager, National Centre for Environmental Data and Surveillance, EA). Decentralisation has begun: 'We're steering very much away from central control, [and that's] just what I'm managing at the moment, that devolution of power' (Paul Deane, EA), with the aim of providing more locally specific information.

The EA website (www.environment-agency.gov.uk) is also used to provide more services, thus bypassing some bureaucratic structures. It was used to display the *State of the Environment* report, which aimed to inform the public of the current situation, what gaps there were in the data-sets and what were the core issues for the environment. One of its aims in using the internet was to facilitate access to their data-sets of environmental information and provide it in an interactive and interesting form. The EA has also tried electronic consultations, and has a feedback section on its website. In these ways the EA is attempting to incorporate public views and to be seen as accountable to the public.

On balance, it is likely that the EA would have moved towards providing better environmental data online without the actions of FoE. However, the CRI did illustrate both the problems and the potential of the internet for public environmental information distribution. The EA's response was not one of hostility; rather, it has examined its own information provision strategies and developed processes to improve its web presence.

Not responding

Kent County Council (KCC) is an example of a statutory body whose staff had sympathies with environmental demands but who did not see it as their role to respond to online activism. In the environmental management department there was a deep and genuine concern for the environment and a general sympathy with the protesters at Lyminge. Any council has a mixed bag of responsibilities, which include the business interests of the county and the environmental concerns of its residents. But KCC's situation was further complicated by the previous activities and affiliations of their county environmental management officer, Pete Raine. Raine, the former director of Kent Wildlife Trust (who had given evidence against the Rank development at Lyminge) and the Centre for Alternative Technology (1980–86), had worked for FoE Birmingham and was a local resident of Lyminge. He acknowledged: 'I've done some fairly radical things in the past' (Pete Raine, KCC).

KCC was involved in Lyminge, according to Pete Raine, by the very fact that it was 'responsible for providing ecological advice, both within and without the county council, when it comes to planning applications'. Although Pete Raine had visited the Forest he had not seen the protesters' website, and KCC was, at the time, using internal email but had problems with its external server. KCC's use of CMC (through an intranet and its website – www.kent.gov.uk) did not appear to be in any way a response to activists' use, but seemed rather to be dictated by slow moving county policy. In terms of environmentalists using CMC to communicate their ideas, Pete Raine was very supportive, but worried that the information was often biased. By 2002, however, KCC was running its own internet campaign, using its website (www.kent.gov.uk/coreinfo/cliffe) to protest against a proposed airport to be constructed (the Cliffe proposal) in the county.

Many components of the State are in an ambiguous position when it comes to dealing with environmentalists' demands. While illegal activity is repressed, some government agencies have a duty to respond to environmentalists' concerns by altering their practices. This variety of response has been illustrated by EA reaction to FoE's criticism in re-organising its system for distributing information, whereas the police are using material from online sources to inform their intelligence gathering operations.

Corporate responses to online activism

The target of many environmentalists is often big business for its involvement in, and profit from, environmental destruction (Brabbs 1999; Scott and Street 2001). Corporate counter-tactics include environmental advertising, adopting the language of the environmental movement (such as 'ozone-friendly' aerosols), influencing the mainstream media, and censoring criticism (often using libel laws[9]). Companies also attempt to isolate the radicals and co-opt the moderates (thus dividing the movement) through public relations strategies, and even by setting up pseudo-green groups which are a front for corporate sponsored anti-environmental propaganda (Rowell 1996; Beder 1997; Janssens 1999; Klein 2000a).

Corporate use of CMC is rapidly expanding as many companies utilise the potential of the technology as an additional advertising tool, an online marketplace (for their brand), or for business-to-business interaction (Rushkoff 1998; Reed 1999). CMC is becoming increasingly commercially commodified (Cleaver 1995; Kellner 1998; Resnick 1998). Such corporate forces threaten to subvert the internet's democratic possibilities by practising censorship to protect their brand image (Vidal 1997a; Klein 2000a). Rushkoff (1998: 226) argues that big business and activists cannot co-exist in cyberspace because companies are pushing the development of the web purely as another selling device: 'the only space left for interactivity will be our freedom to watch a particular movie "on demand" or, better, to use the computer mouse to click on an object or article of clothing we might like to buy'.

The ways in which many ISPs are set up also prioritise certain websites over others. Service providers such as AOL and Microsoft provide recommended 'channels' for CMC users to surf through which categorise certain websites into interests such as shopping or sport. How such sites are chosen, however, is not clear, and not surprisingly they are comprised mainly of the big brand companies rather than independent sites. In this way the ISPs encourage the branding of cyberspace. Filter programs have been developed, such as *Nanny Net*, for parents who are concerned about what their children might view through CMC. However, the process of choosing which websites are listed, and thus restricted through such software, has resulted in discrimination, with not only pornographic sites being chosen, but activist sites for being politically subversive.

Eight companies (Monsanto, BNFL, Unilever, Tarmac, Rank, Nestlé, Shell and McDonald's) were examined to assess their responses to online activism. Seven tactics were identified, with different companies choosing different methods of response. These were: ignoring the issue; monitoring online activity; proactively using CMC to enable debate between a company and its opponents; posting counter-arguments online; reinforcing computer security to prevent online breaches; attempting to remove offending websites; and employing a contractor to tackle anti-corporate online activism.

Burying their heads in the sand

The Rank Group is one such corporation which appears to have opted 'for the head-in-the-sand approach, hoping that if they ignore it, it will go away' (Reed 1999: 2). Rank was the target of Lyminge Forest protesters because it was behind the planned holiday complex development. Rank's website (www.rank.com) contained no mention of the proposed development but did detail the corporation's other portfolios. Rank refused to comment about the way it used the internet, or about the protesters' website.

Monitoring online activity and assessing public opinion

Several companies monitor environmentalists' online activities to understand the extent of the risk to their business: 'The actions and opinions of online communities are beginning to have a serious impact on public relations, investor relations and corporate brand management' (Lubbers 2002a: 118). McDonald's reacted to McSpotlight initially by reading what was posted online – 'in the first week the McDonald's main computer accessed McSpotlight something like 2,500 times' (Jessy, McSpotlight). Unilever used Infonic's services (www.infonic.com). Infonic is a UK-based internet intelligence service which aims to 'explore the internet for content impacting on our clients' business or brands' (Lubbers 2002a).

Some companies have used environmental material posted online to assess the mood of public opinion (Brush 1996). For example, Unilever 'monitors the internet to appreciate how it is viewed by stakeholders and other interests, and to understand how different groups view questions of relevance to Unilever. Internet-derived information, combined with that from other sources, informs Unilever's management of its public reputation' (Anne Weir, corporate relations department, Unilever). Similarly, for Tarmac 'protest groups such as Manchester Airport Runway2 have used the internet and we find the sites very useful in giving us an insight into what the protest groups perceive to be the major issues' (John Davies, group media relations manager, Tarmac). Neither Unilever nor Tarmac, however, mentioned how such information is then used and whether policies or PR are altered as a result.

In contrast, Nestlé was more explicit about its reactions to online opinions. They use the information to gauge any public fears: 'It prepares you in terms of people who will then ask you questions', and if a new criticism emerges it is verified and checked: 'Occasionally something new comes up and we will look into things if we find out information that way' (Nestlé spokesperson). This information is then used as a form of monitoring of its policies, and if necessary it alters its processes. However, Nestlé felt able to dismiss many of the criticisms it received: 'You can't just focus on a small activist group saying something out of turn, because at the end of the day we have to accept as a big company [that] there will always be some people out there who don't like us' (Nestlé spokesperson).

Commercially, there have been several attempts to build up databases of companies' online visitors and customers. Such surveillance is operated predominantly through the deployment of 'cookies' that identify repeat users and their details. However, Intel has developed a processor that can identify online users as they traverse through cyberspace, with each having a unique serial number, further contributing to the mapping of users' 'clickstreams' (Sprenger 1999).

Facilitating debate

Other companies have gone further than simply monitoring what is said through CMC and have deliberately sought to encourage debate online. Although 'one might conclude that this amounts to a fake openness, for show purposes only' (Lubbers 1998: 5), such companies have chosen to interact with their critics rather than ignore them, and have thus become more flexible and fluid in their approach, understanding that the branding and marketing of goods must adapt to the new communications media.

Tarmac has used its website to generate interaction: 'Environmentalists and the public at large have found our internet site to be a most useful method of getting messages [and] questions to us, and we always endeavour to respond with a prompt and informative reply' (John Davies, Tarmac). Shell attempted to dissipate some criticisms by posting information about its environmental practices on its website, including its controversial presence in Nigeria (Reed 1999). Forums were established for open debate, giving the impression that 'dialogue was the core concept, and sensitive issues were not sidestepped' (Lubbers 1998: 4). There were also links to the websites of Shell's opponents, such as FoE and Greenpeace. When asked if these forums had been helpful to Shell, Simon May (internet manager, Shell) responded: 'We were the first multinational to allow open, uncensored forums on their site and the message that that gives out in itself is sometimes stronger than the contents of the forums themselves.' Such attempts to enable debate are indicative of Shell's commitment to communicating with the public and its critics.

Monsanto can also illustrate such engagement with debate. Although initially Monsanto adopted a defensive position (exemplified by its threat of libel against *The Ecologist* in December 1998), the majority of its tactics have attempted to engage the public in debate. Thus Monsanto tried to shift its position from being the focus of public fears to being part of an open debate.

Monsanto launched a major advertising campaign in the UK in June 1998. This included several full-page adverts in national newspapers which included the telephone numbers and web addresses of many of its critics – such as FoE and the Genetics Forum. Monsanto also advertised its own website (www.monsanto.co.uk) as a source for further information on 'the real benefits it [biotechnology] provides for both customers and the environment' (Monsanto 1998: 7). In this way Monsanto was responding to environmentalists' use of CMC by countering their arguments on its own website.

Monsanto continued this tactic of using 'debate' in January 1999 when an online discussion forum was launched on its website. Here it posed a question[10] and asked for responses, which were then posted on the website. This served to enable Monsanto to gauge public opinion and to be seen to welcome and even to host debate. Although sceptics might suggest that Monsanto could screen responses, there were many postings which were hostile towards Monsanto. The extent to which these online discussions are part of a PR strategy rather than a way to take on board criticism is obviously difficult to determine. However, Monsanto did not seem to respond to any of the postings made, despite requests from those involved in the debate. Other contributors noted that Monsanto's website remained very supportive of biotechnology despite the public outcry.

Posting counter-arguments online

Several multinationals have utilised CMC as a tool through which to disseminate their message: 'In a medium where preventing activists from making allegations appears unviable, disarming them by issuing a counter message seems an attractive option' (Reed 1999: 3). To counter claims made by McSpotlight, 'McDonald's offer an extensive file of environmental information with energy saving outlets, reduced packaging and use of recycled materials' (Rumble 1997). Similarly, Tarmac use its web page (www.tarmac.co.uk) to communicate the environmental initiatives which they are undertaking. Nestlé uses the website (www.nestle.co.uk) to promote 'some sides of the company that we want people to know about a bit more' (Nestlé spokesperson). Specifically, Nestlé responded to the criticism over its baby-milk formula by having a dedicated micro-website (www.babymilk.nestle.com), which provides information on 'Nestlé's monitoring and action on compliance with the World Health Organisation (WHO) Code on Marketing of Breast Milk Substitutes'. This use of CMC to respond to specific criticisms has also been employed by British Nuclear Fuels Limited (BNFL). Mark Thomas posed two questions to BNFL about the transporting of nuclear waste through London during his show on Channel 4 television, and BNFL posted its replies the following morning on its website (www.bnfl.com), countering Thomas's assertions.

Reinforce security

Another option available to companies concerned by the threat of online environmental activism is to reinforce the security of the computer networks. Although this will not deter the online criticisms of companies' practices, it will help prevent the execution of online attacks, such as hacking. Companies in the City of London were advised to update their computer security in the wake of the J18 demonstrations, after several had been bombarded with emails.

Attempts to remove offending websites

A more proactive response to environmentalists' internet activism is the attempt to remove an offending website or a discussion list by applying to a court for an injunction. Companies can pursue the relevant ISP who can be held responsible for what it has allowed to be published. Despite this possibility of legal action, however, Nestlé, Shell and McDonald's have taken no action against environmentalists' websites. This is in contrast to the numerous threats from multinationals (for example, Monsanto and McDonald's) of injunctions and litigation for offline activities. This is perhaps because the 'corporate giants are still trying to figure out how to best deal with online criticism. Legal threats and writs are not an effective deterrent when national borders and personal identities dissolve' (Rumble 1997: 55).

Nestlé found that there was little that it could do to legally prevent online activism: 'It's a very unregulated medium which you can't make much effect on in many areas' (Nestlé spokesperson). (S)hell's website (www.kemptown.org/shell), just one of a number which criticised Shell, added dripping blood to the Shell logo. According to (S)hell, Shell reacted by requesting that the site be taken down. However, Simon May denied this and claimed that Shell did not attempt to curtail the protesters' internet broadcast in any way and that the company has never taken action against comments made online about Shell.

Despite the McSpotlight website distributing the same information as that for which activists were being sued, no action was taken against the site. This was perhaps because McDonald's did not want to compound the PR disaster of McLibel by taking on the website, or, alternatively, that it knew of no way to curtail it: 'McDonald's spokesmen say they're concerned with this kind of use of the internet worldwide, but have no way to police it' (Lawrence 1996). The only attempt McDonald's did make to attack the website was to file a case that the McLibel defendants had taken 'part in a 'photo-opportunity' outside McDonald's Leicester Square store' (Lubbers 1996: 5), which was part of the publicity surrounding the launch of the McSpotlight website. McDonald's argued that consequently the defendants took part in publishing further the allegedly libellous factsheet. Despite these early moves, however, no further action was taken against McSpotlight.

Employing a contractor to tackle anti-corporate online activism

As illustrated by Unilever's use of Infonic's online intelligence services, there is a growing number of companies which offer corporate clients online intelligence services. Companies such as eWatch also advise clients how to deal with online activists. eWatch is an American company which tracks discussions in cyberspace about more than 800 of the world largest corporations. Its purpose is to 'safeguard stakeholder value, improve customer service, protect corporate reputation, monitor competition, identify trends, and pinpoint corporate activism' (www.ewatch.com). It has even offered a 'Cybersleuth' service which identifies the entity behind the screen names which have targeted particular organisations (Lubbers 2002a).

A new haven for activism or a temporary space of resistance?

Contrary to reports (such as in Reed 1999 and Vidal 2000a), environmentalists' corporate adversaries have undertaken multifarious actions in response to online activism. Although it is difficult to discern specifically what actions have been taken (as companies prefer not to divulge much detail), most have been in response to activists' use of CMC. This indicates that environmentalists' internet presence had has an impact upon their opponents' operations, though most companies have maintained that online activism was not a serious threat to their activities.

Environmentalists' perceptions of surveillance and the multifarious

means by which state and corporate bodies attempt to counter online activism confirm that CMC is a contested space, a focus of conflict: 'cyberspace
is a site of struggle, rather than a straightforward liberation or domination'
(Froehling 1997: 293). Environmentalists have utilised CMC as a new
public sphere, which they could colonise to their advantage (O'Lear 1997).
The original optimism about the power of CMC, however, has now been
tempered by threats of surveillance and counter-strategies perpetrated by
the State and activists' corporate adversaries. The State and corporate
sources have acknowledged that the threats to environmentalists' online
space of activism are real and practised.

Although some interviewees viewed CMC as a safe haven, the majority
were sceptical of the security of the technology. Interview responses were
split between those who sought to avoid the surveillance and others who,
less optimistically, suggested that environmentalists' use of CMC would
be only temporary. Few of the interviewees were prepared to give up their
use of CMC, and instead made adjustments to it, such as taking basic pre-
cautions against surveillance by restricting what they posted online. A few
took further action, attempting to protect what was online by using
increased computer security, encryption, foreign hosts, their own servers
and mirror-sites. Others again used CMC as a space within which they
could be subversive and break laws. Despite their tactics to avoid surveillance and the optimism of many of the interviewees, several suggested
that their use of CMC was gradually becoming marginalised, that the
space which they could safely and freely use was being narrowed. Thus
some feared that their use of CMC would only be temporary.

The interviewees tended to err on the side of caution in their attitude to
surveillance. While some were quite paranoid, many did not trust even the
use of encryption, such as *PGP*, which has proved quite unbreakable.
Furthermore 'decryption is far, far harder than encryption' (Wood, personal communication, 2002). While this cautiousness plays a part in protecting activists from surveillance, it is also a form of self-censorship which
can negate the advantages of using CMC without adversaries actually
having to be proactive. In this sense, there needs to be some consideration
of whether such cautious attitudes to surveillance are actually productive
for activists in the long run. This quandary can be further articulated by
Lessig's understanding (1999a) of the struggle for control over the code of
cyberspace as the key battle for control over use of CMC. If activists
concede too quickly, then control of the code, and of cyberspace, will be
forever out of their hands.

This struggle for space within CMC technologies, a struggle between
environmentalists and their adversaries, represents both parties attempting to benefit from the opportunities offered by CMC. Gradually, however,
the environmentalists' adversaries have sought to limit these opportu-

nities by imposing legislation and commodifying CMC. Whether they will ultimately be successful in closing such opportunities to environmentalists will be determined in part by how quickly environmentalists respond and with what skills. The interviews illustrated that environmentalists are discovering how security conscious they need to be online and that, as a result, a few were involved in a constant search for innovations to keep ahead of any threats to their security. It is unclear, at this stage, whether sufficient action has been taken.

The realisation that CMC is as infused with threats and hazards as offline space indicates that environmentalists have moved beyond the early stages of technology use. They are no longer oscillating between viewing the technology through utopic or dystopic perspectives, but have a more critical perspective on the technology. It may be that environmentalists will win the battle for space, continuously evolving their tactics to remain one step ahead of their opponents.

Alternatively, there may come a time when CMC use is no longer an attractive option for environmental activism. If, as some interviewees suggested, CMC use by environmentalists will be only temporary, terminated by state legislation and corporate influence, the future of environmentalists' online activism looks bleak. If CMC is only a temporarily contested space, environmentalists will be unable to base their activism on it, and will have either to revert to their old forms of communication, or explore new technologies and techniques. However, once CMC becomes commodified, environmentalists might be able to recreate parallel spaces of resistance in its margins as activists have done in offline society:

> Soon the Net will be a closed mass medium with little or no room for new players. But we can then begin to build parallel networks, underground systems, somewhere in the margins. Wonderful subcultures will blossom . . . There is still enough time to create parallel, independent infrastructures in which cyberculture can re-invent itself. (Lovink 2000: 4)

Environmentalists have already been able to resist this encroachment to an extent, and 'although many battles against the forces to re-craft cyberspace into cyberspace.com have been lost, the fight – and dance – is not over' (Silver 2000).

Notes

1 This is not to say that all environmental activists are targeted for surveillance, but certain cohorts of the movement (such as the more radical or anarchist direct-action environmentalists and the peace activists) and certain activities (such as large-scale marches, road protests, genetic crop destruction or animal liberation) are now routinely observed.

2   The British Government has in the past employed private security firms (such as Brays Detective Agency and Group 4) to undertake surveillance of environmentalists, especially anti-roads protesters (O'Hara 1994; Wall 1999a;). They also have specific forward intelligence teams (or evidence gatherers), established to collect intelligence about activists and groups over a period of time (Bennetto 1998; Lodge 1999).

3   Cornerstone Resource Centre is based in a housing co-operative in Chapeltown, Leeds. The Centre is used by a variety of groups interested in environmental direct action (such as the local Earth First! group), prisoner support, peace camps and co-operative housing. Their website is at www.cornerstone.ukf. net/crc.

4   A visitor to the website actually commended the protesters on giving 'relevant information without telling the visitor anything that could be used to incriminate' (Lyminge Forest questionnaire respondent no. 36).

5   *SchNEWS* produced 'RIP it up!', a three-step guide to avoiding the RIP. This included avoiding the big corporate ISPs, which were part of the 'multinational internet oligarchy', and locating instead either abroad or with a small UK ISP. Second, to use encryption and anonymous web-surfing software. Finally, rather than storing data on a PC hard drive (which can be accessed under warrant using the RIP Act), store data on secure sections of the internet (Anon 2000b).

6   ECHELON is a network capable of tapping international telephone, fax and email communications (Penman 1999). It has since been renamed, though the project continues, and it is known to enable word, phrase and context recognition surveillance of CMC, among other things (Wood 2002). The project is co-ordinated by the USA, but runs through the UKUSA system (Hager 1996). The US National Security Agency's base at Menwith Hill, North Yorkshire, also intercepts emails and is part of the ECHELON project (Fogg and Zobel 1998). There have also been other protests against ECHELON, namely Jam ECHELON Day, co-ordinated by Rtmark, in 1999.

7   The operation is based at the General Communications Headquarters (GCHQ) in the UK that specialises in electronic eavesdropping (Campbell 1981; Murray 1993; Anon 1997g).

8   This was confirmed during an informal chat with public relations at New Scotland Yard.

9   The use of law suits by companies to prevent the public airing of some environmentalists views have been termed 'strategic lawsuits against public participation' (SLAPPs). They are designed to intimidate activists into silence. McLibel was a classic case where McDonald's sued Dave Morris and Helen Steel for handing out anti-McDonald's pamphlets (Beder 1997).

10 Debates included 'Which is better for you – organic, conventional or genetically modified food?', 'Science or public perception?', 'Does the destruction of GM crop-trial sites deny the public the opportunity of finding out their effects on the environment?' and 'Should a centralised European regulatory agency for genetically modified products be created?'

7

Cyberprotest: a new politics of protest?

Protest movements are continually appropriating new technologies. The telephone, stills camera, video camera, mobile phone and fax machine have all been utilised (Harding 1997). In many ways CMC is simply one more addition to this list. The question at the heart of this book, however, is whether the ways in which CMC is being utilised enable fundamental changes in the way environmentalists organise themselves, the tactics they develop and even the influence and success they can achieve.

In *The Internet Galaxy* (2001: 137) Castells asks whether the internet has just an instrumental role for social movements or 'is there a transformation of the rules of the sociopolitical game in cyberspace that ultimately affects the game itself – namely, the forms and goals of movements and political actors?' In response he identifies three components of contemporary social movements for which CMC has been indispensable: the mobilisation around cultural values; organising in a non-hierarchical manner; and activists rooting themselves in their local contexts while acting at the global level.

The empirical evidence explored in this book correlates with such assertions, and suggests additional components. However, the technology use did not trigger such changes. To suggest that it did would be tantamount to unadvisedly advocating technological determinism. As is outlined more clearly in this final chapter, environmentalists' ability to organise non-hierarchically, and their attempts to anchor action in local contexts and initiate diverse tactics simultaneously were, among other trends, existing propensities within the movement. Yet CMC has enabled them to more easily sustain such endeavours and thus more easily achieve their goals. Furthermore, the goals themselves remain familiar. In this context, of reinforcing and maintaining existing forms and processes, it is to be doubted whether, as yet, CMC use has *transformed* the rules of the game. CMC use has reconstituted old ways of operating within the environmental movement, but these have yet to dramatically affect 'the game itself'.[1]

This issue is explored further in four parts. It is pertinent, first, to acknowledge that only the early stages of CMC use have been examined, and yet to emphasise that this was a crucial period which determined future frameworks of technology use. Second, how the changes identified in the preceding chapters have influenced environmental politics is explored, as are the challenges which remain for environmentalists both online and offline. Third, given these changes and challenges, it is possible to extrapolate from this study to the broader implications of CMC use for social movements. Fourth, in the context of these changes the chapter concludes by examining the possibilities for future online activism.

The early stages of technology use

This book has explored the early stages of CMC use by environmentalists in Britain. Many of the activists and organisations examined in this research began utilising the technology only in the mid-1990s. Although it could be argued that a study of these early stages would not amount to a general examination of CMC use, it was in these early stages that some of the key determinants of the technology's use were established, thereafter to impact on CMC use (Pickerill 2001).

As with many other technologies the early stages of use are characterised by a perceived dichotomy between utopic or dystopic possibilities through the use of the technologies. Such forecasts dominated the early stages of CMC use (Breslow 1997). With time, optimism and fears become diluted by the complexity of individuals' experiences of the technology as its use becomes more integrated with everyday life. These experiences serve to *normalise* the use of CMC. Depending upon how use of the technology develops, many of CMCs potential advantages for environmentalists may be restricted (by the imposition of laws and regulations, or the commercialisation of CMC) or expanded (through more numerous and low-cost points of access).

The ways in which the tensions faced by environmentalists in their early use of CMC are resolved are thus of crucial significance to the future use of the technology. The struggles between the corporate and the political disputants, on the one hand, and the activists, on the other (and between the environmental activists themselves), as to how CMC should be used and governed serve not only as an indicator of how CMC might be constituted in the future, but as an example of the way in which society develops, treats and uses new technologies. Furthermore, the catalogue of choices made by environmentalists over how they incorporate CMC into their campaigning, organisation and everyday lives, and the terms on which they accept the technology, are indicative of activists' determination to employ only those tactics or organisational forms which reflect their overall aims (for example, organising in a decentralised manner to achieve a decentralised state). Consequently, although this book is an historical account of CMC use, it is no less relevant for its time-specific context. The examination of these processes of negotiation around the use of CMC as the debates were occurring afforded insight into how CMC use, as now practised in the twenty-first century, was constituted in the decades beforehand.

Altering the forms and processes of environmental politics?

Cyberspace is a site of resistance for environmental activists in Britain – an arena through which a radical democratic form of what Kellner (1999) calls 'technopolitics' could be advanced. The ways in which CMC is used are complexly embedded within existing social relations and attitudes. CMC is not a neutral, value-free, tool waiting to be appropriated, but one with constraints (logistical and legal) that require negotiation.

Environmentalists have enthusiastically adopted CMC but also have had to deal with its limitations. They have had to resolve the tensions of using environmentally damaging technology, and be cautious of online surveillance. Many have secured access to CMC and, despite nuclei of control clustering around its use, have attempted to employ CMC to strengthen their non-hierarchical forms of organisation and to resist the pressure to formalise. Environmentalists have also grasped the opportunities afforded by the technology in aiding participant mobilisation and co-ordination, distributing their alternative media, developing new online tactics of protest and effectively subverting (or mutating) the technology from within. The ways in which environmental activists overcame the barriers and utilised these opportunities (in different ways by distinct groups) illustrate the complex use of cyberspace as a site (and form) of resistance. They illustrate also how interaction between the offline and the virtual can produce practical outcomes for environmental activism.

The forms of British environmental politics changed in the 1990s (Rootes 1992; Scott and Street 2001). The emergent 'new politics' or 'new political culture' (Clark and Hoffman-Martinot 1998) has been marked by novel methods of political communication and action which employ cultural symbols and the mass media to convey their message. Although the extent of the 'newness' of this cultural turn in relation to social movements remains debatable, there have been emerging radical tendencies within environmentalism. The use of direct-action tactics, the emphasis on performance and activists' use of cutting-edge technology are not particularly new in themselves: all have been inherited from past or parallel movements (McKay 1998; Doherty 1999a). Nor does the use of cultural modes of action necessarily lead to new forms of politics (Scott and Street 2001). However, it is the combination of these factors that point to a new direction in environmental politics. Environmentalists have surpassed the criticism of being 'single-issue' activists to exemplify the links between many different issues and to widen them to a general critique of the capitalist system and corporate globalisation. This reflects Melucci's assertion (1994) of a shift towards those social movements most concerned with challenging the dominant logic of society. In addition, many participants of the current movement refuse to be co-opted into formal organisations, or to become government policy advisers, and instead focus on remaining non-integrated and using non-linear forms of organisation.

These and other characteristics of contemporary environmental activism were to the fore prior to the influence of CMC, but the use of CMC has made a significant contribution to the ability of activists to sustain these forms. As documented in this book, CMC use has altered relationships between activists and the mainstream media, between activists and their adversaries and between like-minded activists. CMC has facilitated international networking at a grassroots level (as opposed to the existing plethora of co-ordinating international NGOs), helping to create a more interconnected movement and forging new global solidarities. New tactics are being developed through CMC that may alter the use of existing techniques, and CMC puts new levels of control into the hands of activists. CMC also provides the possibility of a virtual public sphere, a global commons which environmentalists could use to voice their opinions and build allegiances (Kellner 1998; Walch 1999).

The use of CMC is not without its problems, not least the inequality of access, ill-suited organisational logistics and CMC use by adversaries. Cyberspace is likely to be as infused with discrimination, inequality and politics as is offline space. However, its use has opened up opportunities, a temporary space of resistance, which has enabled environmental movements to move in a new direction typified by global grassroots solidarities, multi-issue campaigns and anti-hierarchical forms of organising. CMC alone has not triggered a new form of environmental politics, but it has been a significant contributing factor to the changes observed within the British environmental movement.

There are six key consequences of CMC use for environmental politics. The interviewees were: modifying, not rejecting, the use of high technology; able to extend the control they had; capable of decreasing environmentalists' containability by their opponents; strengthening the cohesion of the movement; better able to 'swarm' opponents; and operating at an increased speed. Environmental groups were able to benefit from these to differing extents and groups played different roles in contributing to and/or exemplifying these opportunities.

Modifying, not rejecting, technology

How interviewees dealt with the paradox of using computers to advance their cause illustrated that environmentalists are pragmatists in respect of technology (and not as they have often been portrayed). By compromising they are able to engage with the populus and campaign for change rather than segregate themselves into isolated communities. Environmentalists' use of modern technology helps challenge the stereotype of the anti-technology, anti-progress, protester, making them more appealing to the populus. This attitude also reflects the desire to trigger change offline, within society, rather than engage solely in online activities.

Extending control

The interviewees were able to foster control over the use of CMC, and so provided an additional (and extensive) channel through which they could proliferate their message(s). They had such control over traditional avenues of alternative media, but CMC was cheaper, quicker and enabled distribution to an international audience. Furthermore, CMC reinforced some environmentalists' aims of organising by employing non-hierarchical structures, enabling less-hierarchical forms of organisation to exist more effectively than previously and reducing the pressure towards professionalisation that many groups faced. Moreover, grassroots groups were able to maintain more control over their operations, and not rely on large NGOs for resources or on mainstream media for coverage.

Decreasing containability

The containability of environmental protest (and politics) by its opponents has been reduced by the use of CMC. Not only did CMC give interviewees ready access to a national and an international audience, but traditional attempts at surveillance have (to some extent) been subverted by the use of CMC. Moreover, interviewees were able to maintain their non-hierarchical forms of organising, sustaining a nomadic form of power and centre-less structure which are hard to target by the centred state authorities and hierarchical multinational organisations. This is especially poignant in that traditionally the State and the multinationals had been able to yield power over some environmental NGO's by threatening to seize or freeze their assets. In contrast, it is a lot harder to locate key individuals of non-hierarchical networks or any of their assets.

Strengthening cohesion

CMC has facilitated the mobilisation of participation for virtual actions and served to strengthen the existing movement networks for physical action. Furthermore, it has been possible using CMC to mobilise those who are already within movement networks without face-to-face contact with them. CMC is simply a quicker, cheaper and more global method of utilising these networks. While CMC has the potential to provide a new method of recruitment, mobilisation remains reliant upon integration with existing networks; and at present CMC is consigned to the role of a strengthener (in terms of reducing the importance of the elements of time and space in communication) of the existing linkages. In these ways, the technology has been used to expedite the interlinking of the British environmental movement.

'Swarming' of opponents

CMC can be used to develop new tactics of protest and thus add to, or change, the activists' repertoire of action. Although many of these were particularly innovative, they were extensions to the existing repertoire, rather than new additions. However, the use of online tactics has added to activists' ability to 'swarm' a target using a variety of techniques simultaneously – physical tactics and electronic attacks through computer systems.

Rapid interaction

The speed at which CMC can operate has enabled environmentalists to communicate more quickly and more often and for the barrier of distance to be reduced. The increased velocity at which activists were able to communicate contributed to the changes outlined above and increased the dynamism of the movement. As processes of interaction were quickened, the process of mobilisation was also speeded up, enabling some actions to become more spontaneous, and consequently less confinable by the authorities.

Challenges for internet activists

Given these six alterations in the practice of environmental politics, and the variety of constraints faced by activists in their use of CMC, the use of the technology implies four further challenges for environmentalists. First, that the use of CMC is a site of political and cultural struggle; second, that cyberspace may only be a temporary space of resistance; third, that environmentalists have maintained the importance of the offline and local; and, finally, that the use of CMC has disproportionately benefited small grassroots groups which often suffer from a lack of resources.

A site of struggle

Cyberspace, and the use of CMC, constitute a contested terrain for environmentalists. Their experiences move the discussion about cyberspace on from the utopic–dystopic debate to illustrate the practical ways in which environmentalists have sought to create a cyberspace which fits their needs and aspirations – rather than the technology being either good or bad. Their struggle is a reflection of the wider discord surrounding the use of new technologies and represents a microcosm of the broader debates about the future of technopolitics and society.

Furthermore, activists at times used the technology in ways which appeared to contradict their principles. Despite broad scepticism of technology, most of the interviewees sought to justify their use of CMC on the condition that they would reject it once they had achieved their goals. This attitude contradicts the forms of prefigurative politics discussed in chapter 3, whereby environmentalists seek to act as they would were they already living their ideal. Thus not only is cyberspace a terrain contested by activists and their adversaries, but CMC use raises areas of contention between environmentalists' principles and their practice.

Temporary space of resistance

Due to the struggle over cyberspace, it may provide only a temporary space of resistance. Environmentalists may be able to secure a corner of cyberspace free from corporatisation and state regulation, but environmentalists' long-term use of CMC is by no means assured. This is due in large part to their own success in using the technology. The increasingly high profile of environmental internet activism in the mainstream media has focused attention on the use of the technology for subversive purposes, and thus has given their opponents cause to constrict activists' use of CMC in the future. It may be that CMC use will level off as its usefulness and freedom from corporate control diminish, or that there will be 'dramatic fluctuations in tactical advantage and in the degree of resistant intensity' (CAE quoted in Little 1999: 196). As yet it is unclear how environmentalists will respond to such threats, though the use of the technology is unlikely to replace existing forms and processes of action.

Offline and mortal, earth-bound life

To environmentalists it may not necessarily matter that their use of CMC is only temporary, because what is most important to them is what is offline: 'This lucid dream of virtual freedom is at odds with the strongest current in our emerging public culture: a sense of the bonds which tie us to nature and each other' (Gray 1995: 17). For each of the uses of CMC, environmentalists have asserted the importance of locality. For online actions and alternative media, the importance of basing actions in the physical world remained.

Environmentalists are not embracing the ideals of an alternative social (virtual) reality, but rather are seeking to locate CMC within their existing world. Their primary concern is for the protection of the earth's natural environment. They have little wish to become 'dissociated from the complexity and gravity of the real world' (Robins 1996: 12). While some have used cyberspace to create a new 'social commons' (cf. Rheingold 1994) to replace the lost public spheres of the physical world, such idealisation of online communities actually involves a denial of difference and the desire to create order, security and sameness. In contrast, environmentalists are less interested in a virtual space that 'is being created as a domain of order, refuge and withdrawal' (Robins 1996: 24), and more interested in using CMC to create a better offline world.

This emphasis on the local reiterates Washbourne's assertion (1999a) that CMC was being used as part of translocalism – the process whereby social networks can operate between and within specific localities to enable collective action, without the requirement for a central organisation or hierarchy. Thus environmentalists were using the global medium of CMC to express their desire for each individual internationally to protect his or her local space. Environmentalists' use of CMC can be viewed as part of a strategy to transpose the debate's focus from the forces of globalism to the importance of localism and the environment. It is at the local level that the importance and significance of the environment to everyday activities and survival are clearest: 'At the end of the day, the world worth fighting for is one in which people control their own lives and communities, and live in a vibrant, sharing, creative, co-operative, face-to-face everyday culture. The role of modern technology in that [culture] is open to question' (Dave Morris, McSpotlight). Despite this emphasis on local context, CMC, as Castells (2001: 143) has argued, has enabled social movements to 'think local and act global'. Thus they are able to generate 'the legitimacy and support provided by their reliance on local groups, yet they cannot remain local or they lose their capacity to act upon the real sources of power in our world'.

'Levelling the playing field': strength without resources

This globalising of social movement concerns and actions has helped reduce the slope in the political playingfield – enabling activists to compete more easily with their corporate adversaries. It has also, however, altered the power relations between groups within the British environmental movement. Traditionally, large centralised NGOs have wielded significant influence within the movement because they had the resources to do so, and resources determined the actions which environmentalists could take. With the use of CMC, however, the need for extensive resources and a centralised organisational structure to co-ordinate actions is reduced. It is not the best-resourced groups which are benefiting most from CMC use, but the more adaptable and inventive groups. Although resources are required to use CMC, it is adaptability, enthusiasm and innovation that are also crucial – and these are fostered by non-hierarchical networks. The use of CMC has disproportionately benefited small grassroots groups which often suffer from a lack of resources, distributing the components within the environmental movement more equally.

CMC use for protest organisation also facilitates disproportionately the work of political activists linked only into fluid networks using cellular structures, not hierarchy, to organise, rather than the larger, more formally structured, political pressure groups. The more informal, non-hierarchical, flexible and often radical are best able to benefit from CMC's ability to aid organisation in a decentralised manner. CMC enables groups to co-ordinate campaigns without the need for a central office, newsletters, or the physical presence of activists, as such groups are unrestricted by bureaucratic organisational procedures. In contrast, the larger NGOs are less able to adapt to the new technology because they appear to require a high degree of control over, and centralisation of, operations and decision making. More formal hierarchical organisations, such as FoE, are slower to adapt. FoE was one of the first environmental groups to use CMC, and it developed several innovative uses of the technology, but some of its staff felt that the organisation had failed to extend this trend.

Such radical activists are able to benefit from the anonymity of CMC, its speed, low cost, and potential for innovation. The consequence is the rise of less-structured environmental groups with significant protest-organising power and an overall strengthening of the British environmental movement. This is not a result of CMC alone, but of the continuation of a process which started in the early 1990s with the rise of small non-violent direct-action groups. CMC has made the process more sustainable and has contributed to the rise of the individual action in protests. Also, as is true of the internet, if any group (node) is removed or suppressed, then a replacement group or individual can emerge using CMC, or else the links to other nodes rejoin. Thus CMC contributes to the building of a robust network of small environmental groups and to the rising importance and power of grassroots groups.

Social movements and technology

While this book has focused on British environmentalists' use of CMC, there is much here that can be extrapolated to the broader consideration of online political activism. If, as documented here, CMC has enabled environmentalists to sustain existing trends for longer than would otherwise have been possible, then use of the technology is liable to do the same for other political movements and their tendencies.

Principally, examination of environmentalists' CMC use has reinforced the assertion of social movement theorists (such as Melucci and Touraine) that in the network age movements are concerned primarily with contesting cultural values. A recurrent theme of the book has been the emphasis on the *need* for communication. Other quandaries about the suitability of CMC for environmentalists – such as concerns about its environmental impact, security (due to surveillance fears), or its capacity for use in an inclusive and participatory manner – were overridden by the mantra that, as activists, they had to be able to communicate their ideas to a wide audience. CMC was perceived to be a crucial conduit via which to contest the dominant codes of society that structure our understanding.

More specifically, analysis of the types of tactic adopted using CMC confirms that repertoires of action are relatively stable and do not alter quickly. As Meikle (2002) has shown, most online tactics are remarkably similar to offline tactics. Furthermore, this similarity was deemed necessary to the tactics' success. Hence the term 'virtual sit-in' being used to refer to electronic civil disobedience, in the hope that activists would more clearly identify with its form and aims (as being similar to those of the traditional sit-in in an office or on the street) and thus adopt it. Similarly, much early culture jamming online was of a similar nature to that which had been done to offline adverts – the subtle alteration of fundamental meaning. The use of CMC, therefore, did not radically alter the repertoires of action, though its main use for tactical advancement may be in increasing the dynamism of the evolving repertoires. With the increasing interaction between activists worldwide who are able to exchange skills and work collaboratively, the cycles of protest, which influence repertoires of action, might begin to quicken.

In relation to forms of participant mobilisation, analysis of CMC use reaffirms that inclusion within movement networks is a vital component of participation. Thus, due to the 'thinner' forms of interaction possible online as compared to face-to-face communication, mobilisation remains a process rooted in a gradual socialisation of an individual into activist networks. Rather, CMC is most useful in connecting those already within some sector of a social movement.

Theorists have made extensive studies of the forms of social movement organisations and their inner functions. Often, it is the non-linear non-hierarchical forms, which can typify the early stages of a movement's evolution, that are deemed temporary, as the need to formalise to co-ordinate resources or maintain momentum becomes imperative. The use of CMC to help sustain fluid forms of organisation, however, might alter our understanding of the way in which social movement organisations develop. Evident as a considerable component of the numerous so-called anti-corporate protests, such loosely structured forms can have significant organising power (Starr 2000). The proliferation of this means of organising could radically alter the forms that social movements take. Furthermore, environmentalists' use of CMC, to provide a network of durable interconnectivity, further confirms the understandings of cyberspace as a rhizomic model through which societal relationships online can be ascribed to the fully interconnected and non-hierarchical structure of a rhizome.

Environmentalists' emphasis on the importance of local context, local identity creation and local action adds further credence to social movement theorists' attempts to locate the meaning of collective action at the personal level. Melucci (2000: 92) suggests that 'individuals' control of action is a necessary condition for the formation of collective mobilization and change'. In other words, collective action has for many become primarily about fulfilling personal needs, with enacting social change a secondary objective. This individuation of action corresponds with an increased emphasis on the local: one's immediate surroundings, personal lifestyle, community networks and other aspects perceived to be within an individual's control and influence (unlike the many global decisions made by faceless institutions). This process further correlates with Willson's assertion that CMC can 'potentially provide the settings for the increased individuation and compartmentalisation of the individual' (2002: 233). Thus, CMC use once more serves to enforce a tendency within contemporary social movements, namely the increasing focus on the individuation and localisation of action. Analysis of such CMC use could further aid our understanding of these processes of individuation. Such analysis could be used to explore the various influences on the construction of collective identities. This has been touched upon here through examinations of CMC use in network cohesion, mobilisation and individuation, but require further exploration.

On a slightly different tack, environmentalists' use of CMC has contributed also to a smudging of the boundaries between the private and public spheres of life, as CMC engages in both. Moreover, the likelihood of a new public sphere being developed through the use of CMC seems limited, given that cyberspace is such a contested terrain (Beslow 1997; Kellner 1998). Consequently, in contrast to the optimism of Castells (2001), the possibility that an improved (and global) civil society will emerge from the use of CMC seems somewhat diminished. Rather, its potential lies, not in creating an improved public sphere, but in the use of CMC to aid the actions of those most marginalised within existing civil society – including environmentalists.

It can be difficult, however, to critique social movement perspectives on the basis solely of an analysis of CMC use. This is because the technology has rarely been central to a group's operation and tends to illuminate the *how* rather than the *why* of social movement operations. A shortcoming in terms of social movement perspectives has been the lack of detailed attention to the implications of CMC use for activism. Virtual communities' literature offers informative examples of virtual interaction leading to personal investment in networks, but little of this work has been undertaken in relation to the potential within social movements more broadly. Furthermore, use of CMC by environmentalists has contributed to the globalising of the movement as evidenced by the increasing number of anti-corporate globalisation protests. The correspondingly diffuse aims, tactics and targets of activists, and the problems of generating collective identities in such large-scale interaction and among contentious participants, are only just beginning to permeate social movement literature. Traditionally it had been assumed that protest would operate at the national level. With increased borderless activism, new understandings need to be explored.

In relation to theories of technology, this research has proved that the utopic–dystopic distinction in analysing technological change is clearly inappropriate. Environmentalists' use of CMC illustrates that the debate is more complex than this division allows, and that CMC will aid different people and groups in different ways. Furthermore, one group of individuals could simultaneously benefit from use of a technology and incur problems by its use. Thus 'the net provides new spaces for new political discussions about democracy, revolution and self-determination but it does not provide solutions to the differences that exist: it is merely a means to accelerate the search for such solutions' (Cleaver 1995: 6).

This critique of utopic–dystopic debates reinforces the theoretical need to examine the interactions between online and offline processes and the social processes through which technology is constructed. It is in the interplay between online existence and offline consequences that the potential for societal change occurs. Furthermore, as technologies become incorporated into mainstream society, they can become less useful to those who wish to employ them innovatively to stimulate change. This is because the 'cracks that appear in the mediascape' (Meikle 2002: 120), which activists previously maximised to their own advantage, become blocked by government or corporate control. Despite this, environmentalists have continued the vision of the situationists and have sought to subvert the use of the technology where possible. This illustrates activists' propensity to use technology in whatever innovative ways are open to them.

Where to now?

Environmental activists' use of CMC has highlighted three areas for potential change – the problems of inclusion in CMC use, the use of hierarchical methods of organisation and the potential for further tactical use of new technologies. While constraints to CMC access may eventually be negotiated, this lack of inclusion reflects a broader area of contention within environmental movements. The importance of there being a balance between practising prefigurative politics (thus acting according to principles and ideals) and the capacity to act with efficiency and speed is accentuated by the use of CMC. While many groups advocate the value of participatory democracy, their ability to be inclusive is tempered by the need to campaign effectively. While in the short run focusing on campaign needs is productive, in the long run a lack of attention to inclusivity will result in a narrow homogenous movement. The challenge remains for activists to resolve such a tension or, more likely, find a suitable balance between ideals and efficiency.

Related to the problematic issues of access and participation, but also to the problems of resolving tensions around use of the technology, is the increased use of open source software by activists. This is the practice of enabling source code to be freely shared, copied and enhanced by a variety of enthusiasts. Not only does this reduce reliance on corporate material, but it instils an ethos of collaboration and sharing into CMC use. Developments in the design of open source systems, making them easier to use, have already been put to good use by alternative media projects such as Indymedia (see Pickerill 2004), and will be an obvious benefit to environmentalists.

The greatest potential for change using CMC was in those groups which organised using non-hierarchical methods. It was these loosely organised and flexible groups that facilitated the necessary experimentation with the technology, and which subsequently enabled activists to use it in innovative ways. CMC is facilitating the decentralisation of the environmental movement and the rise of grassroots activism. All these factors highlight a need for the more formal and bureaucratic environmental groups to reassess their organisational structure and perhaps reform using non-hierarchical and more flexible methods of organisation. This is not to discount the important role that the larger organisations play in coordinating large-scale public information campaigns, parliamentary lobbying or legislative activity. Rather, a greater awareness of the opportunities offered by flexibility would enable them to adapt to the changing social structure and perhaps increase their potential for mobilisation.

Simultaneously, there is greater awareness that innovations in the use of CMC need to be effectively combined with the continuing use of existing media, such as print, telephone and face-to-face engagement, to have greatest effect and benefit. While CMC is unlikely ever to replace these media, it is integration with existing methods that provides the greatest promise. In combination, it has the potential to facilitate international collaboration and new virtual tactics, while traditional media can continue to encourage participation and stimulate local protest.

For state and corporate adversaries, environmentalists' use of CMC has highlighted two key challenges – that they increasingly face a dispersed and global resistance, and that in order to combat these they will have to employ stricter security measures and legislation, or, as Arquilla and Ronfeldt (1998) suggest, adopting network structures in order to target oppositional networks. State and corporate adversaries are increasingly unable to control the way in which these groups communicate and co-ordinate. Furthermore, state and corporate entities face a diffuse (and sometimes global) threat from a source they cannot always identify, especially when activists employ anonymity via CMC. This inability to clearly identify the source of the threat facing them means that environmental groups have become harder to target, prevent or assimilate. Moreover, the use of CMC provides activists with an additional tool with which to swarm their opponents – further complicating any ability of corporate or State targets to ignore or resist attacks. This threat is often the result of the global networking of assorted grassroots groups. The rising prominence of globally co-ordinated protests (such as those in Seattle, Gothenburg, Quebec, Prague and Genoa) that have involved activists travelling from diverse locations has illustrated the usefulness of CMC to international co-ordination.[2] The visibility of such protests, coupled with the terrorist activity in the USA in September 2001 and Bali in October 2002, however, has triggered governments to increase their legislation and surveillance of society, and to reduce some of the freedom once assumed of CMC. The full ramifications of this 'anti-terror' legislation have yet to be understood.

While there remains a novelty (and a degree of hype) about the use of CMC which can distort its worth, its use by environmentalists has had an impact on the forms and processes favoured by the interviewees and their affiliated groups. British environmental activists are a diverse cohort composed of individuals and groups with diverging aims, ideologies and forms of organisation. These differences are exposed in their contrasting attitudes to, and use of CMC. They are united, however, in their struggle to use CMC to their advantage and to continue their protest, activism and resistance (and the creation of positive alternatives) through, and in, cyberspace. The environmental movement is particularly innovative, creative and skilful, and these attributes have been extended to its use of CMC.

CMC use will continue to evolve in the hands of environmentalists, modifying and being modified by social processes. The new interactions triggered by CMC have significantly altered each of the environmental groups considered here, and are likely to aid new collaborations and the development of new forms of environmental protest, particularly internationally. Although problems and restrictions remain in its utilisation, environmentalists continue to weave a green web.

Notes

1 If, at the end of the day, all the attention CMC has received has been unwarranted, then this in itself still needs to be acknowledged. As has been the case with many new technologies, in its early stages CMC appeared to be revolutionary; and if, after time, it is evident that it was not revolutionary, the processes of its use and adoption and the reasons why the 'rules of the game' weren't changed still need to be analysed.
2 Though, of course, it is the proliferation of low-cost air travel that has enabled such activists to travel more easily.

Appendix

Case-study profiles[1]

Centre for Alternative Technology

Opened 1975

Aims

To showcase alternative technology so as to inform, inspire and enable others to utilise sustainable living practices.

Internal structure

The Centre is run by a co-operative and full-time staff (who are all paid the same wage), supplemented by both long- and short-term volunteers. The Alternative Technology Association (ATA) is CAT's supporter group. ATA has approximately 4,000 members, holds annual conferences and produces the *Clean Slate* magazine. The majority of CAT's income is from visitors and donations, and other revenue is raised through publications, mail orders, residential courses and consultancy. The 7-acre site houses the visitor complex, a shop and restaurant, environmental information centre, a mail order service, a consultancy, a publications department, an education department and eco-cabins.

Tactics

Although CAT is primarily a visitor centre, it also runs training courses about alternative technology, publishes a range of books, operates the eco-cabins as an educational centre for school children, provides consultancy to organisations and runs a free information service.

Friends of the Earth UK

Formed 1971

Aims

To take action to change policies or practices that degrade the environment. In 2002 its major campaigns focused on the corporates, real food and transport.

Internal structure

The FoE (England and Wales – FoE Scotland operates as a separate group) network is comprised of the national office and 250 local groups. There are eight regional campaign co-ordinators. The local groups are encouraged to engage in actions of their own, to choose their own campaign priorities and to function as autonomous units. Local groups' reliance on FoE Ltd varies considerably, with some employing full-time staff. Membership at the national level has increased steadily since 1971, with a sharp increase in 1988–89, which then subsided; in the late 1990s numbers were stable. FoE relies on individual supporters' contributions for 96 per cent of its income, with the rest coming from fundraising events, sponsorship, grants and trading.

Tactics

FoE's strategy has been five-pronged:

1   political lobbying and legislative activity;
2   scientific research and information provision;
3   employing the media;
4   mobilising the public through local group activities and mass rallies;
5   co-ordinating and co-operating with other groups.

FoE's aversion to the use of illegal direct action, together with its emphasis on political lobbying, prevent it from being a radical environmental group.

Green Student Network

Formed late 1980s

Aims

To exchange information, debate environmental issues and facilitate local group actions.

Internal structure

GSN's organisational structure was very loose. Initially centred on British university 'green' groups, national gatherings and a newsletter produced by the co-ordinator, any structure that existed was fragmented in 1998. GSN effectively became less of a network with a strategic function and more a non-hierarchical collection of disparate individuals communicating via an email list. Participation was free and unregulated. Users simply sent an email to an specific address that automatically added them to the list. There was a high turnover of participants in the email list. GSN had no source of income.

Tactics

As GSN was not a campaigning group as such, it had no campaign tactics or priorities. However, certain topics on the email list were discussed more than others. The topics very much reflected the immediate concerns of British environmental politics.

McSpotlight

Launched 1996

Aims

To gather information that was critical of or damaging to McDonald's, and to make such material publicly available; to act as a network of support for all those (like the defendants in the McLibel trial) aiming to expose the operations of multinational corporations and to demonstrate that corporate attempts at censorship would fail.

Internal structure

The McInformation Network, a loose coalition of individuals, created the McSpotlight website. Many people joined in to do a small section of work or a specific task, and then left, while others continued to be involved through the peak of the website's popularity. The fifty contributors to the site were spread internationally, and email was used to help co-ordinate their efforts. Many of them have not met in person. McSpotlight was a collaborative but *ad hoc* endeavour, with a core of volunteers who tried not to dominate decisions about content. There was an attempt to organise along non-hierarchical lines. McSpotlight did not have a membership, but participants could sign up to email distribution lists or contribute to the debate forum. McSpotlight relied on donations and sales of its merchandise for its income.

Tactics

The tactic adopted by McSpotlight was to post anti-McDonald's information on its website for all to see. The McSpotlight website contained over 20,000 pages, with many different sections – about the McLibel trial, current issues, campaigning tools, a debating area, media coverage, court transcripts, interviews with key witnesses, and the libellous leaflet, translated into twenty languages, ready to print off.

The Mobile Office

Formed 1997

Aims

To provide activists in on-site protests with access to office facilities. Its various services included:

1   distributing information;
2   assisting with communications;
3   improving on-site safety;
4   acting as an information and resource centre;
5   recording events for archives.

The MO was run by a small group of volunteers, but, once the Office was on-site, others – from the protest camp and the locality – tended to become involved. MO attempted to organise non-hierarchically, though Pete, who spent the most time on the project, was often able to finalise decisions. The van and equipment were acquired on 'tat runs',[2] or were donated or purchased using a grant.

Tactics

MO has been involved in several direct-action campaigns for which it provided the office equipment, communications technology and a resource base for activists.

Save Westwood, Lyminge Forest

Occupation began in 1997

Aims

To prevent the development of a holiday complex in Lyminge Forest.

Internal structure

The campaign was an organic direct-action protest, not an offshoot of an organisation or existing group. Non-hierarchical and decentralised forms of decision-making were practised, involving whatever participants were present. From March 1997 to the final months of 1999, 10–100 protesters lived in several camps situated across the development site. The protesters in the Forest relied on their personal income and on donations.

Tactics

Several tactics have been employed: their occupation of the site (which involved tunnelling, the building of towers and tree-houses, and using lock-ons) was an act of resistance to any attempts at clearing the Forest to build the holiday complex.

Through this occupation and the associated media attention protesters sought to raise the public profile of the development proposals in order to increase support and put pressure on the local council and the Forestry Commission. They also undertook other direct actions, such as the occupation of Rank's boardroom. Finally, on some of their publicity flyers they encouraged people to write to their MP in support of the on-site action.

SchNEWS

Launched 1994

Aims

To distribute the news which is ignored by the mainstream media. It is also anti-copyright, encouraging readers to copy and re-distribute it themselves.

Internal structure

SchNEWS was run entirely by volunteers, roughly twenty-five people at any one time, in a non-hierarchical manner, using consensus decision-making and monthly review meetings to determine courses of action. A weekly timetable for activities and jobs to be done was established so that people knew when copy could be included in an issue and when different volunteers were required. New volunteers were continually sought, and training days arranged to impart the necessary skills to newcomers. Costs were covered by donations and subscriptions.

Tactics

Various tactics were employed to make *SchNEWS'* distribution as wide as possible – it was available via email; it was posted both on its website and via land-mail; and it was distributed by hand on the streets, at festivals and in bookshops. It encouraged other groups to copy and re-distribute *SchNEWS'* original material.

Notes

1 Information supplied by the groups themselves and in Anon. (1998d and 1999a), Atton (2000), Blue (1997), Frisch (1994), George (1999), Gibbs (2000), Greenberg (1985), Jenkins (1995), Krinks (1997), Lamb (1996), Lowe and Goyder (1983), McCormick (1995), Mills (1997), Pipes (1996), Rawcliffe (1998), Reed (1999) and Wapner (1995).
2 'Tat' refers to items which have been appropriated or recycled for free from a variety of sources, such as skips or building sites; in some cases the items were stolen.

References

Alam, S. (1996) 'On-Line Lifeline', *The New Internationalist* (December).

Allen, T. (1996) *West Yorkshire Pilot Project: Summary Report*, Leeds, Friends of the Earth.

Amusing Pseudonym (1999) 'Keep it Up, Don't Let Violence Divide Us', Reflections on J18, Reclaim the Streets, available online: www.infoshop.org/octo/j18_rts 3.html.

Angell, I. (1992) 'Winners and Losers in the Information Age', *Society*, vol. 34, no. 1.

Annis, S. (1992) 'Evolving Connectedness Among Environmental Groups and Grassroots Organisations in Protected Areas of Central America', *World Development*, vol. 20, no. 4.

Anon. (1997a) 'PPS News' www.geocities/RainForest/3081/newspp 3.html.

Anon. (1997b) 'The Luddites' War on Industry; A Story of Machine Smashing and Spies', *Do or Die – Voices from Earth First!*, no. 6.

Anon. (1997c) 'The Evolution of Reclaim the Streets', *Do or Die – Voices from Earth First!*, no. 6.

Anon. (1997d) *McSpotlight: Frequently Asked Questions*, version 3 (June).

Anon. (1997e) *Judge for Yourself* (video), Oxford, Undercurrents 6.

Anon. (1997f) 'AQUA: No Teign-Bovey Diversion!', available online: www.geocities.com/RainForest/3081/newton.html.

Anon. (1997g) 'The Empire Strikes Back', *Do or Die – Voices from Earth First!*, no. 6.

Anon. (1997h) 'Too Close Circuit for Comfort', *Squall*, available online: www.squall.co.uk/squall.cfm?sq=2001061905&ct=2.

Anon. (1998a) 'http://www.cat.org.uk', *Clean Slate*, no. 27 (winter).

Anon. (1998b) *MO Log and News*, available online: www.geocities.com/RainForest/3081/molog.html.

Anon. (1998c) 'Website Success', *Clean Slate*, no. 30 (autumn).

Anon. (1998d) *The Mobile Office*, available online: www.geocities.com/RainForest/3081/mo.html.

Anon. (1999a) 'Fifth Birthday Shocker . . . and the Next Five Years? . . . Wake Up! Wake Up! It's Yer Typical *SchNEWS* Week', *SchNEWS*, available online: www.schnews.org.uk/justice/year 1999.htm.

Anon. (1999b) 'Friday June 18th 1999: Confronting Capital and Smashing the State!', *Do or Die – Voices from the Ecological Resistance*, no. 8.

Anon. (1999c) 'Sabbing Shell: Office Occupation A-Go-Go', *Do or Die-Voices from the Ecological Resistance*, no. 8.

Anon. (1999d) 'Fun with Computers on Office Occupations', *Earth First! Action Update* (April).

Anon. (1999e) 'Hacktivism', *Do or Die – Voices from the Ecological Resistance*, no. 8.

Anon. (1999f) 'Net Closes in on Eight City Riot Suspects', *The Times*, 30 October.

Anon. (2000a) 'Wealthy Man Planned City Demo', *BBC News Online*, 11 April, news.bbc.co.uk.

Anon. (2000b) 'The Empire Bytes Back', *SchNEWS*, 4 August.

Anon. (2000c) 'Legitimising Surveillance: The Regulation of Investigatory Powers Bill', *Statewatch*, available online: www.statewatcyh.org/news.

Anon. (2000d) 'Home Office Attempts to Censor Satirical Website! RIP it Up', *SchNEWS*, 31 March.

Anon. (2000e) 'Radical Internet Users Condemn Tapping Plans', *nonviolent action*, no. 9 (March).

Anzovin, S. (1994) *The Green PC: Practical Choices that Make a Difference*, New York, McGraw-Hill.

Arquilla, J. and D. Ronfeldt (1998) 'Cyberwar Is Coming!', in G. Stocker and C. Schoph (eds) *InfoWar*, Springer Wien, New York.

Arquilla, J. and D. Ronfeldt (2000) *Swarming and the Future of Conflict*, Santa Monica, CA, RAND National Defence Research Institute.

Atton, C. (1996) 'Anarchy on the Internet: Obstacles and Opportunities for Alternative Electronic Publishing', *Anarchist Studies*, vol. 4, no. 2.

Atton, C. (2000) 'Are There Alternative Media After CMC?', *M/C Reviews*, 12 April, available online: www.uq.edu.au/mc/reviews/features/politics/altmedia. html.

Baggott, R. (1995) *Pressure Groups Today*, Manchester, Manchester University Press.

Bagguley, P. (1992) 'Social Change, the Middle Class and the Emergence of "New Social Movements": A Critical Analysis', *Sociological Review*, vol. 40, no. 1.

Ball, G. (1997) 'Framed: Smart Cameras Know Thieves' Faces', *Independent on Sunday*, 13 July.

Barbrook, R. (1995) *Electronic Democracy* (4 pages), available online: http://ma. hrc.wmin.ac.uk/ma.theory.4.5.db.

Barnett, A. (2000) 'Police to Track Mobile Phone Users', *Observer*, 30 July.

Batchelor, W. (1995) 'Financial Information Over the Internet: Legal Issues', paper presented at the International Quality and Productivity Centre Conference, London, 20 September.

Bate, R. (1983) 'Friends of the Earth', in P. Lowe and J. Goyder (eds) *Environmental Groups in Politics*, London, Allen & Unwin.

Bauerlein, M. (1999) 'The Luddites are Back: To Resist or Not to Resist, That Is the Question', *Daily Bleed Calendar*, available online: www.eskimo.com/~recall/ bleed/sinners/LudditesBack.htm.

Beder, S. (1997) *Global Spin: The Corporate Assault on Environmentalism*, Totnes, Devon, Green Books.

Bennetto, J. (1998) 'Police Unit to Target Green Protesters', *Independent*, 7 November.

Bijker, W. E. and J. Law (eds) (1992) General Introduction, *Shaping Technology/ Building Society: Studies in Sociotechnical Change*, London, MIT Press.

Bimber, B. (1998) 'The Internet and Political Transformation: Populism, Community, and Accelerated Pluralism', *Polity*, vol. 31, no. 1.

Bimber, B. (2001) 'Information and Political Engagement in America: The Search for Effects of Information Technology at the Individual Level', *Political Research Quarterly*, vol. 54, no. 1.

Bingham, N., G. Valentine and S. Holloway (2001) 'Life Around the Screen: Reframing Young People's Use of the Internet', in N. Watson and S. Cunningham-Burley (eds) *Reframing the Body*, Palgrave Macmillam, London.

Birkerts, S. (1995) *The Gutenberg Elegies: The Fate of Reading in an Electronic Age*, London, Faber & Faber.

Birkett, P. (1997) 'Party Time for Pagan Army', *Weekend Telegraph*, 27 December.

Blair, T. L. (1971) 'Friends of the Earth', in J. Barr (ed.) *The Environmental Handbook: Action guide for the UK*, London, Ballantine–Friends of the Earth.

Blue (1997) 'Swampy, Eat Your Heart Out', *The Big Issue*, no. 239, 30 June–6 July.

Boal, I. A. (1995) 'A Flow of Monsters: Luddism and Virtual Technologies', in J. Brook and I. Boal (eds) *Resisting the Virtual Life: The Culture and Politics of Information*, San Francisco, CA, City Lights.

Boncheck, M. S. (1995) 'Grassroots in Cyberspace: Using Computer Networks to Facilitate Political Participation', paper presented at the 53rd Annual Meeting of the Midwest Political Science Association, Chicago, IL, 6 April, available online: http://www.ai.mit.edu/people/msb/pubs/grassroots.html.

Bonnett, A. (1999) 'Situationist Strategies and Mutant Technologies', *Angelaki, Journal of Theoretical Humanities*, vol. 4, no. 2.

Bosso, C. J. (1991) 'Adaptation and Change in the Environmental Movement', in J. Ciger and B. Loomis (eds) *Interest Group Politics*, Washington, DC, Congressional Quarterly Press.

Bowden, C. (2000) 'Big Browser Is Watching the Web: Is the Regulation of Investigatory Powers Bill a License for State Snooping?', *Observer*, 25 June.

Bowden, C. and Y. Akdeniz (1999) 'Privacy II: Cryptography and Democracy – Dilemmas of Freedom', in J. Cooper (ed.) *Liberating Cyberspace: Civil Liberties, Human Rights and the Internet*, Pluto Press, London.

Bowlby, R., M. Bowlby and S. Lowe (1992) 'Environmental and Green Movements', in A. Mannion, M. Bowlby and R. Bowlby (eds) *Environmental Issues in the 1990s*, Chichester, John Wiley & Sons.

Boyle, G. and P. Harper (eds) (1976) *Radical Technology*, London, Wildwood House.

Boyle, J. (1997) *Shamans, Software, and Spleens: Law and the Construction of the Information Society*, Cambridge, MA, Harvard University Press.

Brabbs, C. (1999) 'Why Global Brands Are Under Attack', *Marketing*, 9 December.

Brass, E. and S. Poklewski Koziell (1997) *Gathering Force: DIY Culture – Radical Action for Those Tired of Waiting*, London, Big Issue Writers.

Breslow, H. (1997) 'Civil Society, Political Economy and the Internet', in S. Jones. (ed.) *Virtual Culture: Identity and Communication in Cybersociety*, London, SAGE.

Brush, M. (1996) 'Got a Gripe? There Are Plenty of Places to Vent on the "Net"', *Money Daily*, 13–14 July.

Buchanan, D. A. (1993) 'The Organisational Politics of Technological Change', in D.

Medycki-Scott and H. M.Hearnshaw (eds) *Human Factors in Geographical Information Systems*, London, Belhaven Press.

Budge, I. (1996) *The New Challenge of Direct Democracy*, Cambridge, Polity Press.

Byrne, P. (1997) *Social Movements in Britain*, London, Routledge.

CAE (1996) *Electronic Civil Disobedience and Other Unpopular Ideas*, New York, Autonomedia.

CAE (2001) *Digital Resistance*, New York, Autonomedia.

Calhoun, C. (1998) 'Community Without Propinquity Revisited: Communication Technology and the Transformation of the Urban Public Sphere', *Sociological Inquiry*, vol. 68.

Campbell, D. (1981) *Phonetappers and the Security State*, Report no. 2, London, New Statesman.

Campbell-Jones, S. (1998) 'The Future: How Scary Is it Really?', *Earth Matters: Supporters' Magazine of Friends of the Earth, UK*, no. 37.

Carey, P. (1997) 'Defamation, Live Broadcasts and the Internet', *New Law Journal*, vol. 147, no. 6815.

Castells, M. (1996) *The Information Age*, vol. 1: *The Rise of the Network Society*, Oxford, Blackwell.

Castells, M. (1997a) *The Information Age*, vol. 2: *The Power of Identity*, Oxford, Blackwell.

Castells, M. (1997b) 'An Introduction to the Information Age', *City*, no. 7.

Castells, M. (2001) *The Internet Galaxy: Reflections on the Internet, Business and Society*, Oxford, Oxford University Press.

CAT (1997a) *The Centre for Alternative Technology Guide Book*, Centre for Alternative Technology, Machynlleth.

CAT (1997b) *The Power System at CAT – How We Manage Our Renewable Electricity*, Machynlleth, Wales, Centre for Alternative Technology.

CAT (1997c) 'CAT's Man-Made Lake Is the Reservoir for the Water Balanced Cliff Railway', caption on a postcard at CAT.

CAT (1998a) *A Users's Guide to the Centre for Alternative Technology*, Machynlleth, Wales, Centre for Alternative Technology.

CAT (1998b) *ATEIC Appeal*, Machynlleth, Wales, Centre for Alternative Technology.

Charlton, R., R. May and T. Cleobury (1995) 'NGOs in the Politics of Development: Projects as Policy', *Contemporary Politics*, vol. 1, no. 1.

Chartier, D. and J. Deleage (1998) 'The International Environmental NGOs: From the Revolutionary Alternative to the Pragmatism of Reform', *Environmental Politics*, vol. 7, no. 3.

Chesters, G. (2000a) 'Resist to Exist? Radical Environmentalism at the End of the Millennium', *ECOS*, vol. 20, no. 2.

Chesters, G. (2000b) 'The New Intemperance: Protest, Imagination and Carnival', *ECOS*, vol. 21, no. 1.

Chesworth, S. and A. Johnson (1997) 'Police Clampdown on RTS', *Squall*, no. 14.

Chin, C. and J. Mittelman (1997) 'Conceptualising Resistance to Globalisation', *New Political Economy*, vol. 2, no. 1.

Clark, N. (1996) 'Earthing the Ether: The Alternating Currents of Ecology and Cyberculture', in Z. Sardar and J. Ravetz (eds) *Cybersfutures: Culture and Politics on the Information Superhighway*, London, Pluto Press.

Clark, T. N. and V. Hoffmann-Martinot (1998) *The New Political Culture*, Boulder, CO, Westview Press.

Clarke, C. (2000a) 'Big Brother Is Watching the Web: Is the Regulation of Investigatory Powers Bill a License for State Snooping?', *Observer*, 25 June.

Clarke, C. (2000b) 'The Bill Does Not Outlaw Any Form of Encryption' (debate with Caspar Bowden), *Guardian*, Online (supplement), 30 March.

Cleaver, H. (1995) *Cyberspace and 'Ungovernability'*, available online: www.spunk. org/library/comms/sp001000.txt.

Cleaver, H. (1997) *The Zapatista Effect: The Internet and the Rise of an Alternative Political Fabric*, available online: www.eco.utexas.edu/Homepages/Faculty/ Cleaver/zapeffect.html.

Cleaver, H. (1999) *'Computer-linked Social Movements and the Global Threat to Capitalism'* (19 pages), available online: www.eco.utexas.edu/faculty/Cleaver/ polnet.html.

Cohen, R. and S. M. Rai (eds) (2000) *Global Social Movements*, London, Athlone Press.

Colin, B. (1997) 'The Future of Cyberterrorism', *Crime and Justice International* (March).

Collin, M. and J. Godfrey (1997) *Altered State: The Story of Ecstasy Culture and Acid House*, London, Serpent's Tail.

Cramp, J. (1997) 'Wind Power in Lyminge Forest', *Meridian Tonight*, ITV, 18 December.

Dahlberg, L. (2000) 'Democratic Participation Through the Internet: A Brief Survey', *M/C Reviews*, available online: www.uq.edu.au/mc/reviews/fea-tures/politics/participation.html.

Davis, R. (1999) *The Web of Politics*, Oxford, Oxford University Press.

De Silva, S. (2001) 'Free Code and the Divisions Within', in M. Cordell (ed.) *Rogue States*, Melbourne, Media Circus Reader.

Deleuze, G. and F. Guattari (1987) *A Thousand Plateaus: Capitalism and Schizophrenia*, Athlone Press, London.

Della Porta, D. and M. Diani. (1999) *Social Movements: An Introduction*. Oxford, Blackwell.

Denning, D. (1997) 'The Future of Cryptography', in B. Loader (ed.) *The Governance of Cyberspace: Politics, Technology and Global Restructuring*, London, Routledge.

Denning, D. (1999) *Activism, Hacktivism, and Cyberterrorism: The Internet as a Tool for Influencing Foreign Policy*, available online: www.nautilus.org/info-policy/workshop/papers/denning.html.

Diani, M. (1992) 'The Concept of Social Movement', *The Sociological Review*, vol. 40, no. 4.

Diani, M. (2001) 'Social Movement Networks Virtual and Real', in F. Webster (ed.) *Culture and Politics in the Information Age: A New Politics?*, London, Routledge.

Dickson, D. (1974) *Alternative Technology and the Politics of Technical Change*, London, Fontana.

DJNZ (2000) *Client-Side Distributed Denial-of-Service: Valid Campaign Tactic or Terrorist Act?* available online: www.gn.apc.org/pmhp/ehippies/files/op1.htm.

Dobson, A. (1995) *Green Political Thought*, London, HarperCollins Academic.

Dobson, A. (2000) *Green Political Thought*, 2nd edn, London, Routledge.

Doherty, B. (1996) *Paving the Way: The Rise of Direct Action Against Road-Building and the Changing Character of British Environmentalism*, Working Paper 21, Keele University, Department of Politics.

Doherty, B. (1997) 'Direct Action Against Road-Building: Some Implications for the Concept of Protest Repertoires', in J. Stanyer and G. Stoker (eds) *Contemporary Political Studies 1997: Proceedings of the Political Studies Association Annual Conference held at the University of Ulster, Jordanstown*, Dublin, Political Studies Association of Ireland.

Doherty, B. (1998) 'Opposition to Road Building', *Parliamentary Affairs*, vol. 51, no. 3.

Doherty, B. (1999a) 'Manufactured Vulnerability: Eco-Activist Tactics in Britain', *Mobilisation*, vol. 4, no. 1.

Doherty, B. (1999b) 'Change the World via E-Mail', *New Statesman*, 1 November.

Doherty, B. (2002) *Ideas and Actions in the Green Movement*, London, Routledge.

Doherty, B and M. de Geus (1996) *Democracy and Green Political Thought*, London, Routledge.

Dordoy, A. and M. Mellor (2001) 'Grassroots Environmental Movements: Mobilisation in an Information Age', in F. Webster (ed.) *Culture and Politics in the Information Age: A New Politics?*, Routledge, London.

Dosi, G. (1982) 'Technological Paradigms and Technological Trajectories: A Suggested Interpretation of the Determinants and Directions of Technical Change', *Research Policy*, vol. 11.

Doward, J. (2000) 'Father of the Web Lashes Snooping Bill', *Observer*, 11 June.

Doyle, T. (2000) *Green Power. The Environment Movement in Australia*, University of South Wales Press, Sydney, Australia.

Doyle, T. and A. Kellow (1995) *Environmental Politics and Policy Making in Australia*, Melbourne, Macmillan.

Doyle, T. and D. McEachern. (1998) *Environment and Politics*. London, Routledge.

Drew, J. (1995) 'Media Activism and Radical Democracy', in J. Brook and I. Boal (eds) *Resisting the Virtual Life: The Culture and Politics of Information*, San Fransisco, CA, City Light Books.

Edwards, P. N. (1995) 'From "Impact" to Social Process: Computers in Society and Culture', in S. Jasanoff, G. Markle, E. J. Petersen, C. Pinch and T. Pinch (eds) *Handbook of Science and Technology Studies*, Thousand Oaks, CA, SAGE.

Elliott, C. and D. Campbell (1996) 'Police Chiefs Want Anti-Terror Squad to Spy on Green Activists', *Guardian*, 27 March.

Engel, D. (1997a) 'Bad News Travels Fast Out in Cyberspace', *The Times*, 19 August.

Engel, D. (1997b) 'Cyberlibel: The New "Internet Defence"', *International Media Law*, vol. 15, no. 10.

Escobar, A. (1994) 'Welcome to Cyberia: Notes on the Anthropology of Cyberculture', *Current Anthropology*, vol. 35, no. 3.

Escobar, A. (1999) Gender, Place and Networks: A Political Ecology of Cyberculture, in W.Harcourt. (ed.) *Women@internet: Creating New Cultures in Cyberspace*, London, Zed Books.

Ethical Consumer (1996) 'Product Report: Computers and Printers', *Ethical Consumer*, no. 43 (September–October).

Evans, K. (1998) *Copse: The Cartoon Book of Tree Protesting*, Dunford Bridge, Sheffield, Orange Dog Publications.

Express (1999) 'Net Sparks City Riot', *Daily Express*, 19 June.

Eyerman, R. and A. Jamison (1991) *Social Movements: A Cognitive Approach*, Cambridge, Polity Press.

Feenberg, A. (1999) *Questioning Technology*, London, Routledge.

Fernback, J. and B. Thompson (1995) *Virtual Communities: Abort, Retry, Failure?* Available online: www.well.com/user/hlr/texts/Vccivil.html.

Fischer, C. S. (1985) 'Studying Technology and Social Life', in M. Castells (ed.) *High Technology, Space and Society*, London, SAGE.

Fogg, A. and G. Zobel (1998) 'The Hills Have Ears', *Squall*, no. 16 (summer), available online: www.squall.co.uk.

Ford, R. (1998) 'Animal Activists Face Ban as Terrorists', *The Times*, 18 December.

Frederick, H. (1997) 'Mexican NGO Computer Networking Cross-Border Coalition Building', in M. Bailie and D. Winseck (eds) *Democratizing Communication – Comparative Perspectives on Information and Power*, Cresskill, NJ, Hampton Press Inc.

Freeman, J. (1970) 'The Tyranny of Structurelessness', *Berkeley Journal of Sociology*, available online: http://flag.blackened.net/revolt/hist_texts/structurelessness.html.

Friends of the Earth (1990) *Greening the Machinery of Government: A Framework for Governmental Administration in the 1990s and Beyond*, London, Friends of the Earth.

Friends of the Earth (1996) *The Green Office Plan*, London, Friends of the Earth.

Friends of the Earth (1997a) *Look Forward to a Better Future*, London, Friends of the Earth.

Friends of the Earth. (1997b) *Campaign Networks*, London, Friends of the Earth.

Friends of the Earth (1998a) *Where on Earth? Briefing Sheet*, London, Friends of the Earth.

Friends of the Earth (1998b) *Annual Review 1998*, London, Friends of the Earth.

Friends of the Earth (1998c) *Support Survey, November 1997*, London, Friends of the Earth.

Friends of the Earth (1999) 'Electronic Networks', in A. Watson (ed.) *Change Your World*, London, Friends of the Earth.

Friis, C. S. (1996) 'Two Starting Points on the Study of Internet', paper presented at the joint sessions of the European Consortium for Political Research in the workshop 'The International Relations of the Internet', Oslo, Norway, 29 March–3 April.

Frisch, M. (1994) *Directory for the Environment: Organisations, Campaigns and Initiatives in the British Isles*, London, Green Print.

Froehling, O. (1997) 'The Cyberspace "War of Ink and Internet" in Chiapas, Mexico', *The Geographical Review*, vol. 87, no. 2.

Fuller, D. (1999) 'Part of the Action, or "Going Native"? Learning to Cope with the "Politics of Integration"', *Area*, vol. 31, no. 3.

George, P. (1999) 'McSpotlight: Freedom of Speech and the Internet', in J. Cooper (ed.) *Liberating Cyberspace; Civil Liberties, Human Rights and the Internet*, London, Pluto Press.

Gibbs, G. (2000) 'Earth works', *Guardian*, Society (supplement), 1 March.

Glave, J. (1998) 'Anti-Nuke Cracker Strikes Again', *Wired News*, 14 December, available online: www.thing.net/~rdom/ecd/Brithacker.html.

Glendinning, C. (1990a) *When Technology Wounds: The Human Consequences of Progress*, New York, William Morrow.

Glendinning, C. (1990b) 'Notes Toward a Neo-Luddite Manifesto', *Utne Reader* (March–April).

Graham, G. (1999) *The Internet:// A Philosophical Inquiry*, London, Routledge.

Graham, S. and A. Aurigi (1997) 'Virtual Cities, Social Polarization, and the Crisis in Urban Public Space', *Journal of Urban Technology*, vol. 4, no. 1.

Graham, S. and S. Marvin (1996) *Telecommunications and the City: Electronic Spaces, Urban Places*, London, Routledge.

Grant, W. (1989) *Pressure Groups, Politics and Democracy in Britain*, London, Philip Allan.

Gray, J. (1995) 'Virtual Democracy', *Guardian*, 15 September.

Greenberg, D. W. (1985) 'Staging Media Events to Achieve Legitimacy: A Case Study of Britain's Friends of the Earth', *Political Communication and Persuasion*, vol. 2, no. 4.

Greenslade, R. (2000) 'RIP Bill Passed', *Guardian*, 31 July.

Greensword (1997) 'Lyminge Forest – the Facts', *Green World*, no. 19 (autumn).

Grint, K. and S. Woolgar. (1997) *The Machine at Work: Technology, Work and Organization*, Cambridge, Polity Press.

Groombridge, N. (1996) 'The Road to Utopia: Joyriding, Road Rage and Road Protests – Masculinities and Censure', paper presented at the Annual Conference of the British Sociological Association, Reading University.

Gusfield, J. (1981) 'Social Movements and Social Change: Perspectives of Linearity and Fluidity', in L. Kriesberg (ed.) *Research in Social Movements, Conflict and Change*, vol. 4, Greenwich, NY, JAI Press.

Hager, N. (1996) *Secret Power: New Zealand's Role in the International Spy Network*, Nelson, New Zealand, Craig Potton Publishing.

Hamelink, C. (1995) *World Communication: Disempowerment and Self-Empowerment*, London, Zed Books.

Hamilton, J. (2000) 'The Inter-Not?', *M/C Reviews*, 12 April, available online: www.uq.edu.ac/mc/reviews/features/politics/internot.html.

Harasim, L. M. (1993) 'Networlds: Networks as Social Space', *Global Networks: Computers and International Communication*, Cambridge, MA, MIT Press.

Haraway, D. J. (1990) *Simians, Cyborgs, and Women – the Re-invention of Nature*, London, Free Association Press.

Harding, T. (1997) *The Video Activist Handbook*, London, Pluto Press.

Harding, T. (1998) 'Viva Camcordistas! Video Activism and the Protest Movement', in G. McKay (ed.) *DiY Culture: Party and Protest in Nineties' Britain*, London, Verso.

Harper, P. (1995) *The CAT Story: Crazy Idealists! The Why, How, When and What of Europe's Foremost Eco-Centre*, Machynlleth, Wales, Centre for Alternative Technology.

Hartley, P. (1999) *Interpersonal Communication*, London, Routledge.

Haywood, T. (1995) *Info-Rich – Info-Poor: Access and Exchange in the Global Information Society*, London, Bowker-Saur.

Henderson, B. (ed.) (1996) *Minutes of the Lead Pencil Club: Pulling the Plug on the Electronic Revolution*, New York, Pushcart Press.

Hill, K. A and J. E. Hughes (1998) *Cyberpolitics: Citizen Activism in the Age of the Internet*, Oxford, Rowman & Littlefield.

Holden, S. and B. Szerszynski (1999) *Public Participation, Electronic Democracy and the Environment*, Lancaster, Centre for the Study of Environmental Change.

Holderness, M. (1998) 'VCs Reclaim the Sites', available online: www.poptel. org.uk/nuj/mike/censor.htm.

Holloway, J. (1998) '"Undercurrent Affairs": Radical Environmentalism and Alternative News', *Environment and Planning A*, vol. 30.

Ineson, R. (1999) 'Lyminge Forest', section in Open University broadcast *Digital Planet*, 6 March, BBC2.

Jackson, R. (1995) 'The Global Eco-Village Network', in J. Conrad (ed.) *Eco-Villages and Sustainable Communities: Models for 21st Century Living*, Forres, Scotland, FindHorn Press.

Jakubal, M. (2002) 'Fighting to Win: A Movement Without a Past Is a Movement Without a Future', *Earth First! Journal* (February–March).

Janssens, J. (1999) *A Corporate Counterstrategy Near You: Report on the N5M Panel Discussion on Corporate Counterstrategies Against Campaigns* (report available from the author: j.g.janssens@speed.a2000.nl).

Jasper, J. M. and J. D. Poulson (1993) 'Fighting Back: Vulnerabilities, Blunders, and Countermobilization by the Targets in Three Animal Rights Campaigns', *Sociological Forum*, no. 8.

Jasper, J. M. and J. D. Poulson (1995) 'Recruiting Strangers and Friends: Moral Shocks and Social Networks in Animal Rights and Anti-Nuclear Protests', *Social Problems*, vol. 42, no. 4.

Jenkins, D. (1995) *Centre for Alternative Technology: The First Twenty Years* (video), Machynlleth, Wales, Centre for Alternative Technology.

Jim (1999) 'Observations on e-litism', Post-Caravan European Meeting at Exodus, November, email discussion list communication.

Johnston, H., E. Larana and J. R. Gusfield (1994) 'Identities, Grievances and New Social Movements', in E. Larana, H. Johnston and J. R. Gusfield (eds) *New Social Movements: From Ideology to Identity*, Philadelphia, PA, Temple University Press.

Jones, S. (1998) 'Welcome to the World (Wide Web)', *Clean Slate*, no. 28 (spring).

Jordan, G. and W. Maloney (1997) *The Protest Business? Mobilizing Campaign Groups*, Manchester, Manchester University Press.

Jordan, J. (1998) 'The Art of Necessity: The Subversive Imagination of Anti-Road Protest and Reclaim the Streets', in G. McKay (ed.) *DiY Culture; Party and Protest in Nineties' Britain*, Verso, London.

Jordan, T. (1999a) 'New Space, New Politics: The Electronic Frontier Foundation and the Definition of Cyberpolitics', in T. Jordan and A. Lent (eds) *Storming the Millennium: The New Politics of Change*, London, Lawrence & Wishart.

Jordan, T. (1999b) *Cyberpower: The Culture and Politics of Cyberspace and the Internet*, London, Routledge.

Jordan, T. (2002) *Activism! Direct Action, Hacktivism and the Future of Society*, London, Reaktion Books.

Jordan, T. and P. Taylor (1998) 'A Sociology of Hackers', *The Sociological Review*, vol. 46, no. 4.

Juniper, T. (1997) 'Wildplaces', *Earth Matters*, no. 36.

Justice? (1995) *SchNEWSreader* (issues 1–50), Brighton, Justice?

Justice? (1996) *SchNEWSround* (issues 51–100), Brighton, Justice?

Justice? (1998) *SchNEWS Annual* (issues 101–50), Brighton, Justice?

Justice? (1999) *SchNEWS Survival Handbook* (issues 151–200), Brighton, Justice?

Justice? (2000) *SchQUALL*, Brighton, Justice?

Kala (2000) *Earth First! Revolutionary or Racist?* Distributed with *Earth First! Action Update*, no. 70 (August).

Katz, C. (1994) 'Playing the Field: Questions of Fieldwork in Geography', *Professional Geographer*, vol. 46, no. 1.

Kellner, D. (1998) 'Intellectuals, the New Public Spheres and Techno-Politics', in C. Toulouse and T. W. Luke (eds) *The Politics of Cyberspace*, London, Routledge.

Kellner, D. (1999) 'Globalisation from Below? Toward a Radical Democratic Technopolitics', *Angelaki*, vol. 4, no. 2.

Kendall, L. (1999) 'Recontextualizing "Cyberspace": Methodological Considerations for On-line Research', in S. Jones (ed.) *Doing Internet Research: Critical Issues and Methods for Examining the Net*, London, SAGE.

Keogh, G. (1996) 'Webbing the Barricades', *Wired*, no. 4.12 (December).

Kite, M. (2000) 'E-Mail Snooping Will Create Police State, Guru Warns', *The Times*, 7 June.

Klein, N. (2000a) *No Logo*, London, HarperCollins.

Klein, N. (2000b) 'The Vision Thing', *The Nation*, 10 July.

Klien, N. (2001) 'Welcome to the Net Generation', in A. Roddick (ed.) *Take it Personally: How Globalization Affects You and Powerful Ways to Challenge it*, London, HarperCollins.

Kobayashi, A. (1994) 'Coloring the Field: Gender, "Race", and the Politics of Fieldwork', *Professional Geographer*, vol. 46, no. 1.

Kolko, B. and R. Reid (1998) 'Dissolution and Fragmentation: Problems in On-line Communities', in S. Jones. (ed.) *Cybersociety 2.0: Revisiting Computer-Mediated Communication and Community*, Thousand Oaks, CA, SAGE.

Kovel, J. (1983) *Against the State of Nuclear Terror*, London, Pan Books.

Krinks, P. (1997) 'Eco-Warriors "storm" Rank: West Wood Protesters "Occupy" Liesure Giant's London HQ', *Folkestone Herald*, 21 August.

Kyrish, S. (1994) 'Here Comes the Revolution – Again: Evaluating Predictions for the Information Superhighway', *Media Information Australia*, no. 74.

Lamb, R. (1996) *Promising the Earth*, London, Routledge.

Lawrence, M. (1996) 'McSpotlight: Using the Internet as a Tool of Social Activism' (news report), *NBC News*, 17 April, available online: www.mcspotlight.org/media/television/nbc.html.

Lentin, A. (1999) 'Structure, Strategy, Sustainability: What Future for New Social Movement Theory?', *Sociological Research Online*, vol. 4, no. 3, available online: www.socresonline.org.uk/socresonline/4/3/lentin.html.

Lessig, L. (1999a) *Code and Other Laws of Cyberspace*, New York, Basic Books.

Lessig, L. (1999b) 'The Limits in Open Code: Regulatory Standards and the Future of the Net', *Berkeley Technology Law Journal*, vol. 14, no. 2.

Levi, M. (1996) 'Social and Unsocial Capital: A Review Essay of Robert Putnam *et al.*'s *Making Democracy Work*', *Politics and Society*, vol. 24, no. 1.

Levy, S. (2001) *Crypto. How the Code Rebels Beat the Government: Saving Privacy in the Digital Age*, New York, Viking.

Lewis, M. W. (1992) *Green Delusions; An Environmentalist Critique of Radical Environmentalism*, Durham, NC, Duke University Press.

Little, M. (1999) 'Practical Anarchy: An Interview with Critical Art Ensemble', *Angelaki*, vol. 4, no. 2.

Lockard, J. (1997) 'Progressive Politics, Electronic Individualism and the Myth of Virtual Community', in D. Porter (ed.) *Internet Culture*, London, Routledge.

Lodge, A. (1999) 'Surveillance Watch', *SchNEWS Survival Handbook*, Brighton.

Lovink, G. (1998) 'Radical Media Pragmatism Strategies for Techno-Social Movements', in G. Stocker and C. Schopf (eds) *Infowar*, New York, Springer Wien.

Lovink, G. (2000) 'Interview with Geert Lovink', *M/C Reviews*, 3 May, available online: www.uq.edu.au/mc/reviews/features/politics/lovink.html.

Lowe, P. and J. Goyder (eds) (1983) *Environmental Groups in Politics*, London, Allen & Unwin.

Lowe, R. and W. Shaw (1993) *Travellers: Voices of the New Age Nomads*, London, Fourth Estate.

Lubbers, E. (1996) 'Back To The Source! An Archivist Exploring New Dimensions of Netactivism' (5 pages), paper delivered at the Metaforum III Conference, Budapest, November 1996, available online: www.xs4all.nl/~evel/budastk.htm.

Lubbers, E. (1998) 'The Brent Spar Syndrome: Counterstrategies Against Online Activism' (4 pages), available online: www.xs4all.nl/~evel/brenteng.htm.

Lubbers, E. (2002a) 'Cyber-surveillance', in E. Lubbers (ed.) *Battling Big Business*, Totnes, Devon, Greenbooks.

Lubbers, E. (2002b) 'Net.activism', in E. Lubbers. (ed.) *Battling Big Business*, Totnes, Devon, Greenbooks.

Lyon, D. (2001) *Surveillance Society: Monitoring Everyday Life*, Buckingham, Open University Press.

Mackay, H. (1995) 'Technological Reality: Cultured Technology and Technologized Culture', in B. Adam and S. Allan (eds) *Theorizing Culture: An Interdisciplinary Critique After Postmodernism*, London, UCL Press.

MacKenzie, D. and J. Wajcman (1985) Introductory Essay, in D. MacKenzie and J. Wajcman (eds) *The Social Shaping of Technology*, Milton Keynes, Open University Press.

McAdam, D. (1988) *Freedom Summer*, Oxford, Oxford University Press.

McAdam, D. and R. Paulsen (1993) 'Specifying the Relationship Between Social Ties and Activism', *American Journal of Sociology*, vol. 99, no. 3.

McAdam, D. and D. Rucht (1993) 'The Cross-National Diffusion of Movement Ideas', *The Annuals of the American Academy of Political and Social Science*, no. 528.

McAdam, D., S. Tarrow and C. Tilly (2001) *Dynamics of Contention*, Cambridge, Cambridge University Press.

McAllister, I. (1994) 'Dimensions of Environmentalism: Public Opinion, Political Activism and Party Support in Australia', *Environmental Politics*, vol. 3, no. 1.

McCarthy, J. D. (1996) 'Constraints and Opportunities in Adopting, Adapting and Inventing', in D. McAdam, J. D. McCarthy and M. N. Zald (eds) *Comparative*

Perspective on Social Movements. Political Opportunities, Mobilizing Structures and Cultural Framing, Cambridge, Cambridge University Press.

McCormick, J. (1991) *British Politics and the Environment*, London, Earthscan Publications.

McCormick, J. (1995) *The Global Environmental Movement*, Chichester, John Wiley & Sons.

McCormick, N. and J. Leonard (1996) 'Gender and Sexuality in the Cyberspace Frontier', *Women and Therapy*, vol. 19, no. 4.

McKay, G. (1998) 'DiY Culture: Notes Towards an Intro', in G. McKay (ed.) *DiY Culture; Party and Protest in Nineties' Britain*, Verso, London.

McRae, S. (1997) 'Flesh Made Word: Sex, Text and the Virtual Body', in D. Porter (ed.) *Internet Culture*, London, Routledge.

Mander, J. (1994a) 'Tyranny of Technology', *Resurgence*, no. 164 (May–June).

Mander, J. (1994b) 'Return of the Sacred', *Resurgence*, no. 166 (September–October).

Margolis, M. and D. Resnick (2000) *Politics as Usual: The Cyberspace "Revolution"*, Thousand Oaks, CA, SAGE.

Martinson, J. (2000) 'Spider in the Web', *Guardian*, 3 May.

Marx, L. and M. Roe Smith (1994) 'Introduction', in L. Marx and M. Roe Smith (eds) *Does Technology Drive History? The Dilema of Technological Determinism*, Cambridge, MA, MIT Press.

Mastrangelo Gittler, A. (1999) 'Mapping Women's Global Communications and Networking', in W. Harcourt (ed.) *Women@internet: Creating New Cultures in Cyberspace*, London, Zed Books.

Mattausch, J. (1987) 'The Sociology of CND', in C. Creighton and M. Shaw (eds) *The Sociology of War and Peace*, London, MacMillan.

Mattausch, J. (1989) *A Commitment to Campaign: A Sociological Study of CND*, Manchester, Manchester University Press.

Maxey, I. (1999) 'Beyond Boundaries? Activism, Academia, Reflexivity and Research', *Area*, vol. 31, no. 3.

Maynard, R. (1998) 'Vision 2000', in A. Watson (ed.) *Change Your World*, London, Friends of the Earth.

Meikle, G. (2002) *Future Active: Media Activism and the Internet*, Sydney, Pluto Press.

Melucci, A. (1989) *Nomads of the Present: Social Movements and Individuals' Needs in Contemporary Society*, London, Hutchinson Radius.

Melucci, A. (1994) 'A Strange Kind of Newness: What's "New" in New Social Movements?', in E. Larana, H. Johnston and J. R. Gusfied. (eds) *New Social Movements: From Ideology to Identity*, Philadelphia, PA, Temple University Press.

Melucci, A. (1996) *Challenging Codes: Collective Action in the Information Age*, Cambridge, Cambridge University Press.

Melucci, A. (2000) 'Social Movement in Complex Societies', *Area Journal*, no. 15.

Merchant, L. (1992) *Radical Ecology: The Search for a Livable World*, London, Routledge.

Middleton, J. (1997) 'Liability of Service Providers for Defamation in Cyberspace', *European Business Law Review*, vol. 8, no. 4.

Mies, M and V. Shiva (1993) *Ecofeminism*, London, Zed Books.

Mills, D. (1997) 'Making Mincemeat of McDonald's', *ECOS*, vol. 18, no. 2.

Mitchell, W. J. (1996) *City of Bits*, Cambridge, MA, MIT Press.

Mitra, A. and E. Cohen (1999) 'Analyzing the Web: Directions and Challenges', in S. Jones (ed.) *Doing Internet Research: Critical Issues and Methods for Examining the Net*, London, SAGE.

Mobbs, P. (2000) 'The Internet, Disintermediation and Campaign Groups', *ECOS*, vol. 21, no. 1.

Mohan, G. and J. Mohan (2002) 'Placing Social Capital', *Progress in Human Geography*, vol. 26, no. 2.

Monsanto (1998) 'Food Biotechnology is a Matter of Opinions . . .' *Observer*, advertisement, 21 June.

Moody, G. (2002) *Rebel Code: Linux and the Open Source Revolution*, London, Penguin.

Murray, G. (1993) *Enemies of the State*, London, Simon & Schuster.

Myers, D. J. (1994) 'Communication Technology and Social Movements: Contributions of Computer Networks to Activism', *Social Science Computer Review*, vol. 12, no. 2.

Newsome, R. (1997) If You Go Down to the Woods Today . . .', *The Big Issue*, November 3–9.

Norris, P. (2001) *Digital Divide: Civic Engagement, Information Poverty and the Internet Worldwide*, Cambridge, Cambridge University Press.

Norris, P. (2002) *Democratic Phoenix: Reinventing Political Activism*, Cambridge, Cambridge University Press.

Norton-Taylor, R. (1999) 'Straw Bill Widens Terrorism Definition', *Guardian*, 3 December.

Nuthall, K. (1997) 'Eco-Warriors Go Soft and Opt for the Telly', *Independent on Sunday*, 16 November.

Nuthall, N. (1999) 'ICI Heads List of Worst Polluters', *The Times*, 22 March.

O'Donnell, S. (2001) 'Analysing the Internet and the Public Sphere: The Case of Womenslink', *Javnost*, vol. 8, no. 1.

O'Hara, L. (1993) *At War With The Truth*, London, Mina.

O'Hara, L. (1994) *Turning Up the Heat: MI5 After the Cold War*, London, Phoenix Press.

O'Lear, S. (1997) 'Electronic Communication and Environmental Policy in Russia and Estonia', *Geographical Review*, vol. 87, no. 2.

Oliver, P., E. Marwell and G. Marwell (1992) 'Mobilizing Technologies for Collective Action', in A. Morris, D. McClurg Mueller and C. McClurg Mueller (eds) *Frontiers in Social Movement Theory*, London, Yale University Press.

Opie, A. (1992) 'Qualitative Research, Appropriation of the "Other" and Empowerment', *Feminist Review*, no. 40 (spring).

Paehlke, R. (1988) 'Democracy, Bureaucracy and Environmentalism', *Environmental Ethics*, vol. 10, no. 4.

Paquin, B. (1998) 'E-Guerrillas in the Mist' (9 pages), *Ottawa Citizen*, available online: www.ottawacitizen.com/hightech/981026/1964496.html.

Parsons, L. (1997) 'Digging in', *Folkestone Herald*, 17 April.

Paterson, M. and J. Lewis (1998) 'Eco Warriors or Vandals?', *Mail on Sunday*, 21 June.

Pearce, F. (1991) *Green Warriors: The People and the Politics Behind the Environmental Revolution*, London, Bodley Head.

Penman, D. (1999) 'Cops in Your Computer', *Daily Express*, 28 September.

Pepper, D. (1984) *The Roots of Modern Environmentalism*, London, Croom Helm.

Pepper, D. (1996) *Modern Environmentalism: An Introduction*, London, Routledge.

Perry, J. and E. Leigh Vanderklein (1996) 'Environmental Problem Solving in an Age of Electronic Communications: Toward an Integrated or a Reductionist Model?', in J. Lemons (ed.) *Scientific Uncertainty and Environmental Problem Solving*.

Pickerill, J. (2001) 'Weaving a Green Web: Environmental Protest and Computer Mediated Communication in Britain', in F. Webster (ed.) *Culture and Politics in the Information Age*, London, Routledge.

Pickerill, J. (2004) 'Rethinking Political Participation: Experiments in Internet Activism in Australia and Britain', in R. Gibson, A. Römmete and S. Ward (eds) *Electronic Democracy: Mobilisation, Organisation and Participation via new ICTs*, London, Routledge.

Pipes, S. (1996) 'Environmental Information on the Internet', *ECOS*, vol. 17, no. 2.

Pipes, S. (1997) 'Raising the Standard: Access to Environmental Information' (11 pages), available online: www.foe.co.uk/camps/edu/agi97.html.

Porritt, J. (1984) *Seeing Green: The Politics of Ecology Explained*, Oxford, Blackwell.

Poster, M. (1997) 'Cyberdemocracy: Internet and the Public Sphere', in D. Porter (ed.) *Internet Culture: Identity and Community in Cyberspace*, London, Routledge.

Princen, T. and M. Finger (eds) (1994) *Environmental NGOs in World Politics: Linking the Local and the Global*, London, Routledge.

Putnam, R. (2001) *Bowling Alone*, Simon & Schuster.

Putnam, R., R. Leonardi and R. Nanetti (1993) *Making Democracy Work: Civic Traditions in Modern Italy*, Princeton, NJ, Princeton University Press.

Rawcliffe, P. (1998) *Environmental Pressure Groups in Transition*, Manchester, Manchester University Press.

Redden, G. (2001) 'Networking Dissent: The Internet and the Anti-Globalisation Movement', *Mots Pluriels*, no. 18, available online: www.arts.uwa.edu.au/MotsPluriels/MP1801gr.html.

Reed, M. (1999) 'Wide Open to the Web Warriors', *Marketing On-Line*, available online: http://193.133.103.27/feature99/0204a/0204a.htm.

Reid, E. (1999) 'Hierarchy and Power: Social Control in Cyberspace', in M. Smith and P. Kollock (eds) *Communities in Cyberspace*, London, Routledge.

Resnick, D. (1998) 'Politics on the Internet: The Normalization of Cyberspace', in C. Toulouse and T. W. Luke (eds) *The Politics of Cyberspace*, London, Routledge.

Rheingold, H. (1994) *The Virtual Community: Finding Connection in a Computerised World*, London, Secker & Warburg.

Rifkin, J. (1989) *Entropy: Into the Greenhouse World*, New York, Bantam Books.

Ritchie, D. (1999a) 'Welcome to the Traffic-Reduction Email Discussion List', emailed to author, received 8 April.

Ritchie, D. (1999b) 'Electronic Communications', in A. Watson (ed.) *Change Your World*, London, Friends of the Earth.

Riviere, P. (1999) 'How the Americans Spy on All of Us', *Le Monde* (January).

Roach, C. (1995) 'Women and Communications Technology: What Are the Issues?', in P. Lee. (ed.) *The Democratization of Communication*, Cardiff, University of Wales Press.

RoadAlert! (1997) *Road Raging: Top Tips for Wrecking Road Building*, Berkshire, RoadAlert!

Robins, K. (1995) 'Cyberspace and the World We Live in', in K. Robins (ed.) *'Into the Image': Culture and Politics in the Field of Vision*, London, Routledge.

Robins, K. (1996) 'Cyberspace and the World We Live in', in J. Dovey (ed.) *Fractal Dreams: New Media in Social Context*, London, Lawrence & Wishart.

Robins, K. and F. Webster (1999) *Times of the Technoculture*, London, Routledge.

Rochon, T. R. (1988) *Mobilizing for Peace – the Antinuclear Movements of Western Europe*, London, Adamantine.

Rodgers, J. (2001) 'NGOs and E-Activism: Institutionalizing or Extending the Political Potential of the Internet?', paper presented to the ISA Hong Kong Convention of International Studies, 26–8 July, available online: www.isanet.org/archive/rodgers.html.

Rootes, C. (1992) 'The New Politics and the New Social Movements: Accounting for British Exceptionalism', *European Journal of Political Research*, vol. 22.

Rootes, C. (1995) 'A New Class? The Higher Educated and the New Politics', in L. Maheu (ed.) *Social Movements and Social Classes: The Future of Collective Action*, London, SAGE.

Rooum, D. (1992) *What Is Anarchism? An Introduction*, London, Freedom Press.

Rowell, A. (1996) *Green Backlash: Global Subversion of the Environment Movement*, London, Routledge.

Rowell, A. (1999) 'Greenwash: Isolate, Cultivate, Educate. (and Co-Opt)', *Peace News*, no. 2436 (September–November).

Rucht, D. (1993) '"Think Globally, Act Locally"? Needs, Forms and Problems of Cross-National Cooperation Among Environmental Groups', in J. D. Liefferink, P. D. Lowe and A. P. J. Mol (eds) *European Integration and Environmental Policy*, London, Belhaven Press.

Rüdig, W. (1995) 'Between Moderation and Marginalization: Environmental Radicalism in Britain', in B. Taylor (ed.) *Ecological Resistance Movements: The Global Emergence of Radical Popular Environmentalism*, Albany, NY, State University of New York Press.

Rüdig, W., L. Bennie and M. N. Franklin (1991) *Green Party Members: A Profile*, Glasgow, Delta Publications.

Rüdig, W. and P. D. Lowe (1986) 'The Withered "Greening" of British Politics: A Study of the Ecology Party', *Political Studies*, vol. 34, no. 2.

Rüdig, W., J. Mitchell, J. Chapman and P. D. Lowe (1991) 'Social Movements and the Social Sciences in Britain', in D. Rucht (ed.) *Research on Social Movements: The State of the Art in Western Europe and the USA*, Boulder, CO, Westview Press.

Rumble, S. (1997) 'It's Net Time Now', *The Australian*, 29 April.

Rushkoff, D. (1994) *Cyberia: Life in the Trenches of Hyperspace*, London, HarperCollins.

Rushkoff, D. (1998) 'Coercion and Countermeasures: The Information Arms Race', in G. Stocker and C. Schoph, *InfoWar*, New York, Springer Wien.

Sale, K. (1995) *Rebels Against the Future: The Luddites and Their War on the Industrial Revolution. Lessons for the Computer Age*, Reading, MA, Addison-Wesley.

Scalmer, S. (2002) *Dissent Events: Protest, the Media and the Political Gimmick in Australia*, Sydney, University of New South Wales Press.

Schofield, J. (1995) 'Netwatch', *Guardian*, Online (supplement), 17 August.

Schofield Clark, L. (1998) 'Dating on the Net: Teens and the Rise of "Pure" Relationships', in S. Jones (ed.) *Cybersociety 2.0: Revisiting Computer-Mediated Communication and Community*, Thousand Oaks, CA, SAGE.

Schumacher, E. F. (1973) *Small Is Beautiful: A Study of Economics As If People Mattered*, London, Abacus.

Schwartz, E. (1996) *NetActivism: How Citizens Use the Internet*, Sebastopol, CA, Songline Studios.

Schwartz, E. (1998) 'An Internet Resource for Neighbourhoods', in R. Tsagarousianou, D. Tambini and C. Bryan (eds) *Cyberdemocracy: Technology, Cities and Civic Networks*, London, Routledge.

Schwarz, W. (1994) 'Direct Action: Pulling in the Same Direction', *Guardian*, 21 December.

Schwarz, W. (1997) 'Lure of the Luddites', *Guardian*, 3 December.

Scott, A. (1995) *Ideology and the New Social Movements*, London, Routledge.

Scott, A. and J. Street (2001) 'From Media Politics to E-Protest? The Use of Popular Culture and New Media in Parties and Social Movements', in F. Webster (ed.) *Culture and Politics in the Information Age: A New Politics?* Routledge, London.

Secrett, C. and P. Cochrane (1999) 'Are We Hysterical About New Technologies?', *Guardian*, Saturday Review, 12 June.

Seel, B. (1997) '"If Not You, Then Who?" Earth First! in the UK', *Environmental Politics*, vol. 6, no. 4.

Shenk, D. (1997) *Data Smog*, London, Abacus Books.

Sherkat, D., E. Blocker and T. J. Blocker (1993) 'Environmental Activism in the Protest Generation: Differentiating 1960s' Activists', *Youth and Society*, vol. 25, no. 1.

Shurmer-Smith, P. and K. Hannam (1994) *Worlds of Desire. Realms of Power: A Cultural Geography*, London, Edward Arnold.

Siegel, L. and J. Markoff (1985) *The High Cost of High Tech: The Dark Side of the Chip*, New York, Harper & Row.

Silver, D. (2000) 'Setting E-Commerce Aside: A Conference Review', paper presented at the conference 'Directions and Implications of Advanced Computing 2000. Shaping the Network Society: The Future of the Public Sphere in Cyberspace', 20–3 May, Seattle, USA.

Slevin, J. (2000) *The Internet and Society*, Cambridge, Polity Press.

Smith, G. J. H. (1996) *Internet Law and Regulation* (Special Report), London, Financial Times Law and Tax.

Smith, J., J. McCarthy, C. McPhil and B. Augustyn (2001) 'From Protest to Agenda Building: Description Bias in Media Coverage of Protest Events in Washington, DC', *Social Forces*, vol. 79, no. 4.

Smith, P. and E. Smythe (2001) 'Globalisation, Citizenship and Technology: The Multilateral Agreement in Investment (MAI) Meets the Internet', in F. Webster (ed.) *Culture and Politics in the Information Age: A New Politics?* London, Routledge.

Sommer, P. (2000) 'Protection or Persecution?', *Guardian*, Online (supplement), 30 March.

Sprenger, P. (1999) 'Pirates Sneer at Intel Chip', *Wired News*, 22 January.

Stabile, C. A. (1994) *Feminism and the Technological Fix*, Manchester, Manchester University Press.

Starr, A. (2000) *Naming the Enemy: Anti-Corporate Movements Confront Globalization*, Annandale, Pluto Press.

Stefanik, N. (1993) 'Sustainable Dialogue/Sustainable Development: Developing Planetary Consciousness Via Electronic Democracy', in J. Breacher, J. Brown Childs and J. Cutler (eds) *Global Visions: Beyond the New World Order*, Boston, MA, South End Press.

Stoll, C. (1995) *Silicon Snake Oil: Second Thoughts on the Information Highway*, London, Pan Books.

Street, J. (1992) *Politics and Technology*, London, Macmillan.

Swift, R. (2002) *The No-Nonsense Guide to Democracy*, London, Verso–New Internationalist.

Sydenham, M. (1996) *Friends of the Earth Scotland's Green Home Handbook*, Edinburgh, Friends of the Earth Scotland.

Szerszynski, B. (1998) 'Action's Glassy Essence: The Dramatics of Environmental Protest', paper presented at the Annual Conference of the Royal Geographical Society with the Institute of British Geographers, Kingston University, Kingston-on-Thames, 5–8 January.

Tang, P. (1997) 'Multimedia Information Products and Services: A Need for "Cybercops"?', in B. Loader, *The Governance of Cyberspace; Politics, Technology and Global Restructuring*, London, Routledge.

Tarrow, S. (1998a) *Power in Movement: Social Movements and Contentious Politics*, Cambridge, Cambridge University Press.

Tarrow, S. (1998b) 'Fishnets, Internets and Catnets: Globalization and Transnational Collective Action', in M. Hanagan, P. L. Moch, P. te Brake and W. te Brake (eds) *Challenging Authority: The Historical Study of Contentious Politics*, Minneapolis, University of Minnesota Press.

Taylor, P. (1999) *Hackers*, London, Routledge.

Taylor, P. (2001) 'Hacktivism: In Search of Lost Ethics?', in D. Wall (ed.) *Crime and the Internet*, London, Routlege.

Terranova, T. (2001) 'Demonstrating the Globe: Virtual Action in the Network Society', in D. Holmes (ed.) *Virtual Globalization; Virtual Spaces/Tourists' Spaces*, London, Routledge.

Thorpe, D. (1995) 'What Is an Eco-Naut and Is Netsurfing a Truly Sustainable Activity? A Dialogue with a Netsceptic', *Clean Slate*, no. 18 (autumn).

Tilly, C. (1978) *From Mobilisation to Revolution*, Reading, MA, Addison-Wesley.

Tilly, C. (1986) *The Contentious French*, Cambridge, MA, Harvard University Press.

Toby (1997) '*SchNEWS* to do/Ideas', Internal *SchNEWS* memo, 6 June.

Tokar, B. (1992) *The Green Alternative: Creating an Ecological Future*, San Pedro, CA, R. & E. Miles.

Trainer, T. (1991) 'The Technological Fix', in A. Dobson (ed.) *The Green Reader*, London, André Deutsch.

Tranter, B. (1996) 'The Social Bases of Environmentalism in Australia', *Australian and New Zealand Journal of Sociology*, vol. 32, no. 2.

Tsagarousianou, R. (1998) 'Electronic Democracy and the Public Sphere', in R. Tsagarousianou, D. Tambini and C. Bryan (eds) *Cyberdemocracy: Technology, Cities and Civic Networks*, London, Routledge.

Turner, R. and L. Killian (1987) *Collective Behaviour*, Englewood Cliffs, NJ, Prentice-Hall.

Urban75 (1996) 'So, What's Going On in the Internet?', *Urban75*, www.urban75.com/Mag/internet.html.

Vidal, J. (1996) 'You and I Against McWorld', *Guardian*, Weekend Magazine, 9 March.

Vidal, J. (1997a) *McLibel: Burger Culture on Trial*, London, Macmillan.

Vidal, J. (1997b) 'DIY Democracy. Direct Action: When All Else Fails, Is it the Best Solution?', *One Thousand Days: A Special Report on How to Live in the New Millennium*, London, Guardian–WWF-UK.

Vidal, J. (1999) 'Modem Warfare', *Guardian*, Society (supplement), 13 January.

Vidal, J. (2000a) 'Web of Intrigue', *Guardian*, Society (supplement), 28 August.

Vidal, J. (2000b) 'The World@War', *Guardian*, Society (supplement), 19 January.

Virnoche, M and G. Marx (1997) '"Only Connect" – E. M. Forster in An Age Of Electronic Communication: Computer-Mediated Association and Community Networks', *Sociological Inquiry*, vol. 67, no. 1.

Volti, R. (1992) *Society and Technological Change*, New York, St. Martin's Press.

Vranesevich, J. (1999) 'Kaotik Protest Conditions in East Timor', available online: www.antionline.com/SpecialReports/kaotik.

Wadham, J. (1999) 'No, You're Turning Us All into Criminals', *Guardian*, 14 December.

Wakeford, N. S. (1995) 'Researching Diversity on the Net', *Electronic Journal of Virtual Culture*, vol. 3, no. 4.

Walch, J. (1999) *In the Net: An Internet Guide for Activists*, London, Zed Books.

Walcroft, G. (1998) 'Whose Turn Is it to Wash Up? Gender Relations and Stereotypes within Anti-Roads Protest Camps', unpublished undergraduate dissertation, University of Leeds.

Wall, D. (1999a) *Earth First! and the Anti-Roads Movement: Radical Environmentalism and Comparative Social Movements*, London, Routledge.

Wall, D. (1999b) 'Mobilising Earth First! in Britain', *Environmental Politics*, vol. 8, no. 1.

Walters, W. (2002) 'Social Capital and Political Sociology: Re-imagining Politics?', *Sociology*, vol. 36, no. 2.

Wapner, P. (1995) 'Politics Beyond the State: Environmental Activism and World Civic Politics', *World Politics*, vol. 47, no. 3.

Warf, B. and J. Grimes (1997) 'Counterhegemonic Discourses and the Internet', *Geographical Review*, vol. 87, no. 2.

Wark, M. (1994) 'Third Nature', *Cultural Studies*, vol. 8, no. 1.

Warschauer, M. (2002) 'Reconceptualizing the Digital Divide', *First Monday*, vol. 7, no. 7, available online: http://firstmonday.org/issues/issue7_7/warschauer.

Washbourne, N. (1999a) 'Beyond Iron Laws: Information Technology and Social Transformation in the Global Environment Movement', unpublished PhD thesis, University of Surrey.

Washbourne, N. (1999b) 'New Forms of Organizing? Translocalism, Networks and Organizing in FoE', paper presented at the conference 'A New Politics? Representation, Mobilization and Networks in the Information Age', University of Birmingham, 16–17 September.

Weatherley, R. (1994) *Friends of the Earth Information Systems Strategy*, London, Friends of the Earth.

Webster, F. (1995) *Theories of The Information Society*, London, Routledge.

Webster, F. and K. Robins (1986) *Information Technology: A Luddite Analysis*, New Jersey, Ablex.

Which?Online (2002) *Annual Internet Survey 2002*, available: www.which.net/surveys/survey2002.pdf.

White, C. (1999) 'Environmental Activism and the Internet', unpublished MA thesis, Massey University, New Zealand.

Whittikar, M. (1996) *Costing the Earth*, BBC Radio 4, 17 April.

Wilkin, P. (2000) 'Solidarity in a Global Age – Seattle and Beyond', paper presented at Department of Politics Seminar Series, Lancaster University, January.

Willetts, P. (1996) 'From Stockholm to Rio and Beyond: The Impacts of the Environmental Movement on the United Nations' Consultative Arrangements for NGOs', *Review of International Studies*, vol. 199, no. 22.

Wills, M. (1999) 'Net Profit and Lost Innocence', *The Times*, 19 May.

Willson, M. (2002) 'Technically Together: The Implications of Using Communication Technologies for Our Understandings and Experiences of Community', unpublished PhD thesis, Monash University, Australia.

Winner, L. (1986) *The Whale and the Reactor: A Search for Limits in an Age of High Technology*, Chicago, IL, University of Chicago Press.

Winner, L. (1988) 'Mythinformation', in J. Zerzan and A. Carnes (eds) *Questioning Technology – a Critical Anthology*, London, Freedom Press.

Witherspoon, S. (1994) 'The Greening of Britain: Romance and Rationality', in R. Jowell, J. Curtice, L. Brook and D. Ahrendt (eds) *British Social Attitudes: The 11th Report*, Aldershot, Dartmouth .

Wood, D. (2002) Personal communication with the author, August.

Woolf, M. (1995) 'Green Protesters Give Up Scraps of Paper for the Internet', *Independent on Sunday*, 20 February.

Woolley, B. (1992) *Virtual Worlds: A Journey in Hype and Hyperreality*, Oxford, Blackwell.

Wray, S. (1998a) 'Electronic Civil Disobedience and the World Wide Web of Hacktivism: A Mapping of Extraparliamentarian Direct Action Net Politics' (13 pages), available online: www.nyu.edu/projects/wray/wwwhack.html.

Wray, S. (1998b) 'Transforming Luddite Resistance into Virtual Luddite Resistance: Weaving a World Wide Web of Electronic Civil Disobedience' (3 pages), available online: www.gn.apc.org/pmhp/dc/activism/srway.htm.

Young, I. M. (1990) *Justice and the Politics of Difference*, Princeton, NJ, Princeton University Press.

Young, J. E. (1993) *Global Network: Computers in a Sustainable Society*, World Watch Paper 115, Washington, DC.

Zelwietro, J. (1998) 'The Politicization of Environmental Organizations Through the Internet', *The Information Society*, vol. 14, no. 1.

Index